Continuous Computing Technologies for Enhancing Business Continuity

Nijaz Bajgoric
University of Sarajevo, Bosnia and Herzegovina

INFORMATION SCIENCE REFERENCE

Hershey · New York

Director of Editorial Content:	Kristin Klinger
Director of Production:	Jennifer Neidig
Managing Editor:	Jamie Snavely
Assistant Managing Editor:	Carole Coulson
Typesetter:	Cindy Consonery
Cover Design:	Lisa Tosheff
Printed at:	Yurchak Printing Inc.

Published in the United States of America by
    Information Science Reference (an imprint of IGI Global)
    701 E. Chocolate Avenue, Suite 200
    Hershey PA 17033
    Tel: 717-533-8845
    Fax: 717-533-8661
    E-mail: cust@igi-global.com
    Web site: http://www.igi-global.com/reference

and in the United Kingdom by
    Information Science Reference (an imprint of IGI Global)
    3 Henrietta Street
    Covent Garden
    London WC2E 8LU
    Tel: 44 20 7240 0856
    Fax: 44 20 7379 0609
    Web site: http://www.eurospanbookstore.com

Library of Congress Cataloging-in-Publication Data

Bajgoric, Nijaz.

  Continuous computing technologies for enhancing business continuity / Nijaz Bajgoric.

    p. cm.

  Includes bibliographical references and index.

  Summary: "The main objective of this book is to assist managers in becoming aware and more knowledgeable on the economics of downtime and continuous computing technologies that help in achieving business continuity and managing efficiently information resources"--Provided by publisher.

  ISBN 978-1-60566-160-5 (hbk.) -- ISBN 978-1-60566-161-2 (ebook)

  1. Information technology--Management. 2. Client/server computing. I. Title.

  HD30.2.B3474 2009

  658.5'67--dc22

                  2008023188

British Cataloguing in Publication Data
A Cataloguing in Publication record for this book is available from the British Library.

All work contributed to this book is original material. The views expressed in this book set are those of the authors, but not necessarily of the publisher.

To my wife Ermina and son Adnan.
and
To the memory of my parents.

Table of Contents

Foreword

Information technologies help businesses in achieving their goals in today's highly competitive economy. However, the implementation of information technologies may bring some business risks as well. Some businesses had experienced IT-based horror stories due to wrong implementations of enterprise information systems or some sort of data loss.

Information technologies have opened new opportunities for businesses in their efforts to cope with increasing competition, reduce the costs of doing business, increase the profits, improve the quality of products and services, improve relations with customers.

The main objective of this book is to assist managers and IT managers in becoming aware and more knowledgable on the economics of downtime and continuous computing technologies that help in achieving business continuity and managing efficiently information resources.

The book has three main goals. The first goal is to provide clear and precise understanding of several information technologies that can be used in order to enhance business continuity. The second goal is to help managers and IT managers in understanding how important are information technologies in modern business. The third goal is to explore in more details the role of enterprise servers, server operating systems and serverware solutions within the form of integrated server operating environment in improving both continuous computing and business continuity dimensions.

This book is aimed at providing the framework for using and managing information technologies in order to enhance the availability ratios of business computing platforms. It is not the intention of the book to provide the reader with enough specific and detailed technological knowledge on each continuous computing technology to make them business continuity experts on that particular technology.

What makes this book different when compared to other books in this area is in a systemic approach that explores a set of continuous computing technologies for enhancing business continuity and in exploring the role of server operating environmnets for enhancing business continuity. The methodological approach used in the book is also distinctive.

The book consists of three parts and includes fourteen chapters. Each chapter includes a list of discusssion questions, and one or more case studies related to that chapter.

The first four chapters (I–IV) build a foundation for understanding modern business, business computing, economics of downtime, and business continuity. The second part (subsequent eight chapters, V–XII) describes the major continuous computing technologies that can be implemented for enhancing business continuity. The third part of the book contains two chapters dealing with business continuity management (Chapter XIII) and relations between business continuity and business agility (Chapter XIV).

I strongly recommend this book for both researchers and practitioners in the area of information systems.

Angappa Gunasekaran

Professor and Chairperson

Department of Decision and Information Sciences

Charlton College of Business

University of Massachusetts – Dartmouth

Preface

Forrester recently introduced the term "business technology" pointing out that this represents one of the major shifts in the way people think about computers in IT history. Forrester's business technology is based on two key ideas: IT risks are business risks, and IT opportunities are now business opportunities.

Modern business owes a lot to information technology (IT). IT helps businesses in achieving business goals and, in general, in becoming more efficient, effective and competitive on a highly competitive market. On the other hand, however, the implementation of information technologies may bring some business risks as well. It is well known that some businesses had experienced "IT-based horror stories" due to wrong implementations of enterprise information systems or because of some sort of data loss and/or disruption. As contemporary business is becoming more and more bound to IT, this dependence may become critical for business itself in case of data lost, data unavailability, wrong IT-implementation, and so on.

Information technologies, particularly during the last decade, after introducing Internet and Web, have opened new opportunities for businesses in their efforts to cope with increasing competititon, reduce the costs of doing business, increase the profits, improve the quality of products and services, improve relations with customers, and ease data access. In general, information technologies are used to enhance both efficiency and effectivenness of a business. IT plays crucial role in both "Doing the Things Right" and "Doing the Right Things" as Peter Drucker defined the terms of "efficiency" and "effectiveness.

However, at the same time, organizations may face several situations in which their business may suffer due to some IT-related problems, such as: unavailable data, lost data, data exposed to competition and unauthorized usage, stolen or lost computers, stolen backup tapes, hardware error on any computer component that causes system downtime, broken LAN/WAN connection, destroyed computers or computer center due to any type of disaster, hackers' activities over Internet, and so forth. Organizational management can not be effective if it does not integrate organization-wide information management as well. This is in particular important for contemporary businesses which require continuous computing platform as a main prerequisite for business continuance. Therefore, modern business needs an efficient integration of business continuity management into organizational management, the process which is done by integrating the continuous computing technologies into enterprise information system.

In today's information age, information management comprises numerous activities with data processing/data management being the core component. In addition to core data management implemented in one or more databases, information management includes the following components as well: system management, network management, security management, and so forth. Recently, with advances in Internet technologies and e-business, the need for achieving "a near 100%" level of business computing availability was brought up yet again. Consequently, the term of "business continuity management" was coined up and became a significant part of organizational information management. Business continuity management (BCM) has become an integral part of organizational management. It involves several measures (activities) that have to be implemented in order to achieve higher levels of the system/application availability ratios.

Business continuity has been treated as both IT and managerial issue during the last ten years particularly after the e-business boom and the "9/11" event. In that sense, an enterprise information system should be managed from business continuity perspective in a way that this process includes managerial and system administration activities related to managing the integration of business continuity drivers.

The main objective of this book is to assist managers and IT managers in becoming aware and more knowledgable on the economics of downtime and continuous computing technologies that help in achieving business continuity and managing efficiently information resources.

The book has three main goals. The first and foremost goal is to provide clear and precise understanding of several information technologies that can be used in order to enhance business continuity. The second goal is to help managers and IT managers in understanding how important are information technologies in modern business. The third goal is to explore in more details the role of enterprise servers, server operating systems and serverware solutions within the form of integrated server operating environment in improving availability ratios, continuous computing dimensions and business continuity in general. Other continuous computing technologies are explained as well, however, an emphasis was given on server operating platforms and this is the main distinctive point of this book.

This manuscript is intended to provide the reader with a foundation of concepts relevant to using and managing information technologies in order to enhance the availability ratios of business computing platforms. However, it is not intended to provide a comprehensive description of all aspects of numerous continuous computing technologies that are listed in the book. This is because of the fact that each continuous computing technology described in the book is itself a topic for one or many books. That is the reason why the book is not intended to provide the reader with enough specific and detailed technological knowledge on each continuous computing technology to make them continuous computing and business continuity experts on that particular technology.

What makes this book different when compared to other books is in the following aspects: a) systemic approach that considers a set of continuous computing technologies for enhancing business continuity and b) in exploring the role of enterprise servers, server operating systems and serverware solutions for enhancing business continuity. The methodological approach used in the book is also distinctive. It is based on one of the main system's definitions provided by C.W. Churchman, one of the founders of the systems approach, operations research and systems science. His five-dimensions systemic view has been used as a framework for identifying the role of today's enterprise information systems and business computing in general in modern business.

The book consists of three parts and includes fourteen chapters. Each chapter includes a list of discusssion questions, and one or more case studies related to that chapter.

The first part of the book (Chapters I–IV) builds a foundation for understanding modern business, business computing, economics of downtime and business continuity. The second part (subsequent eight chapters, V–XII) describe the major continuous computing technologies that can be implemented for enhancing business continuity. The third part of the book contains two chapters: one dealing with business continuity management (Chapter XIII), and Chapter XIV that provides some relations between business continuity and business agility.

Chapter I introduces the main framework of business computing in Internet era. It has been evident that businesses today, more than ever, are faced with tremendous competition in a rapidly changing environment. Companies are operating on highly competitive markets that have become global, more dynamic and customer-oriented. Customers are more powerful and ask for customized products and services, while governments issue more and more compliance regulations. In today's e-business and e-economy world, in many cases the whole business is IT-dependent and data-driven. Therefore, such businesses need to be able to continuously run their mission critical applications. This implies that data operations activities and operations such as backup, update, upgrade, and hardware maintenance have be done without bringing the system down. Businesses employ information technologies in order to provide responses to business pressures and business risks, by enhancing productivity levels, reducing costs and improving the quality of products and services. In this chapter, the following concepts are introduced: business pressures and IT-based responses, business technology, business risks.

Chapter II introduces the terms "downtime" and "uptime" and their importance in modern business. The concept of the "economics of downtime" is explained as well, having in mind the fact that in modern business, even a few minutes of system downtime may cause thousands or even millions in lost revenues. In addition, such situations may result in bad decisions, unsatisfied customers, broken image of the company. Simply put, when mission-critical applications are considered, system downtime (both planned and unplanned) should be avoided or minimized. This fact emphasizes the need for system's reliability, availability and scalability.

The implications of downtime can be expressed in financial terms and easily bound to a company's economic results. Therefore, the terms such as "economics of availability," "economics of uptime/downtime" have become topics of interests in the field of the economics of enterprise information systems. Different types of businesses, different business functions and accompanying applications, require different levels of availability. Today, it is possible to measure or estimate losses in financial terms of each hour, even minute of downtime. These losses vary depending on the type of business (e.g., online banking systems, call centers, airline reservation systems, point-of-sale systems, dispatching systems, online shops, e-mail servers, etc.).

Chapter III defines the main framework for the book. The systems approach defined by C. W. Churchman (1968), one of the founders of operations research and systems approach, is used as a main methodological framework. Several dimensions of business continuity, continuous computing are defined by using Churchman's systemic model that contains five dimensions: objectives, environment, resources, components, and management. An attempt was made to apply Churchman's concept of systems approach to developing a framework for implementation of continuous computing technologies for enhancing business continuity.

By following Churchman's systemic model, the objective of a continuous computing platform in an organization are identified as achieving the business continuity or business resilience. In other words, this means the following: continuous data processing, continuous data access and delivery, multi-platform data access, on-time IT-services and better decisions through better data access. The system's measures of performances are defined in the form of several continuous computing attributes such as scalability, reliability, availability, fault-tolerance, disaster tolerance, automatic failover. The model is re-shaped into "the onion model" of high availability information architecture.

Business continuity relies on several continuous computing technologies that provide an efficient operating environment for continuous computing. Implementation of continuous computing technologies provides a platform for "keeping business in business" since business-critical applications are installed on enterprise servers, run by server operating systems that include serverware components, backed-up by data storage systems and supported by several fault-tolerant and disaster-tolerant technologies.

The term "high availability" is associated with high system/application uptime which is measured in terms of "nines." The more nines in a number that represents availability ratio of a specific platform, the higher level of availability is provided by that operating platfom. In addition to the term "availability," two additional dimensions of server operating platform are used as well: reliability and scalability.

Chapter IV identifies the main information architectures that are used in designing and implementing of enterprise information systems and business computing in general.

These systems are designed, developed and implemented by using several approaches and methodologies. No matter which information system development methodology is used, business information system comprises several information technologies such as servers, desktop computers, portable/mobile computing devices, systems software, application software, data communication technologies, computer networks, and so forth. Information systems employ several profiles of IT specialists including those who are dealing with business continuity.

Contemporary business computing is mainly based on a client/server architecture or one of its several modifications such as "Thin" or "Thick" c/s, two-tier c/s, three-tier, "n-tier client-server," while several types of old-style mainframe-based architectures still exist. Client-server architectures consist of servers and clients (desktop and portable computers) with applications being installed and running on server computers. There are also specific types of servers still named mainframe computers (e.g., IBM's mainframes, Hitachi's mainframes, Amdal's mainframes), but they are installed, implemented and used within client-server architecture and without dumb terminals.

Recently introduced new computing paradigms and models such as Web-enabled legacy systems, utility or on-demand computing, software-as-a-service (SaaS), Web-based software agents and services, subscription computing, grid computing, clustering, and ubiquitous or pervasive computing use the combination of the previous configurations and newly developed technologies.

Chapter V describes server configurations or enterprise servers that play crucial role in modern computing environments especially from business continuity and business agility perspectives. Servers are identified as integrated operating environments consisting of server hardware, server operating system (SOS), server applications, and server-based utilities called serverware. Servers are expected to provide such an operating environment that must meet much more rigorous requirements than a standard desktop operating system can provide. Such platforms are of special interest for businesses that require "always-on" or "online-all-the-time" computing environments. Therefore, server operating systems that provide zero-downtime or 100% uptime or some solution which is "near it" are of extreme importance for such businesses.

Purchasing a server is not a simple task, even when it is done for small business and even in a case when a high availability is not critical requirement. It happens to be a strategic decision having in mind all kinds of the factors including: processor type and vendor, operating system, commercial versus open-source dilema, and so forth. The selection of a server or server configuration is explained in more details having in mind the server's business continuity perspective consisting of the measures of performances such as availability, reliability, and scalability. A framework consisting of several questions and suggested options has been defined.

In **Chapter VI**, server operating systems are explained from the business continuity perspective. Modern server operating systems are expected to provide a set of features and functions that are critical in achieving business continuance. These features and functions usually come bundled (pre-installed) together with core operating system. A "built-in support" includes a number of features, functions or business continuity drivers that aim at enhancing the performances of continuous computing. In addition to standardcore operating system features that come within the core server operating system, a new approach in developing server operating environments for running business critical applications brings several enhancements called "serverware." Some of these applications come in the form of pre-installed or pre-integrated software "bundles" while some others are operating system—independent but very close to that specific SOS platform. As a result, both IT-vendors and IT-specialists have introduced newbroader term called "server operating environment" or "server operating platform."

A conceptual model to illustrate the role of server operating system and server operating platforms in the design of an information system for continuous computing infrastructure is presented in this chapter.

Chapter VII explores advanced server technologies for business continuity such as: fault tolerance and disaster tolerance technologies, fault-tolerant servers, server virtualization technology, server management software, and so forth. Server configurations may include several types of additional hardware and software features that may enhance availability ratios. These technologies include: SMP/Clustering, support for 64-bit computing, support for storage scalability, online reconfiguration, bundled servers, reloadable kernel and online upgrade features, crash-handling technologies, workload management.

Fault-tolerant servers are such servers that are able to continue to operate properly even when one or more faults within their hardware components occur. This feature helps in achieving higher levels of application availability. Such configurations called fault-tolerant servers differ from traditional clustering systems in which a specific failure (hardware failure, communication failure, system software failure, application software failure) on one server causes moving (transferring) the partial or the whole application processing to a second server within a cluster configuration.

Standard server configurations usually include redundant components such as: hot-swappable power supplies, ECC (error-correcting code) memory units, hot-swappable disk units, redundant processor components that perform the processing instructions in lockstep, while self-checking technology can detect and isolate errors at the component level. Server virtualization technology is explained in Chapter VII.

Chapter VIII deals with the selection of the server operating platform for business continuity. It identifies first the main attributes of server operating systems that are of interests from business continuity perspective. As many as 22 attributes or selection criteria are identified and short explanation was given for each of them. This list include criteria such as: TCO, multiplatform support, multiprocessing support, support for 64-bit processing, support for VLM (very large memory) and VLDB (very large data base) concepts and technologies, support for fault-tolerance and disaster tolerance, support for virtualization, integrated system management features, patch management, applications availability and integratibility, application development tools (integrated suites) availability for a specific server operating system platform, DBMS support, availability of enterprise resource planning (ERP) suites, availability of system integration tools (middleware support), support for file/print services, support for Internet, communication, networking, security protocols, support for application-programming protocols, availability of serverware products (messaging servers, Web servers, etc.), PC-client and mobile/portable support (PC-X, CIFS, PC-NFS support, and WAP support), availability of specialists (system administrators) for a specific platform, GUI and Web-based interface, and Viability of OS vendor.

In addition, this chapter presents some empirical studies on the performances of most widely used server operating systems such as several UNIX versions, several Linux flavors, Windows Server versions, some proprietary server operating systems such as OpenVMS, OS/390, and so forth.

Chapter IX explains the roles of system administration and system administrator in enhancing availability ratios of server operating platforms. Core system administration techniques on HP-UX operating systems are explained as well as advanced system administration tools, routines and features that are important in enhancing server's availability ratios.

This issue is very important in business continuity because super-user account is one of the most exploited vulnerabilities on IT platforms. This so-called "root" account or "super-user" (su) on UNIX/Linux servers and System Administrator on Windows servers posses all permissions and unrestricted access to all the files. Should the root account fall into the wrong hands, the security of the whole server configuration becomes compromised.

In addition to most commonly used system administration utilities, some additional and more advanced technologies, tools, routines and utilities that can be used in order to ensure higher levels of availability are explained on HP-UX as an example of server operating system.

As continuous computing and business continuity become more and more important in modern business, a number of new IT-professions have been introduced. It has become evident that employing only traditional system and network administrators is not enough for ensuring a comprehensive business continuity solution on enterprise-wide platform. Therefore, businesses that tend to implement a comprehensive business continuity solution seek for specialists such as Business Continuity Manager, Enterprise Business Continuity Manager, Director of Business Continuity Program, Business Resilience Architect, Business Continuity Analyst, Business Analyst for Business Continuity Program, Business Continuity Specialist, Business Continuity Administrator, Disaster Recovery Specialist, Emergency Preparedness Specialist, and so forth.

Chapter X describes major backup and recovery technologies that are used in enhancing business continuity. Several information technologies are used in order to store data in data centers in an efficient and effective way and protect it such that business does not suffer if data is lost. Primarily, this set comprises the following three main groups: data storage, data backup and data recovery technologies. Efficient and effective organizational data management represents one of the main prerequisites for assuring continuous computing and business continuity. Information technology provides a number of data storage and backup solutions for achieving continuous computing as a basis for business continuity. Technologies used for storing data (data storage), data backup and data recovery are of highest importance for business continuance.

Backup concept is presented and traditional tape-based and disk-based backup technologies are first explored. However, traditional backup is just the first stage toward an integrated storage solution that can enhance availability ratios and business continuity. Continuous computing requires even more comprehensive solutions than traditional tape-based backup. Having mission critical data on a tape in the form of traditional backup is much better than loosing data completely, however, recovering from hardware/software glitch or any kind of failure that caused interrupting data processing in the form of restoring data from a tape usually take a significant time, depending on the amount of data. Therefore, businesses are seeking higher levels of application availability and continuous computing need more sophisticated and, with regard to data backup and data recovery speed, much faster solutions.

In **Chapter XI** advanced data protection technologies such as RAID technology, direct access storage, storage area network (SAN), network attached storage (NAS), off-site data storage, data vaulting, data mirroring and data replication, snapshoot technology, clustering, continuous data protection are shortly explained.

From business continuity perspective, SAN technology provides several advantages such as: enhancing application and data availability, increasing storage capacity, allowing booting and rebooting servers from the SAN environment, enabling duplication features such as "business continuity Volumes," "data-volume cloning," and other real-time duplication technologies, reducing hardware costs. One of the most important characteristics of the NAS infrastructure from business continuity perspective is that data stored within NAS filers remains available even if server is down.

Mirroring and data replication are new technologies that emerged some 5–6 years ago. They are most frequently used as additional, second-level backup technologies, in addition to standard tape-based backups.

Data vaulting is an advanced data archiving technology that permits an automated backup of data to a remote location, archiving and recovery. Data transfer is made via high-speed communication lines that connect business' data centers with "data vaults" as purpose built vaults.

Cluster configurations have the abilitiy of adding computers and other devices and resources in order to increase the overall performances of the system. This is especially important from scalability perspective: the system can be scaled up by adding more hardware resources (processors, RAM), or by adding new computers. A most common use of clustering today is to load balance traffic on Web sites organized and managed by Internet service providers.

Chapter XII discusses computer network technologies within the context of business continuity as an integrated networking infrastructure is a prerequisite for any kind of e-business in a networked economy. It consists of several data communications and computer network technologies that are implemented in order to come up with appropriate data communications—computer network platform.

Network technologies make the third layer of an information system that enables continuous computing. They include technologies such as communication devices, communication media, communication protocols, network operating systems, networking protocols, data protection, and security standards. Network cards, modems, cable modems, DSL modems, routers, bridges, switches, hubs, firewalls, and so forth, are used to connect computers within local area networks, wide area networks, virtual private networks, campus networks, metropolitan networks.

Several communication media, guided and non-guided, such as leased lines, ISDN, ATM, frame-relay, wireless communications devices and protocols, satellite communications, and so forth, are used in order to establish several types of computer networks. These networks are in turn basis for networked enterprises, e-business, e-government and e-economy.

In modern Internet era, in what is called "networked business," the network security in an organization that operates in such a kind of environment represents a business continuity problem. The famous saying, "A chain is only as strong as its weakest link" applies as a rule in modern e-business. Network downtime caused by security attacks is costing large enterprises more than $30 million a year, according to a recent study by Infonetics Research. According to the study, "The Costs of Network Security Attacks: North America 2007," large organizations are losing an average of 2.2% of their annual revenue because of security attacks.

Chapter XIII describes business continuity management (BCM) that involves several measures (activities) that have to be planed in order to achieve higher levels of the system/application availability ratios.

Business continuity management consists of strategies, policies, activities and measures that business undertakes in order to survive when some sort of catastrophic event occurs. Even though it represents a managerial activity, at the end, business continuity in information age relies on high-ratios of application/data availability, reliability and scalability that should be provided by server operating environment. Therefore, business continuity management, being a part of the fifth dimension of Churchman's definition of the system, as defined in introduction, should be based on continuous efforts of integrating business continuity drivers into contemporary enterprise information systems.

Chapter XIV provides some insights on the relations between continuous computing, business continuity and business agility. Business agility is an enterprise-wide response to an increasingly competitive and changing business environment, based on: customer orientation and satisfaction, enriching the customer, reducing time-to-market, increasing profitability, mastering the uncertainty, improving efficiency and effectiveness by continuous process improvement, enterprise-wide collaboration, and improving information access. Continuous computing technologies are employed in order to achieve business continuity from the business operations perspective. In the same time, these technologies are the main prerequisite for business agility as agility relies on available information and "always-on" information system that generates it. Several IT-based agility drivers and their features that are critical for enhancing the enterprise-wide agility are identified.

At the end, the reader should keep in mind that, when continuous computing technologies and information technologies in general are considered, no text is current, be it a book, chapter in the book, or paper published in a scientific journal.

The dynamics of changes in IT industry makes the writing of IT-related texts some sort of "risky business" due to the fact that some sections become obsolete and/or out-of-date sometimes even prior to publication.

Nijaz Bajgoric

Acknowledgment

I would like to acknowledge the contributions made by the following individuals: I am grateful to Ms. Julia Mosemann, development editor, for her continuous help during the process of working on the book.

A further special note of thanks goes to managerial, acquisition, editorial, publishing and marketing teams at IGI Global who provided support and whose contributions throughout the whole process, from the book proposal to final publication, have been valuable.

- Dr. Mehdi Khosrow-Pour, Executive Editor
- Jan Travers, Vice President of Editorial
- Kristin M. Klinger, Director of Editorial Content
- Kristin Roth, Managing Development Editor
- Megan Childs, Marketing Communications Coordinator

I would like to thank three anonymous reviewers for their valuable comments and suggestions on my manuscript.

My special thanks go to Professor A. Gunasekaran, Chairperson of the Department of Decision and Information Sciences, Charlton College of Business, University of Massachusetts – Dartmouth for his foreword.

I am grateful to my wife Ermina and son Adnan for their understanding during this book project.

Nijaz Bajgoric

Chapter I
Business Computing in the Internet Era

CHAPTER OVERVIEW

The first chapter aims at defining a "big picture" of contemporary business and business computing. Business pressures and business risks are explored in order to identify the main factors affecting the functioning of modern organizations in the Internet era. IT-related risks are identified as well, showing some sort of paradox in today's e-business and e-economy era: information technologies are used in order to provide answers to several types of business pressures and reduce the risks, however, in the same time, IT can be a risk by itself, if not implemented and/or managed properly.

BUSINESS AND BUSINESS COMPUTING

This section introduces some basic facts on contemporary business, pressures that exist in business environment, and IT-based responses that organizations employ in order to respond to the ever-growing requirements. Today's business is described by using ten major attributes.

Contemporary businesses today, more than ever, are faced with tremendous competition in a rapidly changing environment. Companies are operating on highly competitive markets that have become global, more dynamic, and customer oriented. Customers are more powerful and ask for customized products and services, while governments issue more and more compliance regulations. Recently, IDC introduced the term of "the velocity of business change" and emphasized the fact that "business is changing at a greater velocity than ever" (Hammond, 2007).

Due to all changes and pressures, businesses are seeking new ways to respond to these requirements. Applying several information technologies in order to find appropriate responses is considered as one of most widely used approach. Organizations try to design modern information architectures and implement enterprise information systems (EIS) in order to fulfill these requirements and create competitive advantage (see Figure 1.1).

Within such a context, contemporary business can be described by the following ten major attributes:

1. Today's business is operating under ever growing set of **business pressures** coming from its environment: competitors, markets, customers, governmental regulatory requirements, and so forth. Many large corporations have product (services) development or manufacturing centers in many countries.
2. Business has to be **proactive,** rather than reactive, in finding the ways to recognize, predict and respond to incoming business pressures.
3. Businesses employ **information technologies in order to provide responses** to business pressures and business risks, by enhancing productivity levels, reducing costs, and improving the quality of products and services.
4. Businesses apply IT-based techniques and methods **in order to improve both efficiency and effectiveness** of decision making and business processes.

Figure 1.1. Modern business, its enterprise information system and relations with environment

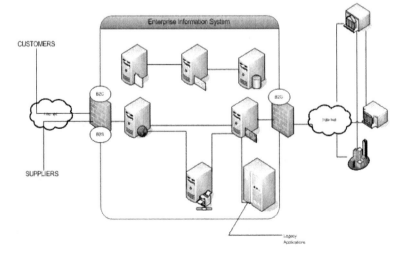

5. They seek for more efficient and more effective ways to **store, manage, analyze, and use data** in order to become and remain competitive.
6. They are constantly exposed to several types of **business risks.**
7. Business has to admit that application of information technologies bring specific **IT-related business risks** as well.
8. It has to integrate itself into a **networked business environment (networked economy, highly interconnected global economy)**, which forces businesses to have a well established data communications-networking platform and a platform for virtual business. The highly interconnected global business is operating at the lightning speed. Improved and well-integrated data and voice communication technologies during the last twenty years enabled businesses to establish customer services in "low-cost" and "Native-English speaking" countries.
9. It has to be **resilient (continuous)** and operational on "always-on" basis: 24 hours a day, 7 days a week, 365 days a year. This is particularly important for multinational companies because theier customers, suppliers, partners, employees, are located in many different time zones. Business critical applications such as enterprise resource planning (ERP), customer relationships management (CRM), supply chain management (SCM), e-commerce applications, financial applications and services, call centers, Web servers, and e-mail servers must be up at all times. The leading multinational companies seek for highly available, reliable and scalable operating environments because their customers, suppliers, employees, are located in many different time zones. Their mission-critical e-business applications such as ERP, CRM, and SCM must be up at all times.
10. Finally, modern business has to be **agile, adaptive and responsive** in increasingly competitive and changing business environment.

In the past, information technologies were used within traditional computer centers organized as "behind-the-scenes" organizational units for performing transaction-processing operations. However, in today's e-business and e-economy world, in many cases **the whole business is IT-dependent and data-driven.** Businesses need to be able to continuously run their mission critical applications. This implies that data operations activities and operations such as backup, update, upgrade, and hardware maintenance must be done without bringing the system down.

Modern business seeks for such a kind of IT platform, which will provide:

•   A highly reliable, available and scalable operating platform designed and implemented for high availability, reliability, and scalability
•   Integrated enterprise applications designed for high availability, reliability, and scalability

- Redundant hardware and redundant networking capabilities
- Fault tolerant technologies
- Data replication capabilities
- Disaster resilient technologies
- Remote system administration
- Remote diagnostics
- More secure environment with respect to user authentication, intrusion detection, secure transactions.

Business computing supported by the concepts and technologies of enterprise information systems such as enterprise resource planning, supply chain management, customer relationship management, electronic commerce (EC), and business intelligence (BI) has evolved into an organizational engine that drives business and provides a powerful source for competitive advantage. Modern business computing must be continuous in order to provide an operating platform for business continuance.

BUSINESS TECHNOLOGY

Business Technology represents a new term coined recently by Forrester. This term implies two important facts: IT risks are business risks, and IT opportunities and now business opportunities. An IT versus BT framework is provided.

New buzzword coined recently by Forrester analysts (Forrester, 2007) namely "business technology" (Figure 1.2) represents one of the major shifts in the way people think about computers in IT history. Business technology is based on two key ideas:

a. IT risks are business risks, and
b. IT opportunities are now business opportunities.

Forrester predicts that "The IT-to-BT" change will produce markedly different approaches to managing technology (Figure 1.2 and 1.3). Business technology management will grow to span multiple organizations embracing:

- **Technology management beyond the technology department.** BT capabilities—from collaboration, to workflow, to content management—will increasingly be acquired as business services driven by business users and not just by traditional tech staffers

Figure 1.2. From IT towards BT—the BT tipping point (Source: addapted from Forrester Report, 2007)

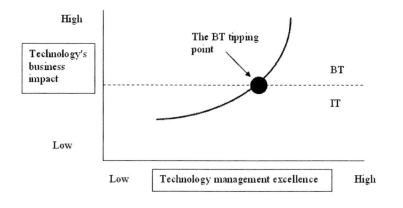

- **Technology governance beyond the steering committee.** IT-business alignment will be replaced by continuous BT scrutiny by top management looking for opportunities—better and smarter ways to use technology to grow earnings per share—the same way top execs think about sales, R&D, and manufacturing strategies.
- **Technology language beyond geek speak.** Business executives will speak easily about BT initiatives as contributions to profit, customer benefits, or revenue. Techno-acronyms like SOA (service-oriented architecture) and SaaS (software as a service) that alienate the very people technology purportedly serves—will be submerged in the BT-world as an MBA-level business expertise permeates the management ranks of the BT management department.

To be truly competitive contemporary business must be continuous and agile (adaptive, responsive). It needs an information system that enables both continuous computing and agile data access. The term of "Business Continuance" (Business ContinuityBC) has been introduced in order to emphasize the ability of a business to continue with its operations even if some sort of disaster on its computing resources occurs. In the same time, business has to be agile in order to cope with increasing complexity in its environment.

Figure 1.3. IT versus BT framework (Source: Adapted from Forrester Report, 2007)

Technology Management	IT	BT
Organizations - across the enterprise	• The IT organization does all technology management • IT is viewed as cost • IT is risk averse • IT is focused on delivery	• The technology department persists • BT is an agent of change • But technology management spans the firm • BT is essential to business • BT success is measured only by business results
Use of technology	• Identified by IT • Deployed as projects • Configured by IT	• Shared and cared for by all business users • Deployed as needed
Industry	Marketed by feature	Marketed by business outcome

BUSINESS PRESSURES AND ORGANIZATIONAL IT-BASED RESPONSES

Business pressures and organizational responses are briefly introduced, as defined by Turban, Rainer, and Potter (2005). However, in today's e-business environment that is usually called "e-economy," additional requirements need to be added as well, the ones that relate to so-called "business resilience," "business continuance," or "always-on business." Today's business has to be "resilient" or "always-on" with an emphasis on continuous, always-on and uninterruptible computing support and data availability.

Turban, Rainer, and Potter (2005) defined a framework for so-called business pressures and IT-based organizational responses.

Market Pressures include:

- *The global economy and strong competition*
- *The changing nature of the workforce*
- *Powerful customers*

Technology Pressures consist of:

- Technological Innovation and Obsolescence
- Information Overload

Societal Pressures comprise:

- Social responsibility
- Government regulation and deregulation
- Spending for social programs
- Protection against terrorist attacks
- Ethical issues

Turban, Rainer, and Potter (2005) defined a number of IT-based responses, technologies and solutions, that can be used and implemented by an organization in order to cope with business pressures coming from its environment:

- Establishing Strategic Systems and Business Alliances in the forms of ERP, SCM, and Electronic Commerce systems
- Customer Focus based on the concept of mass customization
- Continuous Improvement Efforts based on Just-In-Time (JIT) and Total Quality Management (TQM) approaches
- Business Process Reengineering
- Empowering Employees, Fostering Collaborative Work, establishing Team-based Structure

Information and communication technologies are implemented within business information systems. Major capabilities of information systems, as defined by Turban, Rainer, and Potter (2005) are as follows:

- Perform high-speed, high-volume, numerical computation.
- Provide fast, accurate, and inexpensive communication within and between organizations.
- Automate both semiautomatic business processes and manual tasks.
- Store huge amounts of information in an easy-to-access, yet small space.
- Allow quick and inexpensive access to vast amount of information, world-wide.
- Facilitate the interpretation of vast amounts of data.
- Enable communication and collaboration anywhere, any time.
- Increase the effectiveness and efficiency of people working in groups in one place or in several locations, anywhere.
- Facilitate work in hazardous environment.

However, in today's e-business environment that is usually called "e-economy," additional requirements need to be added as well, the ones which relate to so-called "business resilience," "business continuance," or "always-on business" (Figure 1.4).

Today's business has to be "resilient" or "always-on" with an emphasis on continuous, always-on and uninterruptible computing support and data availability. The main prerequisite for such a kind of business is an information system or an integrated IT platform, which operates on "always-on" basis or which is characterized by a high availability ratio.

In his book "Planning for Business Resilience" (IBM & Likeview Technologies, February 2007) Bill Hammond provides a framework for an Information Availability Continuum to Business Continuity."

Different levels of the business continuity continuum are defined according to two major dimensions: a) level of enterprise protection and b) functionality—cost-recovery time objective. These BC levels include the following capabilities: Disaster Recovery, High Availability, Continuous Operations and Continuous Availability. The lower recovery time (days–hours–minutes–seconds–continuous) the higher level of enterprise protection is achieved.

Turban, Rainer, and Potter (2005) defined the traditional and new (additional) major IS-functions in the forms of:

a.   Traditional major IS functions:
   •   Managing systems development and systems project management
   •   Managing computer operations, including the computer center

Figure 1.4. Business resilience: An Internet era's requirement and business pressure

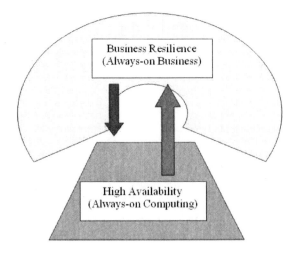

- Staffing, training, and developing IS skills
- Providing technical services

b. New (additional) major IS functions are identified as follows:
- Initiating and designing specific strategic information systems
- Infrastructure planning, development, and control
- Incorporating the Internet and electronic commerce into the business
- Managing system integration including the Internet, intranets, and extranets
- Educating the non-IS managers about IT
- Educating the IS staff about the business
- Supporting end-user computing
- Partnering with the executive level that runs the business
- Actively participating in business processes reengineering
- Proactively using business and technical knowledge to the line with innovative ideas about IT
- Creating business alliances with vendors and IS departments in other organizations

However, this list of "additional" major IS functions as defined by Turban, Rainer, and Potter (2005) needs to be "updated" or "upgraded" by adding a function that can be identified as "business continuance" or "business resiliance." This function should provide a continuous computing platform for business continuity or business resiliance. Such a function must include the following IS capabilities:

- Planning, managing and administering business continuity
- Assuring a platform for "keeping business in business"
- Integrated business continuity drivers into enterprise information system
- Integrated information management into organizational management
- Ensuring business continuity compliances.

BUSINESS RISKS IN INTERNET ERA

Today's business is bound to its information system and dependent on information technology. In addition to standard business risks, the dependence on IT platforms produces the IT-based business risks as well. The IT-related threats that may cause system unavailability are identified and briefly explained. Identifying the IT-related threats has become an important part of managing information resources in an organization. Moreover, it has to be considered as a standard threat that may cause problems to a business just like any other threat (physical, commercial, competition, etc.).

In today's business, information technology plays a critical role in almost every organization. Therefore so-called "mission-critical" applications or "business-critical" applications have become a standard—core IT subsystem in virtually every organization. The attribute "Business-Critical" implies the importance of these applications for "keeping business in business." These applications are implemented in several ways depending on the type of information architecture (legacy—mainframe, thick client-server, thin client-server).

Information technologies, particularly during the last decade, after introducing Internet and Web technologies, have opened new opportunities for businesses in their efforts to:

- cope with increasing competition
- reduce the costs of doing business
- increase the profits
- improve the quality of products and services
- improve relations with customers
- ease data access

In general, information technologies are used to enhance both efficiency and effectiveness of a business. IT plays crucial role in both "Doing the Things Right" and "Doing the Right Things" as Peter Drucker defined the terms of "efficiency" and "effectiveness."

However, at the same time, organizations may face several situations in which their business may suffer due to some IT-related problems, such as:

- Unavailable data—a situation when managers, employees, customers, and so forth, are unable to access data, for any reason.
- Lost data in the form of data exposed to competition and unauthorized usage.
- Stolen or lost computers, including some devices in separate form such as tapes. This may result in the forms of a stolen/lost computer/device as a financial asset, and what is more important, lost data on it.
- Hardware error on any computer component.
- Lost Internet connection or broken LAN/WAN line.
- Destroyed computers due to any type of disaster: destroyed computer(s) as an asset and lost data stored on them.
- Hackers' activities over the Net.

Recent IT Risk Management Report (Schmidt, 2007), examined the IT risks based on interviews with more than 500 IT executives and professionals worldwide. According to this report:

- 62% of organizations expect a regulatory breach and major information loss in the next five years.
- 66% of organizations perceive high/critical operational risk in finance and administration.
- 61% of organizations are not highly effective at governance, compliance, and continuous improvement.
- 24% of IT staff time is devoted to addressing business application performance delays.

Pearlson and Saunders (2006) argue that when information systems are chosen as the tool to outpace the firm's competitors (within the framework of Michael Porter's "Five Competitive Forces" model), executives should be aware of some additional risks that include the following:

- Awaking a sleeping giant. A firm can implement IS to gain competitive advantage, only to find that it nudged a larger competitor with deeper pockets into implementing an IS with even better features.
- Demonstrating bad timing. Sometimes customers are not ready to use the technology designed to gain strategic advantage.
- Implementing IS poorly.
- Failing to deliver what users want. Systems that do not meet the needs of the firm's target market are likely to fail.
- Running afoul of the law. Using IS strategically may promote litigation if the IS results in the violation of laws or regulations.

In addition, serious natural disasters such as floods, fires, storms, earthquakes, and terrorist attacks may completely paralyze the whole business system by shutting down information processing facilities and/or data communication lines, in some cases the whole enterprise-wide information infrastructures.

During the spring of 2006, Continuity Central (2006) conducted a detailed survey into business continuity practices across the world (Figure 1.5).

Respondents were asked to consider application downtime and to rank various causes of unscheduled application downtime, based on which would have the greatest impact on their organization's ability to function. The overall results show that general network and IT failures are considered of more importance than external events, such as natural disasters and terrorism. However, according to this report,

Figure 1.5. Application downtime causes: More–less impact (Source: adapted from Continuity Central, 2006)

Rank these causes of unscheduled application downtime based on which would have the greatest impact on your organization's ability to function	More impact	Less impact
Application Failure	46%	1%
OS Failure	33%	2%
Hardware Failure	36%	3%
Network Outage	53%	1%
Power Outage	38%	5%
Natural Disaster	32%	13%
Denial of Service Attack	21%	16%
Terrorism	32%	23%

North American organizations seem to be more concerned about external factors than their European counterparts, especially when it comes to terrorism and the impacts of natural disasters.

According to this report, for the services which had been ranked as important to protect in business continuity plans, respondents were asked how long these services could be unavailable before the downtime becomes a potentially fatal issue for their organization. For many respondents downtime would become a critical problem very quickly, with 32% of all respondents saying that just four hours downtime, or less, could be fatal for their organization.

Data may be unavailable due to several reasons. However, in all circumstances of data unavailability, if necessary peace of data is missing, decision cannot be made, prospective customer cannot access data about a specific product, services

Figure 1.6. Application downtime—Business criticality (Source: adapted from Continuity Central, 2006)

How long could your most important services be unavailable before the downtime becomes a potentially fatal issue for your organization?	Response percent
Less than 4 hours	32%
Between 4 and 8 hours	17.1%
Between 8 and 24 hours	23.8%
Between 1 day and 1 week	21%
Between 1 week and 1 month	4.4%
More that 1 month	0%

cannot be delivered, and so forth. If all data is lost, the company can go completely out of business.

In addition, if company data is lost for any reason, be it due to a stolen computer, lost manager's notebook, error on backup tape, and so forth, not only company may suffer but its competition can misuse the data. Schmidt (2007) lists four main types of IT risk that organizations today must address:

- **Security** - the risk that internal or external threats may result in unauthorized access to information. This includes such things as data leakage, data privacy, fraud, and endpoint security. It includes broad external threats, such as viruses, as well as more targeted attacks upon specific applications, specific users and specific information—attacks to steal money and to attack the systems that your people are relying on every day.
- **Availability** - the risk that information might be inaccessible due to unplanned system outages. You have a responsibility to customers, employees, and stake-holders to keep your business running. As a result, you need to reduce the risk of application or data loss or data corruption. And, in case of a disaster, you need to be able to recover in the times required by your business.
- **Performance** - the risk that information might be inaccessible due to scalability limitations or throughput bottlenecks. Your business needs to accommodate volume and performance requirements—even during peak times. As a result, you need to proactively identify performance issues before end users or applications are impacted. And, to minimize costs, you need to optimize resources and avoid unnecessary hardware expenditures.
- **Compliance** - the risk of violating regulatory mandates or failing to meet internal policy requirements. Your business needs to comply with federal and state regulations, such as Sarbanes-Oxley, ISO 9000, or the British Standards Institute PAS56 framework. You need to retain information and provide a highly efficient search and discovery engine to find content in emails as required. In addition, you need to ensure that your employees are meeting your own internal best practices and policies to keep your business operating in the most efficient manner.

The IT-related problems may bring some very tangible business risks, such as:

- Revenue loss
- Failures in products and/or services
- Product recalls
- Loss of customers

- Damaged reputation
- Lower end-user productivity
- Better position for competitor
- Unpredicted expenses.

As Adams (2007) pointed out "Risk Management—It's Not Rocket Science…It's Much More Complicated."

Identifying the IT-related threats has become an important part of managing information resources in an organization. Moreover, it has to be considered as a standard threat that may cause problems to a business just like any other threat (physical, commercial, competition, etc.).

The IT-related threats that may cause system unavailability can be classified into the following major categories:

- **Physical threats** that result from any kind of physical damage/theft on IT centers, servers, client computers, mobile devices, communication-networking devices, and so forth. For instance, someone can break into the computer center and steal any or all of the servers. In addition, an employee can steal a computer. Physical threat is also a situation when an unauthorised person enters server room and intentionally press the reset or on-off button on it.
- **Natural threats** such as: fire, lightning strike, flood, earthquake, hurricane, tornado, snow, wind, and so forth.
- **Logical threats** can be of different forms such as: corrupted file, broken proces or program, file system corruption, crashed operating system, hackers' breaches from Internet, and so forth.
- **Technical glitches and/or hardware component failures** that may occur either on any computer component/device or the component within the IT infrastructure (memory chips, fans, system mainboards, hard disks, disk controllers, tapes and tape drivers, network cards, switches, routers, communication lines, power supplies, etc.). These hazards include also the following: power outage, electrical shortage, gas leak, sevage failure, and so forth. If, for instance, a hard disk crashes, the data may or may not be recoverable. Even if data is recoverable, the cost to recover it from the crashed hard disk or backup tape varies inversely with how quickly we want to get that data back to our server. Also, the whole IT infrastructure of a business can go "off" in case of the connection problem with its ISP or its inadequate network-bandwith capacity.
- **Application software defects, failures, and crashes** (bugs in programs, non-integrated or badly integrated applications, user interventions on desktop computers, file corruptions).

- **WAN/Internet-specific** infrastructure problems such as problems with Domain Controllers, Active Directory, DNS servers (Domain Name Services).
- **Human errors,** accidental or intentional file deletion, unskilled operations, intentional hazardous activities including sabotage, strikes, epidemic situations, vandalism. Accidental or even in some cases intentional deleting (removing) files by so-called super users or system administrators can make operating system out of function. For example, just by using a very simple "delete" command on server systems, system administrator can remove all the files on that system, including programs, program files, data, user info, and so forth. These two characters (rm) can destroy the whole business.
- **Loss of key IT personal or leaving of expert** staff due to several reasons, for instance, managerial faults or bad decisions on IT-staffing policy, both on IT manager level (CIO) and general manager (CEO). For instance, neglecting the request for higher salary of a system administrator from CIO/CEO side can lead to a situation when admin guy (UNIX, Linux, or Windows Server system administrator) decides to leave organization over night with all admin/root passwords in his head. In addition, managerial bad decisions in staffing, insufficient training, bad backup policies, lack of disaster recovery plan. In general, disgruntled IT specialists can always be found in any business.

These threats are shown in Figure 1.7.

For instance, an accidental or in some cases intentional deleting (removing) files by a super user or system administrator on any server platform. Just by using a very simple command **rm** on UNIX or Linux server systems on the root level:

 # rm *.*

system administrator (a person holding "su" or "root" password) can remove all the files on that system, including programs, program files, data, user info, and so forth.

Super-user or sys-admin account is said to be one of the most exploited vulnerabilities on server systems because of the unlimited power of system administrator's commands. This so-called "root" account or super-user (su) on UNIX/Linux servers and System Administrator on Windows server machines has all kind of permissions including unrestricted access to all the files.

Several disastrous events in recent years have made it clear that businesses that do not have effective business continuity plans or programs place themselves in a very vulnerable position. These catastrophic events may completely paralyze a business by shutting down fully or even partially their IT-infrastructures. A disaster or disastrous event is an event that can cause several types of IT-infrastructure

Figure 1.7. Major threats (glitches, faults, failures, disasters) that may cause problems on IT infrastructure

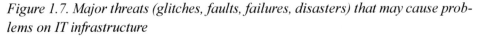
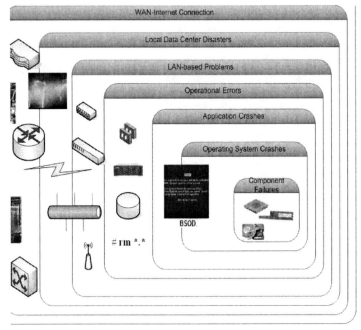

malfunctions as a result of one or more inside-the-system glitches or failures or outside-the-system catastrophic events.

The failures can be single-point or multi-point failures that can occur simultaneously or nearly simultaneously. The system-outside disaster can occur as the result of the occurrence of a natural disaster. In that sense, fault-tolerant and disaster-tolerant IT-based and data communications systems refer to the ability of these systems to maintain the pre-failure or pre-disaster functionality throughout the occurrence of a failure or disaster. Addressing these problems should be based on a systemic approach having in mind the costs of downtime that failures of computer/communication hardware and software, operating systems, database management systems, application software in terms of lost revenues, lost customers, worse image, and so forth. this is particularly important for business-critical applications.

Because downtime affects businesses differently, it is important to select the proper response for the organization. The following table (Figure 1.8) lists different impact levels (based on severity), including the impact each level has on the organization.

Lewis, Watson, and Pickren (2003) noted that, "…some risks faced by the firm are either so remote, such as data center destruction by meteorite impact, or so

Figure 1.8. Downtime impact levels and corresponding effect on business (Source: adapted from Microsoft White Paper, 2005)

Impact level	Description	Business impact
Impact level 1	Minor impact on business results.	Low: Minimal availability requirement.
Impact level 2	Disrupts the normal business processes. Minimal loss of revenue, low recovery cost.	Low: Prevention of business loss improves return on investment and profitability.
Impact level 3	Substantial revenue is lost; some is recoverable.	Medium: Prevention of business loss improves return on investment and profitability.
Impact level 4	Significant impact on core business activities. Affects medium-term results.	High: Prevention of lost revenue improves business results. Business risk outweighs the cost of the solution.
Impact level 5	Strong impact on core business activities. Affects medium-term results. Company's survival may be at risk.	High: Business risk outweighs the cost of the solution.
Impact level 6	Very strong impact on core business activities. Immediate threat to the company's survival.	Extreme: Management of the business risk is essential. Cost of the solution is secondary.

routinely small, such as a corrupted floppy disk, that they are minor concerns to managers. Between these two extremes lie risks of sufficient probability and severity to impose significant threat and uncertainty." They pointed out that, "…the strategic design of information systems should include hardware, software, and network solutions that minimize the impact of IT disasters. The increasing need for uninterrupted information processing capability makes IT availability vital for corporate survival." They argue that managers use quantitative assessments of the level of severity associated with these events in order to achieve more efficient management the IT function.

CHAPTER SUMMARY

Faced with several requirements and pressures coming from their environment, businesses are seeking the ways in order to proactively respond. Applying information technologies in order to find appropriate responses represents one of most widely used approaches. Organizations try to apply information architectures and implement enterprise information systems in order to achieve competitive advantage. The first chapter introduced some basic terms such as business computing, business risks, business technology. The IT-related threats that may cause business disruption are briefly introduced.

REFERENCES

Adams. J. (2007). Risk Management: It's Not Rocket Science...It's Much More Complicated. *Risk Management*, May 2007, 54(5), ABI/INFORM Global, pp. 36-40.

Continuity Central (2006).Retrieved on April 2, 2008, from http://www.continuitycentral.com/feature0358.htm.

Forrester Report (May 7, 2007). Business Technology Defined: Technology Management Is Changing To Deliver Business Results by Laurie M. Orlov and Bobby Cameron with George F. Colony, Mike Gilpin, Craig Symons, Marc Cecere, and Alex Cullen

Hammond, B. (2007). Planning for Business Resilience, IBM and Likeview Technologies. *February 2007*

IDC Report, Business Process Agility: The Next ERP Imperative, March 2007.

Lewis, W., Watson, R., & Pickren, A. An Empirical Assessment of IT Disaster Risk. *Communication of ACM*, September 2003, pp. 201-206.

Microsoft White Paper (2005). Exchange Server 2003, Understanding Downtime, Retrieved on April 2, 2008 from http://technet.microsoft.com/en-us/library/aa998704.aspx.

Pearlson, K. E. & Saunders, C. S. (2006). Managing and Using Information Systems: A Strategic Approach. Wiley

Schmidt, T., (2007). Managing IT Risk. Retrieved on September 14, 2007, from http://www.ciostrategycenter.com/cmpwallstreettech/Res/res_strategies/managing_it_risk/index.html.

Turban, Rainer, & Potter (2005). Introduction to Information Technology, Wiley

REAL WORLD CASES: EXAMPLES OF IT-RELATED BUSINESS RISKS

(25 Terrifying Information Technology Horror Stories: Retrieved from http://www. cio.com/special-reports/horror/index)

1. **The Day the Beepers Died: Satellite Failure**. Galaxy 4 spins out of control! Indeed, on May 19, 1998, in what many consider the most widespread digital failure in history, the Galaxy 4 telecommunication satellite—which hosted paging services, television networks and financial services applications—conked out. A very intense flux of electrons may have caused failure of the attitude control systems and their backup. The outage pulled the rug out from under CIOs and IT managers dependent on beepers and similar devices for instant communications with employees and suppliers. Roughly 45 million pagers went beep-less until providers were able to find capacity on other satellites.

2. **Black Monday: New York Stock Exchange.** Better living through technology. Yes, that's what we're after. But in the "Black Monday" stock market crash on Oct. 19, 1987, technology made life much worse. The Dow Jones average fell by 508 points, or 22.6%. Normal market conditions had set off the downturn, but a Securities and Exchange Commission report later noted that computer-directed strategies used by institutional investors trading large volumes of stock accounted for up to 68% of New York Stock Exchange trades at times during the Black Monday debacle. The day ended with an hour-long panic sell-off.

3. **The Purloined Letters: PlusNet.** We've all lost an important e-mail message or two. A casual click of the delete button. A misconfigured office server. It happens. But, 700GB of e-mail? Gone for eternity? It happened. In 2006, British ISP PlusNet lost 700GB of customer e-mails forever. An engineer accidentally deleted the e-mails and then tried an old admin trick to retrieve them. The trick backfired, and instead made the mail irretrievable, despite PlusNet's efforts.

4. **Nightmare Before Christmas: Comair.** Since at least 1997, Comair knew it needed to replace a creaky old flight-crew management system. The options for new systems were rather raw and unproven. "Let's wait til something better comes along," they said. Here's where the foreshadowing creepy music begins. They kept waiting, postponing, nursing the legacy system along, and finally signed a deal to replace the whole thing in 2005. Too late. It gave up the ghost with a dramatic failure on Christmas Eve 2004. It brought down the entire airline, cancelling or delaying 3,900 flights and stranding nearly 200,000 passengers. The network crash cost Comair and its parent company,

Delta Air Lines, $20 million, damaged the airline's reputation and prompted an investigation by the Department of Transportation

5. **Terrorism: 9/11.** The all-too-real attacks on New York City's World Trade Center towers on September 11, 2001, horrified people across the globe. Thousands were slaughtered. Tens of thousands more were left jobless. When terrorists boarded airplanes on that day, their intention was not simply to kill people and destroy buildings; rather, the attacks were an assault on the American economy. Nowhere was their impact on IT systems felt more strongly than in New York City's financial district, specifically on Wall Street. IT executives from three multinational financial services firms located near ground zero in September 2001—American Express, Lehman Brothers, and Merrill Lynch—told CIO the lessons they learned about disaster recovery, about how their businesses reacted, and why they decided to stay or not to stay in lower Manhattan. "A CIO I worked for a long time ago used to say, 'You lose a whole data center every 10,000 years,' which was his excuse for not having disaster recovery, which was stupid then. …You have to assume it's more likely to happen now."
    — Glen Salow, then CIO of American Express

6. **All Systems Down: CareGroup Health.** CareGroup had developed a well-deserved reputation for being a leader in using information technology to drive improvements in health care. But in November 2002, CareGroup's flagship hospital—Beth Israel Deaconess—was driven back to the dark ages of paper-based patient records by a debilitating series of network crashes. Over five days, the IT department for Beth Israel would frantically try to track down the cause of the problem.

7. **ERP I: Exercise in Agony.** A $400 million investment in upgrading your supply chain systems should buy you a lot. Back in 2000, what it bought Nike was $100 million in lost sales, a 20% stock dip and an assortment of class-action lawsuits. These came thanks to a fumbled attempt to integrate ERP, supply chain planning and CRM into a single superstar system. The setback was a big black eye for one of the United States' premier corporations that lives on as a tale of woe and warning.

8. **ERP II: Sweet Misery.** Spend a dollar to lose a dollar. What? That is not the way information systems are supposed to work. But that was the early outcome of Hershey's 1999 attempt to create a snazzy new order-taking and distribution system. Problem was, it did not initially work—and it prevented Hershey from delivering $100 million in pre-Halloween toothrot. The poor suckers also caught it in the kisser when investors bailed on the stock—to the tune of an 8% drop—on the day former CEO Kenneth Wolf announced the system problem.

9. **ERP III: Sudden Death.** The ultimate cautionary tale for any IT manager about to pull the trigger on a new ERP implementation? FoxMeyer Drug. Following an SAP R/3 implementation in the mid- to late-1990s, the company's bankruptcy trustees filed a $500 million lawsuit in 1998 against SAP, and another $500 million suit against co-implementer Andersen Consulting, claiming the companies' software and installation efforts had contributed to the drug company's demise. "On June 23, 2004, SAP reached a settlement agreement with FoxMeyer pursuant to which SAP was required to pay a specified amount to FoxMeyer and to which all outstanding disputes and litigation were dismissed by order of the United States Bankruptcy Court for the District of Delaware dated August 30, 2004. SAP paid FoxMeyer the settlement amount on September 9, 2004." — Quote from 2004 SAP annual report.

10. **Storm of the Century: Katrina.** Wind-wracked shelters, waterlogged homes, soaked vehicles, drenched pets and haggard people. The public knows those scenes of Hurricane Katrina and sister Rita, which roared ashore along the United States' Gulf Coast in late summer 2005. Hidden just out of view, though, is the role IT played in both collapse and recovery. In the networked world, IT systems fall like dominoes. Executives with organizations based along the Gulf Coast give harrowing accounts of how they dealt with the Storm of the Century, and how they got their operations back up and running.

DISCUSSION QUESTIONS

1. Describe the major business pressures that modern business is coping with.
2. For a business, why is it more important to be proactive that reactive in finding ways to react to business pressures?
3. Information technologies are used in order to provide responses to business pressures. What are the most widely used organizational and managerial techniques and methods?
4. How information technology improve business processes? List some examples.
5. How to explain new IT-paradox: information technologies are used to reduce the uncertainty of a business, while in the same time, having all business data and business processes on vulnerable IT platforms poses a risk as well.
6. Explain the concept of "mission-critical" applications, what are these in your business?
7. Which term is the most appropriate one in explaining the role of IT in modern business: "business resilience," "always-on business," "continuous business?"

8. Explain the term "business technology."
9. Explain the term "keeping business in business."
10. Identify at least ten IT-related problems that might cause a situation in which business suffers.

Discussion Questions: Lessons Learned from Cases

1. What advantages does an ERP system bring to a business?
2. Using an organization with which you are familiar, describe the major pressures and your organization's responses.
3. Why do ERP horror stories exist?
4. When does implementing an ERP system make sense for a large company, when for a small business?
5. How to avoid wrong approach in ERP implementation?

Chapter II
Economics of Downtime

CHAPTER OVERVIEW

After introducing some basic facts on how today's businesses are faced with several types of business risks, the second chapter tends to explain one of the major problems that a contemporary business may face in regard to the impact of its computing infrastructure to business results. System downtime is briefly explained and the resulting "economics of downtime" is elaborated in order to demonstrate the direct financial impacts of the unavailability of so-called "business-critical applications" to business results.

DOWNTIME AND UPTIME

This section introduces basic terms of continuous computing and business continuity: downtime and uptime. It introduces the main framework for so-called "economics of downtime" by providing several empirical data on negative financial effects of system downtime.

A serious glitch on computer system, human error, or any kind of natural disaster (fire, flood, earthquake) can halt or shutdown company's application environment operated and supported by that computer system, in most cases enterprise server (servers). Such an event can cause partial or full unavailability of enterprise data and applications. When system is not operational for any reason, it is said to be down and the time in which it does not operate is called "downtime."

Downtime refers to a period of time or a percentage of timespan that a machine or system (usually a computer server) is offline or not functioning, usually as a result of either system failure (such as a crash) or routine maintenance (Downtime, Wikipedia). The opposite is uptime.

Even in the very beginning of the e-business era, more than a decade ago, Datamation (1995) emphasized how important the system downtime is. In August 1995, Datamation quoted the results of a survey of 400 large companies, which unveiled that, "…downtime costs a company $1400 per minute, on average. Based on these figures, 43 hours of downtime per year would cost $3.6 million. One hour of downtime per year amounts to $84,000 per year. "

Uptime is a measure of the time a computer system has been "up" and running. It is often used as a measure of computer operating system reliability and stability, in that this time represents the time a computer can be left unattended without crashing, or needing to be rebooted for many administrative or maintenance purposes. Long uptime can also indicate negligence as many critical updates require reboot on same operating systems (Downtime, Wikipedia).

In modern business, even a few minutes of system downtime may cause thousands or even millions in lost revenues. In addition, such situations may result in bad decisions, unsatisfied customers, broken image of the company. Simply put, when mission-critical applications are considered, system downtime (both planned and unplanned) should be avoided or minimized. This fact emphasizes the need for system's reliability, availability and scalability. IDC (2006) underscores the fact that a true high availability model expands the concept of availability beyond an infrastructure perspective in terms of system or servers.

There are many definitions for availability. Some consider availability of the data only, while others speak on applications availability or availability of the server or storage subsystem. Many "buzzwords" are in use, such as:

- high availability
- business continuity
- business continuance
- business resilience
- always-on computing
- 24x7x365 computing
- fault tolerant computing
- disaster tolerant computing
- disaster recovery
- disaster resiliency
- real-time computing
- zero latency enterprise, and so forth.

As said before, implications of downtime can be expressed in financial terms and easily bound to company's economic results. Therefore, the terms such as "economics of availability," "economics of uptime/downtime" have become topics of interests in the field of the economics of enterprise information systems. Different types of businesses, different business functions and accompanying applications, require different levels of availability. Today, it is possible to measure or estimate losses in financial terms of each hour, even minute of downtime. These losses vary depending on the type of business (e.g., online banking systems, call centres, airline reservation systems, point-of-sale systems, dispatching systems, online shops, e-mail servers, etc.).

According to Graham & Sherman (2003) each hour of downtime is estimated to cost an average company $44,000. Using that estimate, the cost to move from a level of 99.9% availability to 99.999% availability is far less than the estimated $435,600 reduction in downtime-related costs over a five-year life cycle. In a survey of 450 Fortune 1000 companies, Find/SVP found that the average hourly downtime cost is $82,500 (Barraza, 2002). As stated by Stanton (2005), "It can take less than 60 seconds for a company's reputation to be ruined and its business to be crippled. In just one minute a server failure or hacker can knock out vital applications and lead to a catastrophic series of events." According to the report unveiled by Adam Associates (Stanton, 2005), in the UK alone the annual cost of business interruption is estimated to be £3.9 billion. The average outage time following a fire is 28 days, 26 days for a theft and 10 for flood damage. IT failures take an average of 10 days to recover from, and even a power failure can take up to 24 hours.

Most frequently used measure of the availability is expressed in "number of nines." This number translates into the percentage of time that a given system is active and working properly. For instance, an operating platform with a 99.999% uptime is said to have "five nines" of availability, which in turn means up to five minutes of downtime a year. The following table (see Figure 2.1) correlates the number of nines to calendar time equivalents.

Figure 2.1. Acceptable uptime percentage and downtime relationship (Source: adapted from http://technet2.microsoft.com/windowsserver/WSS/en/library/965b2f19-4c88-4e85-af16-32531223aec71033.mspx?mfr=true, March 19, 2008)

Acceptable uptime percentage	Downtime per day	Downtime per month	Downtime per year
95	72.00 minutes	36 hours	18.26 days
99	14.40 minutes	7 hours	3.65 days
99.9	86.40 seconds	43 minutes	8.77 hours
99.99	8.64 seconds	4 minutes	52.60 minutes
99.999	0.86 seconds	26 seconds	5.26 minutes

Zero downtime means that the server was available all the time. For servers having downtime above 1% per year this can be regarded as unacceptable as this means a downtime of more than 3 days per year. A 2002 Standish Group study of downtime numbers (Graham & Sherman, 2003) found that the average mission-critical application had the following availability experience:

- 9% - greater than 99.99% (less than one hour down per month)
- 24% - 99.91% to 99.99% (one hour to less than nine hours)
- 67% - 99.9% or less (nine hours or greater).

Importance of available data varies by application with business-critical applications having higher levels of "data criticality." Therefore, these applications require recovery time expressed in minutes or even seconds, while some other applications may experience downtime in hours and recovery times in days.

In short, contemporary business has to be continuous from data availability perspective and agile with regard to data access. Therefore, system downtime is not an option in modern business since each hour, even minute, of downtime may generate negative financial effects. As stated by Barraza (2002), "...with worldwide buyers and sellers operating on a 24/7/365 basis, the need for building information systems that approach 100% uptime and data availability is more acute that ever. Simply put, the global economy runs on information. More importantly, it runs on available information." Major causes of system downtime are given as follows (Szelong, 2002).

System can go down due to the following reasons: a) planned—expected and b) unplanned—unexpected (undesired).

Planned shutdown operations comprise several administrative tasks or reasons for shutting application and/or operating system down. Shutting down a desktop computer in general does not cause major problems as it is performed by its user

Figure 2.2. Major causes of system downtime (Source: adapted from Szelong, 2002)

Major Causes of System Downtime (in order of frequency)
1, Software defects/failures
2. Planned administrative downtime
3. Operator error
4. Hardware outage/maintenance
5. Building/site disaster (fire)
6. Metropolitan disaster (storm, flood, etc.)

or desktop system administrator. That user is the only person who will be off with regard to his/her desktop activities during the desktop downtime. Single user may also experience unplanned shutdown operations for the reasons such as: applications and/or operating systems bugs, hardware components failures, and so forth.

Server side of the client-server model of the computing can also have both planned and unplanned downtime. Planned downtime on server side again includes administrative tasks on server, server operating system, application, LAN, and WAN networks. However, advances in information technologies allow several administrative operations on servers, both hardware and software interventions, even without halting the system down.

PLANNED AND UNPLANNED DOWNTIME

Two categories of downtime are briefly explained: planned and unplanned downtime as well as the costs of downtime. The principal risks of a breakdown in business continuity are: loss of revenue, loss of data, deterioration of brand, defection of customers, loss of shareholder value, and so forth.

Planned downtime is scheduled, usually duration-fixed downtime due to planned operations such as: regular data backups, hardware maintenance and upgrade, operating system upgrades and updates, application updates, periodic events such as different types of hardware and software testings, and so forth.

Unplanned downtime is unanticipated, duration-variable downtime of a computing-system due to several types of natural disasters, power outages, infrastructure failures, hardware or software failures, human errors, lack of proper skills, and so forth. Server which is running mission critical application can be halted (shutdown) if somebody trips over the power cable or cable connecting the server to the disk.

A study by Nielsen Media Research and NetRatings Inc. (Dembeck, 1999), which measured Web site usage of Yahoo and eBay indicated that the average time spent per person at Yahoo's auction site increased to 18 minutes Friday from seven minutes Thursday—the night eBay's site crashed. The number of people using Yahoo's site also skyrocketed to 135,000 Saturday from 62,000 Thursday. But the number of users fell to 90,000 Monday. Financial losses to eBay were estimated at $3 million to $5 million.

According to a survey provided by Gartner Dataquest (2003), the top three business risks from downtime continue to be:

- lost revenue,
- increased customer dissatisfaction, and
- decreased employee productivity.

This report unveiled that companies with more that 2500 employees experience approximately 135 minutes of downtime per month, while the acceptable amount of downtime for companies of this size is less than 5 minutes per month. Research results unveiled by META Group (Manning, 2004) indicate that IT system downtime costs American businesses $1 million an hour. MetaGroup estimated the average hourly revenue loss caused by downtime as follows (Vanston, 2004):

According to a recent survey made by AT&T/Economist Intelligence Unit (Ernest-Jones, 2005) the principal risks of a breakdown in business continuity are:

- Loss of revenue
- Loss of data
- Deterioration of brand
- Defection of customers
- Loss of shareholder value
- Higher insurance costs

Figure 2.3. Revenue loss caused by downtime (Source: adapted from Vanston, 2004)

Industry	Hourly revenue loss
Energy	$2,817,846
Telecommunications	$2,066,245
Utilities	$643,250
Manufacturing	$1,610,645
Financial	$1,495,134
Retails	$1,107,274

Figure 2.4. Industry downtime costs per minute (Source: adapted from Standish Group Report, 2001)

Application	Cost per minute
Call location	$27,000
Number portability	$14,000
Enterprise Resource Planning	$13,000
Supply Chain Management	$11,000
Electronic commerce	$10,000
Internet banking	$7,000
Universal personal services	$6,000
Customer service center	$3,700
ATM-POS-EFT	$3,500
Messaging	$1,000

In the same research (Manning, 2004), META Group estimates that by 2008, 45% of Global 2000 users will utilize two data centres to deliver continuous availability; of these, 25% will support real-time recovery. Through 2008, more than 50% of G2000 users will utilize a single "hardened" data centre augmented by third-party services to deliver traditional, cost-effective disaster recovery services (48 to 72-hour recovery).

Infonetics Research (Infonetics, 2006) found recently that medium businesses (101 to 1,000 employees) are losing an average of 1% of their annual revenue, or $867,000, to downtime.

The study says that companies experience an average of nearly 140 hours of downtime every year, with 56% of that caused by pure outages. Applications are the biggest source of downtime, accounting for roughly one-quarter, or $213,000 annually, split 65/35 between outages and degradations. Focusing on the source of application outages could save many organizations a significant amount of money, the report concludes.

Gartner (2003) lists five areas of loss that should be included in a calculation of downtime costs:

- **Revenue:** Direct loss, lost future revenues, compensatory payments, lost future revenue, billing losses, and investment losses.
- **Productivity:** Number of employees affected by downtime multiplied by the number of hours downtime burdened hourly rate.
- **Damaged Reputation:** Customers, suppliers, financial markets, banks, and business partners.
- **Financial Performance:** Revenue recognition, cash flow, lost discounts, payment guarantees, credit rating, and stock price.
- **Other Expenses:** Temporary employees, equipment rental, overtime costs, additional shipping costs, travel expenses, legal obligations.

There are several categories that represent the varieties of cost of downtime. It is also important because several types of cost of downtime stand for different problems in business. The categories of the cost and its involved are as follows:

Because of the fact that cost of downtime is a vital issue in business continuity, calculating the cost is also important and business world focus on this field.

An example of a downtime calculator, as a product of NetworksFirst can be found at: http://www.networksfirst.com/calculator/index.htm.

Another example is IBM's online business continuity self-assessment tool (http://www-935.ibm.com/services/us/bcrs/self-assessment) that can be used in order to identify potential gaps, data, and event threat areas. The tool provides information on IBM's technologies and solutions that relate to this problem.

Figure 2.5. Categories of cost and cost involved (Source: adapted from http://technet. microsoft.com/en-us/library/aa998704.aspx, March 19, 2008)

Category	Cost involved
Productivity	• Number of employees affected by loss of messaging functionality and other IT assets • Number of administrators needed to manage a site increases with frequency of downtime
Revenue	• Direct losses • Compensatory payments • Lost future revenues • Billing losses • Investment losses
Financial performance	• Revenue recognition • Cash flow • Lost discounts (A/P) • Payment guarantees • Credit rating • Stock price
Damaged reputation	• Customers • Suppliers • Financial markets • Banks • Business partners
Other expenses	• Temporary employees • Equipment rental • Overtime costs • Extra shipping costs • Travel expenses

IBM classifies all threats into the three categories (IBM, 2007):

- Business driven threats: how to manage addressing government and industry regulations, how to get prepared to mitigate risks to non-compliance, and so forth;
- Data driven threats: storing data backup without being compromised, data restoration process, back-up plun if the original backup is destroyed, data on-demand in audit situations, and so forth;

- Event driven threats: how to resolve the problems when employees cannot or will not come to work, when normal communications are not available, when normal commnications are limited, and so forth.

However, not every business must have high availability ratios such as 99.999% or even 99.99% for its mission-critical applications, it depends on the type of business. Therefore, an appropriate cost-benefits or return-on-investment analysis should be used before making decisions on increasing the levels of availability just because of the fact that the applications are mission-critical.

Hill (2006) suggests not to equate high availability with high value when mission-critical applications are considered. Infonetics Research (2005) has revealed results of their study of five large organizations in different vertical markets: finance, transportation and logistics, healthcare, manufacturing and retail (North American Companies). They proposed a metrics for revenues loss calculation and productivity loss calculation. With regard to specific enterprise applications, Aberdeen Group (2006) reported that, "...while 82% of companies are concerned about supply chain resiliency, just 11% are actively managing this risk. This action gap is one of the greatest weaknesses of current corporate global supply chain strategies; it threatens the continuity of a company's business and sets the stage for gross margin erosion due to under-managed supply chain uncertainty and risk."

Recent IDC report (2006) indicates that priorities and spending intentions are aligned around the central theme of improving application availability and recovery from different failure types on increasing numbers of applications and services. According to this report, it's not uncommon for availability and business continuity requirements to be published in a company's corporate goals. An emphasis is given also on a continued user productivity and connectivity, a platform in which the users remain seamlessly connected to critical applications and services. As stated by Michael Croy (Ybarra, 2006), "After Katrina, companies need a different paradigm. The heart of American business is now IT. Business continuity needs to be part of daily operations. It's not an IT issue, it's a business issue, it's a corporate governance issue."

Another research provided by the National Archives and Records Administration in Washington DC identified that "Ninety-three percent of companies that lost their data center for 10 days or more due to a disaster filed for bankruptcy within one year of the disaster (Schraeder, 2004). Fifty percent of businesses that found themselves without data management for this same time period filed for bankruptcy immediately."

According to the 2007 AT&T annual study on business continuity and disaster recovery preparedness for US businesses in the private sector, **key findings include:**

- 72% of US companies have a business continuity plan in place, compared to 73% in 2006.
- Of the 10 cities surveyed this year, businesses in New York ranked first in terms of being the most prepared for natural and man-made disasters, and businesses in Cleveland came in last.
- With 30% of companies citing that business continuity planning is not a priority, the results suggest that companies may have a false sense of security. Fifteen percent believe that their systems currently in place are sufficient; 14% believe that the probability of a disaster causing business disruption is small, and 13% believe that the probability of a major disaster is small.
- Businesses are not heeding government warnings. The private sector does not give much credence to warnings issued by the government. Of businesses hit by a disaster, only 41% take action when the federal or state government issues an alert. This is compared with an even lower figure of 33% for those companies that have not been affected before.
- Overall, a majority (57%) have updated business continuity plans in the past 12 months; however, fewer than half (41%) had actually tested the plan in the same period.
- Man-made disasters are a real threat. Roughly 82% of executives surveyed say that cyber security is part of their overall business continuity plan in 2007. Key security threats cited by companies included viruses and worms (nearly 75%), hackers (45%) and spam (37%).
- More than one-third (36%) of small/medium-sized businesses indicate that business continuity planning is not a priority/not important. Smaller businesses are also less likely to have a business continuity plan in place. More than one-third (34%) of small/medium-sized companies surveyed do not have a business continuity plan compared to one-fifth (21%) of large companies.

In short, an IT-infrastructure of a contemporary business in the form of an enterprise information system must be able to meet the requirements for continuous or "24x7x365" computing—an operating platform that represents main prerequisite for business continuance. Such an infrastructure must be ready for any kind of possible downtime causes, both planned and unplanned, such as: daily glitches of hardware and software, systems/application software updates and/or upgrades, hardware upgrades, partial or full-scale disasters, business mergers or acquisitions, and so forth. It should employ several information technologies that help ensure business critical operations be continuously available, in order to meet customers' needs. These technologies provide a basis to ensure cost-effective business availability, reliability and stability in all kinds of events of disruption. They are planned and implemented in organizations within so-called "Business Continuity Planning" projects.

According to Forrester's Enterprise and SMB Hardware Survey, North America And Europe, Q3 2007 (Forrester Research, 2007), approximately 27% of enterprises do not have a recovery site in the event of data center site failure; 23% of enterprises never test their disaster recovery plans, and 40% test their plans once per year. These results show that some enterprises still struggle to create convincing business cases for disaster recovery investment while others struggle with the ability to schedule business and application downtime to conduct adequate disaster recovery testing.

CHAPTER SUMMARY

Computer system running business-critical applications may experience several problems that may, in turn, cause unavailability of applications from end-users' computer devices. These problems include: hardware and system software glitches, bugs in application software, human errors, natural disasters (fire, flood, earthquake), and so forth. Such an event can cause partial or full unavailability of enterprise data and applications. When system is not operational for any reason, it is said to be down and the time in which it does not operate is called "downtime." Several categories of downtime exist; they are briefly explained in this chapter. In addition, the term of "economics of downtime" is introduced.

REFERENCES

Aberdeen Report. (2006). Global Supply Chain Benchmark Report, June 2006, Retrieved on July 29, 2006 from http://www.aberdeen.com/summary/report/benchmark/RA_GlobalTrade_BE_3172.asp.

AT&T Study (2007). AT&T's Business Continuity Study http://www.continuity-central.com/news03284.htm

Barraza, O. (2002). Achieving 99,9998 % + Storage Uptime and Availability. DotHill Systems, Retrieved on August 7, 2006 from http://www.dothill.com/products/whitepapers/5-9s_wp.pdf.

Datamation, August 15, 1995

Dembeck, C. (1999). Yahoo cashes in on Ebay's outage. *E-commerce Times*, June 18, 1999, Retrieved on September 24, 2007 from http://www.ecommercetimes.com/perl/story/545.html.

Downtime. Wikipedia, Retrieved on April 2, 2008 from http://en.wikipedia.org/wiki/Downtime.

Ernest-Jones, T. (2005). Business continuity strategy—the life line. *Network Security*, 2005(8), pp. 5-9, Retrieved on July 18, 2006.

Forrester Research (2007). http://www.forrester.com/ER/Research/Survey/Excerpt/0,,641,00.html.

Gartner Dataquest (2003). North America Customers Reveal Preferred Services for Mission Critical Systems, Users Wants and Needs, Retrieved on August 4, 2006 from http://ftp.hp.com/pub/services/continuity/info/continuity_availabilitywp.pdf.

Graham, S. & Sherman, L. (2003). Opinion: Windows can mean dependable uptime, Retrieved on July 25, 2006 from http://www.computerworld.com/softwaretopics/os/story/0,10801,80574,00.html.

Hill, D. (2006). Storage Tip: Don't Equate High Availability with High Value, Retrieved on July 25, 2006 from http://storage.itworld.com/5002/nls_storage_hill060724/pfindex.html.

IBM (2007), Business Continuity Tool, Retrieved on April 2, 2008 from http://www-935.ibm.com/services/us/bcrs/self-assessment/index.html.

IDC Report (2006), True High Availability: Business Advantage Through Continuous User Productivity, May 2006.

Infonetics Research Report (2005). The Costs of Enterprise Downtime: North American Vertical Markets 2005. *Infonetics Research*, Retrieved on July 28, 2006 from http://www.optrics.com/emprisa_networks/2005_UPNA05_DWN_ToC_Excerpts.pdf.

Infonetics (2006) *The Costs of Downtime: North American Medium Businesses 2006, Retrieved on July 27, 2007 from* http://www.infonetics.com/resources/purple.shtml?upna06.dwn.nr.shtml.

Manning, R. (2004). Managing the Costs of System Downtime, Retrieved on July 21, 2006 from http://www.cioupdate.com/budgets/article.php/3404651.

Schraeder, J. (2004). Served-Based Computing - Old Concept Meets New Technology, Retrieved on August 6, 2006 from http://209.116.252.254/7_2004_focus/f_14.shtml.

Stanton, R. (2005). Beyond Disaster Recovery: The Benefits of Business Continuity, Computer Fraud & Security, July 2005, pp. 18-19.

Szelong, M. (2002). Assuring Reliable Enterprise Data Availability, Retrieved on August 7, 2006 from http://www.netapp.com/library/tr/3170.pdf.

Uptime. Wikipedia, Retrieved on April 2, 2008 from http://en.wikipedia.org/wiki/Uptime.

Vanston, M. (2004). Disaster Recovery: Reaction, Not Reality, ZDNET, Retreived on July 28, 2006 from http://techupdate.zdnet.com/techupdate/stories/main/Disaster_Recovery_Reaction_Not_Reality.html.

Ybarra, M. (2006). The Long Road Back, CIO Decisions magazine, January 2006, Retrieved on July 31, 2006 from http://searchcio.techtarget.com/magItem/0,291266,sid19_gci1154418_idx3,00.html.

REAL WORLD CASE STUDY

HP AlphaServer technology helps Commerzbank tolerate disaster on September 11   (Compiled from: http://h71000.www7.hp.com/openvms/brochures/commerzbank/commerzbank.pdf)

While most large organizations today have plans for Disaster Tolerance (DT), few have to put them to the test. The North American headquarters of Commerzbank, located less than 100 yards from the World Trade Center in New York City, put its DT plan into action on September 11, 2001. Because Commerzbank relies on OpenVMS wide-area clustering, volume shadowing and AlphaServer GS160 systems from HP, the bank was able to function on September 11 because its critical banking applications continued to run at the primary site and were available from the bank's remote site.

Foresight has long been an asset of Commerzbank AG, the parent bank, which was founded in 1870. Frankfurt-based Commerzbank has experienced and helped shape 130 years of German economic history—from empire to monetary union, from the gold mark to the euro. With consolidated total assets of roughly 500 billion euros, Commerzbank is one of Germany's—and Europe's—leading banks. The Commerzbank AG Group includes numerous subsidiaries in Germany and in 45 countries around the world. The New York branch, set up in 1971, was the first to be established in the U.S. by a German bank. Commerzbank, North America is a wholesale bank that serves approximately 500 clients, many of whom are Fortune 500 companies. The bank specializes in areas such as corporate banking, syndications, real estate financing and public financing.

According to Werner Boensch, Executive Vice President of Commerzbank, North America, "Our tolerance for downtime is zero. That imperative creates a challenge for the bank. Gene Batan, Vice President of the Systems and Information Technology Department of Commerzbank, North America, explains, "My primary concern is to minimize downtime to the point of zero—and ascertain that there is a redundancy of data in several locations. We need to ensure that there is no downtime on any critical production system at any point in time."

Zero downtime is why the bank has run its critical systems on the OpenVMS operating system since the 1980s. According to Batan, "OpenVMS is the most secure and reliable operating system we have ever experienced."

Like most enterprises today, Commerzbank has a multi-vendor computing environment. However, the bank runs its most critical banking applications on AlphaServer GS160 platforms. These applications include a money transfer system responsible for the bank's connection to the Federal Reserve and the New York Clearing House, a trading system, a banking system that handles internal banking requirements, a letter of credit system, a futures and options system, and much more—all running under OpenVMS. The bank uses StorageWorks systems to store an impressive two terabytes of data utilizing RAID 0, RAID 1 and RAID 5 technology in a SAN environment. HP fibre switches are utilized to form the SANs.

To ensure constant uptime, the bank has one AlphaServer GS160 system at its primary site in downtown Manhattan and another at its remote site, which is 30 miles away in Rye, New York. Also at the remote site is a pair of AlphaServer 4100 systems. These servers are part of the OpenVMS cluster at the primary site, and their only role is to serve the remote drives to the primary location using Mass Storage Control Program (MSCP), a part of the OpenVMS operating system. The disk drives are either RAID configured or mirrored at local and remote sites, as well as volume shadowed. Batan says, "Because of OpenVMS wide-area clustering, the storage at our remote site is always available and updated in real time."

Boensch explains what happened to the bank on September 11. "From a technology point of view, the first thing we lost was our communication link to the Federal Reserve and the New York Clearing House. One of our staff switched the links to our remote site. Since our AlphaServer GS160 system at our primary site was running, we started to receive payment messages from the Federal Reserve Bank of New York and the New York Clearing House."

Commerzbank is located on floors 31 to 34 at the World Financial Center, which is west of the World Trade Center and across the West Side Highway. When the second jet hit, the bank personnel evacuated the area immediately.

"Our main challenge was to get people from downtown to Rye, because the subways, trains and bridges were closed," states Boensch. "The bank has a staff of over 400 people, but if we have about 10 people we can run the bank for about two days—that's how we're organized. We were able to get 16 people out to Rye that day, and then, as transportation became available, we had more people." For the next eight months, approximately two-thirds of the bank's staff worked in Rye, and the other third worked at a subsidiary in mid-town Manhattan until the primary site was ready for re-occupancy in mid-May 2002.

In addition to having a remote operation site, the bank's DT plan includes comprehensive protection of its primary site. Boensch explains, "In our primary site, we have our own generator, fuel storage tank, cooling tower, uninterrupted power supply, battery backup system and fire suppression system—as well as extra CPUs and redundant drives. As a result, when the World Trade Center area lost power, our generator and cooling tower kicked in, so none of our systems were down initially. However, dust and debris from the collapse of the World Trade Center towers caused our AC units to fail during the day."

From the remote site in Rye, the Systems team was able to monitor its primary data center back near Ground Zero. Boensch describes what happened after the staff evacuated the Manhattan site. "Because of the intense heat in our data center, all systems crashed except for our AlphaServer GS160. We lost one partition in this system due to the heat condition, which was 104 degrees in the QBBs (Quad Building Blocks). The other partition kept on running with remote drives only, since the local drives became unavailable as well. OpenVMS wide-area clustering and volume-shadowing technology kept our primary system running off the drives at our remote site 30 miles away."

Batan describes the OpenVMS Galaxy Software, the technology that allows the bank to run multiple instances of OpenVMS in each of the AlphaServer system's hard partitions. The OpenVMS instances simultaneously run different applications. "One hard partition failed, but the other—whose OpenVMS instances run the more critical applications—kept on running. With GS Series systems, one hard partition can fail without bringing down the whole system. So while most computers were having difficulties in the data center, OpenVMS Galaxy and the AlphaServer GS160 were so robust that even though one of the hard partitions, housed in the upper two QBBs, crashed due to heat, the other hard partition, housed in the lower two QBBs, kept on running multiple instances of OpenVMS. The money transfer system never went down and we actually remained operational that day."

Boensch said that all of Commerzbank's vendors extended their help. "Compaq, now part of the new HP, was there for us, asking if there was anything they could do. They were willing to offer hardware, but because of our remote site, we were OK."

The bank's DT environment is part of a larger business continuity plan, which was designed and maintained by the Systems and IT Department. "We not only test our systems and applications on a regular basis involving business users," explains

Boensch, "but we also have a call tree system to make sure that every member of Commerzbank, North America is aware of the process we have to go through in case there is a contingency condition. This plan was in place before September 11."

According to Boensch, a survey from the Federal Reserve showed that banks that had their own DT sites handled September 11 much better than those that did not. "OpenVMS wide-area clustering and remote shadowing, which allow you to locate a remote site up to 500 miles away, greatly reduce your risk in case of a disaster."

Batan maintains that the OpenVMS AlphaServer platform is the ideal way for Commerzbank to run its critical applications. "OpenVMS, with its clustering, volume shadowing, security and resilience, ensures high availability. The AlphaServer GS160 system, which we divided into two hard partitions and clustered the OpenVMS instances with our remote site 30 miles away, is a very robust machine and the Galaxy software provides the ability to share CPUs among the OpenVMS instances within each hard partition. The combination provides unbeatable tolerance, reliability and redundancy."

Boensch describes the activities of Commerzbank's Disaster Recovery (DR) site in non-disaster mode. "Our DR site is really dual purpose. The AlphaServer GS160 system is a standby production site in case of a disaster. But on a regular day-to-day basis, it's up and running as a test and development system. Actually, the only things that are redundant in an active/active configuration are the StorageWorks data disks—they are truly dedicated both locally and remotely. We also use the site for training."

As things return to normal for businesses around the World Trade Center area—and indeed around the world—OpenVMS on AlphaServer systems will continue to be the gold standard of availability, reliability and security—backed by people who will be there whenever they are needed.

DISCUSSION QUESTIONS

1. Define the concepts: downtime and uptime.
2. What is a meaning of high availability?
3. What is the difference between continuous computing and business continuity?
4. Explain the concept of the "economics of downtime."
5. What is the difference between "planned" and "unplanned" downtime?
6. How do we calculate the high availability ratio?
7. Does every business need a high availability ratio?
8. What are the levels of the fault tolerant computing?

9. Why disaster recovery and disaster tolerance are not the same concepts?
10. Explain the principal IT risks of the downtime for your company.

Discussion Questions: Lessons Learned from CASES

1. Make an Internet survey on how many companies did not survive after September 11 terrorist attack; how many of them used to have a disaster recovery plan?
2. HP OpenVMS operating system is said to be one of the most reliable and available operating systems ever developed. Find on the Internet the story, which explains an experience on OpenVMS system that worked for more than 16 years without shutdown operation.
3. Disaster recovery sites and clustering technologies are used for disaster management: which one was more appropriate in the Commerzebank case?

Chapter III
Business Continuity and Business Continuity Drivers

CHAPTER OVERVIEW

The previous chapter introduced the two major concepts of continuous comput-ing: downtime and uptime. Chapter three goes a step further and aims at defining business continuity (business continuance) and several measures of performances such as availability, reliability, and scalability. The main framework for research is defined. Based on this framework, a systemic model of business continuity, continuous computing and continuous computing technologies has been created. In addition, the "Onion" model of an information architecture for business continuity, IT-based business continuity drivers and technologies are identified in this chapter.

BUSINESS CONTINUITY: INTRODUCTION

Most of today's businesses are under continuous pressure to keep their information systems running 24/7/365 and ensure data and applications are continously available. Basic business continuity terms are introduced in this section.

Business continuance, business resilience, fault-tolerance, disaster tolerance, fast and reliable data access, are just a few of the objectives of contemporary business. Business continuity strategy has become No1 item for both CEO's and CIO's priority list. Business continuity today relies on continuous computing technologies that provide an efficient operating environment for continuous computing. Implementation of continuous computing technologies provides a platform for "keeping business in business" since business-critical applications are installed on enterprise servers, run by server operating systems that include ServerWare components, backed-up by data storage systems and supported by several fault-tolerant and disaster-tolerant technologies.

The term "high availability" is associated with high system/application uptime which is measured in terms of "nines." The more nines that represent availability ratio, the higher level of availability is provieed by the operating platfom. In addition to the term "availability," two additional dimensions of server operating platform are used as well: reliability and scalability.

High availability refers to the ability of a server operating environment to provide end users an efficient access to data, applications and services for a high percentage of system uptime while minimizing both planned and unplanned downtime. As said before, the more "nines" in availability ratio, the higher availability is provided, the better business continuity is served.

High reliability refers to the ability of a server operating environment to minimize (reduce) the occurrences of system failures (both hardware and software) including some fault tolerance capabilities. Reliability goals are achieved by using standard redundant components and advanced fault tolerant solutions (hardware, systems software, application software). Butler and Gray (2006) underscore the question on how system reliability translates into reliable organizational performance. They identify the paradox of "relying on complex systems composed of unreliable components for reliable outcomes."

High scalability refers to the ability of a server operating environment of scaling up and out. Servers can be scaled up by adding more processors, RAM, and so forth, while scaling out means additional computers and forming cluster or grid configurations.

Figure 3.1. IDC classification of availability scenarios (Source: adapted from IDC, 2006)

	Availability	Average Annual Downtime	User Tolerance to Downtime
Fault Tolerant Continuous Availability	99.999%	5 minutes	None
Cluster High Availability	99.9%	8 Hours 45 Minutes	Business Interruption Lost Transaction
Stand-alone GP or Blade Server w/RAID	99.5%	43 Hours 23 Minutes	Tomorrow is Okay

According to IDC (2006), high availability systems are defined as having 99% or more uptime. IDC defined a set of different availability scenarios according to availability ratio, annual downtime, user tolerance to downtime with regard to several continuous computing technologies that are available today:

Dataquest Perspective (Gartner) provides a similar classification shown in Figure 3.2.

Some vendors claim even "zero downtime." Compaq (now part of HP), for instance, claimed in 2001 that 96% of its installed NonStop Himalaya servers had zero downtime. HP, for instance, claims that its Integrity NonStop servers can provide "seven-nines" 99.99999% availability, an uptime level which translates to less than three seconds of unplanned downtime a year (Boulton, 2005).

Aberdeen (2007) defined the accronym "Best in Class" (BIC) companies that leverage a high availability strategy:

a.   the overall ability to recover critical applications (application data) in less than two hours, and
b.   Year-over-year improvement in ability to recover data.

This approach suggests the companies to take the following actions to achieve Best in Class performance:

*   Focus on managing high availability, business continuance, and disaster recovery as a combined initiative;
*   Reduce dependency on tape for data recovery needs by deploying disk-based storage to enable quicker data access and recovery; and
*   Leverage technologies, such as continuous data protection, that enable continuous data recovery.

Figure 3.2. Availability classification (Source: adapted from Dataquest Perspective—High Availability, http://www.itsmsolutions.com/newsletters/DITYvol2iss47. htm, accessed March 18, 2008)

Availability Classification	Level of Availability	Annual Downtime
Continuous Processing	100%	0 minutes
Fault Tolerant	99.999%	5 minutes
Fault Resilient	99.99%	53 minutes
High Availability	99.9%	8.8 hours
Normal Commercial Availability	99-99.5%	87.6 – 43.8 hours

MAIN FRAMEWORK FOR THE BOOK

The main framework for research in the book is defined. Methodological framework used in the book is based on a systems definition provided by C. W. Churchman (1968), one of the founders of OR/MS. An attempt is made to apply Churchman's concept of systems approach to developing a framework for implementation of continuous computing technologies for enhancing business continuity. In addition, this framework is used to define a systemic view of an "always-on" enterprise information system as an information system platform for business continuance or business resilience.

Framework for research on continuous computing technologies for enhancing business continuity (the methodological framework) used in this book is based on the systems approach, more precisely, a MS/OR-based definition of a system given by C. W. Churchman (1968). C. W. Churchman was one of the founders of Operational Research/Management Science and the systems approach. He died on March 21, 2004.

The fundamental concept of systems approach as defined by Churchman is that all systems can be defined by a common set of elements. These elements (dimensions or attributes) are as follows:

1. System is teleological and has a **measure of performance**. The **objective** of the system represents its intended impact on its environment.
2. The **environment** of a system—is the set of entities that exist outside of the system boundary. The entities affect the system or are affected by it.
3. System **resources** are the elements that are used in building and operating the system. Resources may include people, row materials, capital, technologies, and so forth.
4. The system has teleological **components,** which co-produce the measure of performance of the system. These are the elements of the system that exist within its boundary.
5. **Management** of the system as a set of activities intended for effective management.

Churchman continues his examination of this issue in a subsequent book "The Design of Inquiring Systems" (1971). He gives the necessary conditions that something S be conceived as a system, as follows:

1. S is **teleological.**
2. S has **a measure of performance.**

3. There exists **a client** whose interests (values) are served by S in such a manner that the higher the measure of performance, the better the interests are served, and more generally, the client is the standard of the measure of performance.
4. S has teleological **components** which co-produce the measure of performance of S.
5. S has **an environment** (defined either teleologically or ateleologically), which also co-produces the measure of performance of S.
6. There exists **a decision maker** who—via his resources—can produce changes in the measures of performance of S's components and hence changes in the measure of performance of S.
7. There exists **a designer**, who conceptualizes the nature of S in such a manner that the designer's concepts potentially produce actions in the decision maker, and hence changes in the measures of performance of S's components, and hence changes in the measure of performance of S.
8. The designer's intention is to **change S so as to maximize S's value to the client.**
9. S is stable" with respect to the designer, in the sense that there is a built-in guarantee that the **designer's intention is ultimately realizable**.

The first Churchman's definition will be used as a framework for developing a systemic view of an "always-on" enterprise information system. Additional dimensions from the second definition (client, decision maker, designer) will be elaborated as well.

A conceptual model used in the book, based on Churchman's systems approach to illustrate the concepts of business continuity, continuous computing and continuous computing technologies, is given in Figure 3.3. As can be seen from the Figure 3.3, several information technologies can be applied in the form of continuous computing technologies. However, the book will put more emphasis on the role of server platforms and associated technologies such as: server operating systems, ServerWare, server clustering, server virtualization, server-based fault-tolerant technologies when compared to other technologies that can also be used in order to enhance the availability ratios.

Following Churchman's systemic model, the objective of a continuous computing platform in an organization can be defined as achieving the business continuity or business resilience. In other words, this is meant the following: continuous data processing, continuous data access and delivery, multi-platform data access, on-time IT-services and better decisions through better data access. The system's measures of performances are defined in the form of several continuous computing attributes such as: uptime, scalability, reliability, availability, fault-tolerance, disaster tolerance, and automatic failover.

The model is then re-shaped into "the onion model" of high availability information architecture (see Figure 3.4).

Continuous computing technologies as identified in the previous figures are considered as business continuity drivers having in mind their role in assuring a continuous computing as a main prerequisite for business continuity. This set of information technologies include several IT-based solutions that can be implemented in enhancing continuous computing ratios such as availability, reliability, scalability, and so forth.

These solutions include the following ten major technologies:

1. **Servers or server configurations**. Having in mind the dominance of the client-server architecture in modern computing, the role of server configurations has become crucial from the business continuity perspective. Simply put, having a system, which runs mission-critical applications down equals to being out-of-business. Server processors and server configurations are designed and configured in the form of integrated hardware platforms and implemented in order to enhance availability ratios.

Figure 3.3. A systemic model of business continuity, continuous computing and continuous computing technologies

OBJECTIVE

BUSINESS CONTINUITY - BUSINESS RESILIENCE

Continuous data processing
Continuous data access and delivery
Multi-platform data access
On-time IT-services

MEASURES OF PERFORMANCES

CONTINUOUS COMPUTING ATTRIBUTES:

Uptime, Scalability, Reliability, Availability, Fault-tolerance

COMPONENTS

CONTINUOUS COMPUTING TECHNOLOGIES

| Server Platforms | Server Operating Systems | Server Ware | Server Clusters | Data Backup and Recovery Technologies | Regulations and Compliances |
| Server Virtualization | Server System Admin Skills | Server-based Fault Tolerance | | Networking and Security | Other Advanced |

Figure 3.4. The "Onion" model of an information architecture for business continuity

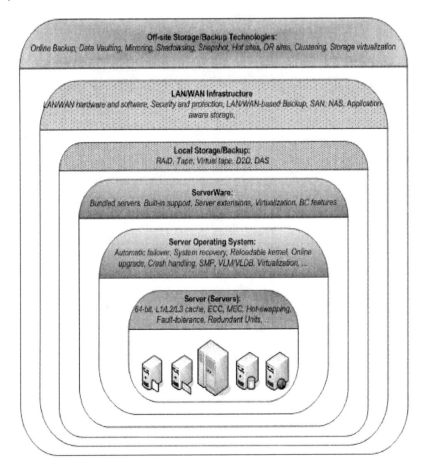

2. **Server operating systems.** Server platforms are run by server operating systems. Unlike a desktop operating system which is intended to be used by a single person at a time, server operating system has to provide access to several dozens, hundreds and thousands of users on concurrent basis (at the same time). For instance, Windows XP operating system as most widely used desktop OS can be halted or reset by a typical shutdown or reset operation several times a day, while Windows Server as a server operating system which is running business critical applications should be kept working without halting as long as possible. Server operating systems are expected to provide high ratios in terms of availability, reliability, and scalability for server configurations running business-critical applications.

3. **ServerWare solutions**. In addition to the core server operating system, server operating system vendors include (bundle) several modules in order to enhance the capabilities of their operating systems. Therefore, modern server operating systems provide several additional components (software modules) called ServerWare solutions, in addition to the core operating platform. HP, for example, has recently officially renamed its HP-UX operating platform from "HP-UX Operating System" (up to version HP-UX 11.0) into "HP-UX Operating Environment" (HP-UX11v1 – HP-UX11v3).

4. **System administration knowledge and skills.** Even though not being a standard "continuous computing technology," system administration knowledge and skills are included into this list with the aim to emphasize the importance of this IT profession in the light of business continuity. IT skilled and experienced system administrator, also known as "sys-admin" or "root," can resolve a lot of problems that occur on operating system level during the process of data processing. Several "tips-and-tricks" that are related to the operating system troubleshooting and system administration as a whole, are very important in reducing the time of system recovery. The same applies for network administrators as well.

5. **Server-based fault-tolerance and disaster-tolerance technologies**. In IT industry, fault-tolerance technology describes a technology (device, component) that can continue to operate even if some sort of defect occurred on it. Physical RAM memory errors, processor errors, hard disk crashes, and so forth, can lead to significant system downtime if they have to be repaired or replaced in a standard way. If an IT platform uses fault-tolerant technology, system can continue to operate even in case of some component's failure. Similar to fault-tolerance, IT-platforms are subject to several types of disasters: floods, fires, earthquakes, and so forth. In either case, if the whole data centre is affected by a disaster, it may lead to the situation when all business data is destroyed and business put into "out of business" mode.

6. **Server clustering** is used as a way of reaching high availability, but not continuous high availability. Clustering is based on defining multiple systems as nodes and connecting them into a cluster system that functions as a single system. Clustering approach is used also in order to resolve the problems of heavy workload and improve scalability performances of server configurations.

7. **Data Storage and Backup solutions**. Technologies used for data storage, data backup and data recovery play crucial role in data management in the form of a secondary layer, in addition to primary data storage (hard disk). *"Your data is your business?"* is a saying that comes originally from IT world. However, in many cases, this warning is not understood well by business world. Having data backed up on the tape, for instance, is not enough in case of hard disk

crash. The time needed to restore data and recover from the crash can even be more important for a business if it takes hours or even days.

8. **Redundant units** are used in order to reduce (minimize) downtime in a way that redundant components are purchased, stored and used to replace the broken ones. These technologies vary from redundant disks (RAID) when data is stored on several disks, to redundant components such as network cards, modems, switches, and routers, including redundant Internet connections as well.

9. **Networking and security technologies.** Several data communications and computer network technologies are implemented in contemporary business. It is already named "networked business" with whole economy renamed to "networked economy." If a company operates at several locations, its information system includes several local and remote IT facilities, remote offices and remote users. Again, in case of any kind of glitch on data communication platform, be it network card, modem, router, broken communication line, as a result, the system is unable to transfer data, users can not access their vital data, customers can not get product information. As a result, the whole business suffers. Therefore, network downtime is also considered as crucial problem in modern computing.

10. **Advanced technologies**. In addition to standard continuous computing technologies, IT world developed new approaches and solutions in dealing with system administrator's horror messages such as: "system-is-down," "network-is-unreachable," "data-is-lost," "core-dump," "file-system-corrupted." These include technologies such as snapshoot mirroring, data vaulting, virtual tape backup, online backup, and so forth.

Apart from these core business continuity technologies, some contemporary business drivers can be considered as business continuity drivers as well:

*   Compliance Regulations (Sarbanes-Oxley and other compliance regulations).
*   Business Agility.
*   Business Competitiveness.

All continuous computing technologies can be grouped into the following major groups:

*   Server-operating environment—related technologies.
*   Data storage, data backup, and recovery technologies.
*   Data communications—networking technologies.

The first group mainly deals with those information technologies, hardware and software features, human skills, that aim at preventing downtime and keeping system uptime as higher as possible.

The second group of continuous computing technologies relate to those solutions that help in recovering from some sort of failure and disaster that caused system and application downtime.

The third group consists of data communications and networking technologies that are used to connect business units and its information system's subsystems and to keep them connected in order to have continuous data exchange.

In the sections that follow, this model will be used as a framework for presenting major continuous computing technologies for enhancing business continuity.

As already mentioned, an emphasis will be given to the first level (the first three "rings" in the onion model presented in Figure 3.4) of continuous computing technologies that are based on server operating platforms and include business continuity solutions related to server hardware, server operating systems, ServerWare solutions, server virtualization technologies, server clustering, system administrator's skills.

BUSINESS CONTINUITY DRIVERS AND CONTINUOUS COMPUTING TECHNOLOGIES: MAIN FRAMEWORK

Businesses today operate in a networked, 24x7x365 global economy. Both business continuance and business agility today rely on high-levels of application/data availability, reliability and scalability. Operating environment for continuous computing is a dimension, which encompasses several technologies that are necessary for an efficient business-critical application platform. Several information technologies are identified in the form of business continuity drivers.

Contemporary business computing is mainly based on client/server architecture and its several modifications (thin/thick, two-tier/three tier). Server's side of such architecture is called "Operating Environment Infrastructure." It consists of standard server-based and additional continuous computing technologies that are used to enhance key server platform features such as reliability, availability, and scalability.

Both business continuance and business agility today rely on high-levels of application/data availability, reliability and scalability. Operating environment for continuous computing is a dimension which encompasses several technologies that are necessary for an efficient business-critical application platform. High availability is the ability of a system (server, operating system, application, network) to continue with its operation even in cases of hardware/software failures and/or disasters.

While the concept of continuous computing is simple, a number of terms has arisen over the years to describe various approaches and solutions. These terms include: mission critical applications, business critical applications, fault tolerancefault tolerant systems, high availability, disaster tolerance, disaster resilient, disaster recovery, 24x7x365, and so forth.

The term "continuous computing" will be defined in the following way:

- By computing, we refer to an information system implemented by using information and communication technologies.
- By continuous, we refer to the ability of an information system to have both applications and data available on continuous basis for end-users, other applications, customers, suppliers, and other business subjects.

In short, the concept of continuous computing is all about "having IT-systems up and running," "always-on," and consequently keeping "business in business."

The term of "business continuance" (Business Continuity - BC) emphasizes the ability of a business to continue with its operations even if some sort of failure or disaster on its computing platform occurs. Several factors affect the level of business continuity such as:

- data availability
- application availability
- network reliability
- operating system reliability, availability, and scalability
- server hardware reliability, and so forth.

All these components can be affected by several types of failures and/or disasters (e.g., hardware/software glitches and failures, thefts, malicious acts, mistakes, floods, fires, earthquakes, hurricanes, terrorist attacks).

High availability is the ability of a system (server, operating system, application, network) to continue with its operation even in cases of hardware/software failures and/or disasters.

Business continuance, fault-tolerance, disaster tolerance and recovery, fast and reliable data access, are just a few of the objectives of contemporary business. Business continuity strategy has become No1 item for both CEO's and CIO's priority list. Business continuity today relies on continuous computing technologies that provide an efficient operating environment for continuous computing. Implementation of continuous computing technologies provides a platform for "keeping business in business" since business-critical applications are installed on enterprise servers, run by server operating systems that include ServerWare components, backed-up by data storage systems and supported by several fault-tolerant and disaster-tolerant technologies.

Server-based technologies include several types of hardware and software features that support so-called "high-availability" technologies: SMP/Clustering, support for 64-bit computing, Storage Scalability, RAID Technology, Fault Tolerance, Online Reconfiguration, N1 Grid Containers, Dynamic System Domains, Virtual Machine Managers, and so forth. In addition, server platforms-based ServerWare suites include: bundled servers, reloadable kernel and online upgrade features, crash-handling technologies, workload management, Windows/UNIX integration, and so forth.

Fault-tolerant and Disaster-tolerant systems include the following technologies: Redundant Units, Data Replication, Hot Sites, Data Vaulting, Disaster Recovery Sites. Some of these technologies overlap with Data Storage Systems which comprise: standard tape backup technology, Storage Area Networks (SAN), Network Attached Storage (NAS), Off-site Data Protection, Fibre Channel, iSCSI, Serial ATA, and so forth.

Typical technologies used to provide high availability include:

- Redundant power supplies and fans
- RAID for disks
- Clusters of servers
- Multiple network interface cards (NICs); redundant routers
- Facilities which include dual power feeds, n+1 air conditioning units, Uninterruptible power supply (UPS) units, or a generator.

As can be seen on Figure 3.4, the main technologies that are used to provide high availability ratios can be classified into the following categories:

- Server-based technologies (processor and RAM technologies, hot-swappable components, servers and server operating systems), enhanced by ServerWare solutions.
- Data Storage and Backup Technologies.
- Data Communications and Networking Technologies.
- Fault-tolerance and disaster-tolerance technologies.
- Redundant units and/or devices such as power supplies and fans, hard disks, network interface cards, routers, and other communication devices.
- Facilities such as: UPS units, dual power feeds or generators, air conditioning units.
- Advanced technologies, such as: virtualization, mirroring, snapshooting, clustering, data vaulting, and so forth.

- Security and Protection technologies.
- Predictive system-monitoring capabilities that are aimed at eliminating failures before they occur.

These technologies are presented here in the form of business continuity driversBCD (see Figure 3.5).

Implementation of continuous computing technologies depends on the type of information architecture, which is in use in an organization system. Chapter four that follows explains most widely used information architectures.

Figure 3.5. IT-based business continuity drivers, attributes, and technologies

Business Continuity Drivers	CC/BC Attributes	CC/BC Enhancing Technologies
Server Processor and Memory Technologies	• Reliability • Availability • Scalability	• Multi Core Processors • Data Bus Recovering • ECC • Hot—swappable components • Cache Reliability • Bad Data Containment • Memory Error Correct • Memory Spares • Hardware Partitioning • Scale-Out and Scale-Up Systems
Server Operating Systems, ServerWare	• Uptime • Reliability and availability • Automatic failover • Disaster recovery • Fault-tolerance • VLM and VLDB • TCP/IP connections failover • HTML/XML support • Dynamic page caching • Bandwidth allocation	• Reloadable kernel and online upgrade • Crash-handling techniques • Workload management solutions • Server consolidation • Internet bundled servers • Server Virtualization • Support for Windows/Unix integration • Transaction prioritization • Encryption accelerator support • HA clustering functions
Data Storage and Backup Technologies	• Uptime • Scalability • Backup • Disaster recovery • Recovery Time Objective (RTO) • Recovery Point Objective (RPO)	• Standard tape backup • RAID and disk-based backup • iSCSI • Serial ATA • Direct Attached Storage • Network Attached Storage • Storage Area Network • Application-aware Storage

continued on following page

Figure 3.5. continued

Fault-tolerance Technologies Redundant Units	• Uptime • Fault-tolerance • Disaster tolerance/ Disaster recovery	• ECC • Cache Reliability • Memory Error Correct • Memory Spares • Redundant units • Hot sites • Disaster recovery sites
Networking Technologies	• Availability of networking services • Continuous support for remote offices and distributed operations	• Integrated Messaging and Collaboration • IP Telephony • Videoconferencing • Network Protocols—services (IP, DNS, DHCP, RADIUS)
Security and Protection Technologies	• Uptime • Secure access • Secure data transfer and transactions	• SSL
Advanced Technologies	• Backup • Disaster recovery • Recovery Time Objective (RTO) • Recovery Point Objective (RPO)	• Storage Virtualization • Online Backup • Electronic Vaulting and Journaling • Mirroring, Shadowing, Snapshot • Hot Standby, Replication

CHAPTER SUMMARY

Contemporary businesses are under continuous pressure to keep their information systems running 24/7/365 and ensure continuous data and applications availability. Business continuance and business resilience are main objectives of contemporary business; they have become number one item for both CEO and CIO. Business continuity relies on an effective implementation of continuous computing technologies.

The main framework for research in the book is defined. Methodological framework used in the book is based on a systems definition provided by C.W. Churchman (1968), one of the founders of OR/MS. An attempt is made to apply Churchman's concept of systems approach to developing a framework for implementation of continuous computing technologies for enhancing business continuity. As a result, a systemic model of business continuity, continuous computing and continuous computing technologies is defined. This model was used as a basis for creating the "Onion" model of an information architecture for business continuity.

REFERENCES

Aberdeen report (2007). The Importance of High Availability, Aberdeen Group

Butler, B. S, & Gray, P. H. (2006). Reliability, Mindfulness, and Information Systems. *MIS Quarterly*, 30(2), pp. 211-224.

Boulton, C. (2005), HP Moves NonStop to Itanium, Retrieved on April 2, 2008 from http://itmanagement.earthweb.com/erp/article.php/3508861.

Churchman, C. W. (1968). *The Systems Approach*. Delacorte Press, NY.

Churchman, C. W. (1971). *The Design of Inquiring Systems: Basic Concepts of Systems and Organisations*. Basic Books, NY.

IDC Report (2006). True High Availability: Business Advantage Through Continuous User Productivity, *May 2006*.

REAL WORLD CASES

Sun – eBay (Compiled from: http://www.sun.com/customers/index.xml?c=ebay. xml)

Business Issues

- Grow infrastructure to keep up with explosive growth in transaction volume
- Minimize administrative costs of managing the data center
- Reduce facilities costs for cooling, power and space
- Ensure high availability of infrastructure
- Manage rapidly expanding volume of data

Solution

To power its massively-scaled resource tiers including both commercial and custom databases, eBay relies on a spectrum of Sun servers, storage and software solutions, which reduce the company's total cost of ownership, optimize application performance and help eBay manage its rapidly growing and massive volume of data. Sun Managed Services provides around-the-clock responsiveness for all data center issues related to the database and search tiers, while Sun Educational Services delivers customized training courses for IT teams worldwide.

Products/Services/Solutions

- Sun Fire X4100 server
- Sun Fire T2000 server
- Solaris 8 Operating System
- Solaris 10 Operating System
- Sun Java System Identity Manager
- Sun Java System Web Server
- Sun StorageTek 9990 system
- Sun StorageTek L700e tape library
- Sun Managed Services
- Sun training on Solaris 10
- Java Platform, Enterprise Edition (Java EE)

Business Results

- Reduced TCO for database farm by using Sun Fire T2000 servers
- Reduced TCO for search farm by using Sun Fire X4100 servers
- 20% improvement in application performance with Solaris 10
- More efficient storage management, several times industry average

HP – Citrix (Compiled from: http://h71028.www7.hp.com/ERC/downloads/4AA0-9023ENW.pdf)

Objective

Ensure Citrix Systems' ability to continue processing customer orders in the event of temporary closure of its south Florida headquarters complex.

When Hurricane Wilma closed down Citrix Systems' main office in Fort Lauderdale, FL, in September 2005, the business never missed a beat, thanks to its HP Software Publishing Services agreement, including disaster recovery services.

"We were shut down for 15 days in October, but did not miss a single customer shipment," says Michael Martin, Citrix Senior Manager for Customer Care. Why? Because Citrix had the worldwide resources of HP Services backing up its operations and fulfillment organizations. The service so effectively kept Citrix on track that it was recognized with the Outsourcing Journal's Outsourcing Excellence Award for Best Business Challenge in 2006

Approach

HP established a Software Library populated with all Citrix software content, a Delivery Center for Software Replication and Fulfillment, and onsite office/SAP access for Citrix Order Processing and Invoicing.

Business Benefits

- Continuous processing of customer orders
- Maintenance of major revenue streams
- No interruption in customer service

IBM - ABN AMRO (Compiled from: http://www-306.ibm.com/software/success/cssdb. nsf/CS/DNSD-6KAH6Y?OpenDocument&Site=eserverzseries&cty=en_us)

ABN AMRO is a prominent international bank that traces its history back to 1824. ABN AMRO ranks 11th in Europe and 20th in the world based on tier 1 capital, with over 3,000 branches in more than 60 countries, a staff of more than 97,000 full-time equivalents and total assets of EUR 855.7 billion (as at 30 June 2005). ABN AMRO Private Banking operates in 60 countries, and has a particularly strong presence in Switzerland, where a significant proportion of the world's private funds are managed. Its Swiss operations had built up a highly robust datacentre to ensure high availability for core systems, and this Lugano site was already hosting data and applications for other divisions of ABN AMRO.

When the private bank made a strategic decision to consolidate and standardise its banking systems, the Swiss datacentre operation was chosen to be the nerve-centre of the new architecture. This placed even greater emphasis on the need to maintain high-availability and to keep systems running at all times—and ABN AMRO selected IBM as its key technology provider for a new dual datacentre architecture.

"We were chosen ahead of other datacentre operations within ABN AMRO's global organisation," says Giorgio Massarotti, Senior Vice President. "When the decision was made, we needed to move very quickly to meet the new requirements, and IBM was the ideal partner."

ABN AMRO Bank Switzerland planned to implement a robust disaster recovery and backup centre in Lugano, around 40km from its main production site in Morbio. The aim was to improve the resilience of its systems in preparation for additional workload, and to reduce long-term costs—both through server and storage consolidation, and through the modernisation of legacy systems. The key to the whole solution was the choice of data replication mechanism. ABN AMRO needed to ensure that data from its banking systems—mainframe, UNIX and Windows alike—could be accurately and permanently mirrored to the backup datacentre.

The bank chose an IBM solution based on two IBM TotalStorage Enterprise Storage Servers, with IBM TotalStorage Metro Mirror software providing synchronous peer-to-peer remote copy (PPRC) services between the two datacentres.

IBM Global Services played a key role in the creation of the new datacentre architecture, and particularly so in the configuration of the Metro Mirror solution. This solution allows ABN AMRO to synchronise data between the production and backup sites, over a distance of 42km.

"As the consolidated datacentre for the global private banking operations, we needed to have the highest possible levels of resilience," says Massarotti. "The IBM team successfully delivered a very complex technical solution that works with outstanding reliability—giving us full confidence in our business continuity plans."

Shortly after the decision to build a dual datacentre architecture in Switzerland, ABN AMRO made a strategic decision to implement a new standard global platform for its private banking operations. The highly resilient Swiss datacentres were chosen to host the consolidated operational platform on new IBM @**server** p5 and @**server**i5 systems.

Each datacentre now has one 8-way IBM @**server**p5 570 system, running CRM and anti-money-laundering applications in logical partitions. Says Massarotti, "The IBM p5 server was selected as our future strategic platform for UNIX applications. As our older servers reach their end of life, we are migrating their applications to AIX 5L on the new p5 systems."

Two new IBM @**server**i5 595 systems were also deployed, one in each datacentre, running ABN AMRO's new core banking application under i5/OS. The private bank is now consolidating to the new platform on a country-by-country basis. When the process is complete, each i5 system will have ten logical partitions, each running a different, country-specific instance of the new core banking software, for a total of 2,500 users.

To provide high-availability storage resources for the i5 environment, ABN AMRO implemented two more Enterprise Storage Servers, and an IBM TotalStorage DS6800 with up to 3TB capacity for test data. Says Massarotti, "The DS6800 gives us high performance and resiliency in a low-cost and very compact package."

ABN AMRO Bank Switzerland has now standardised on IBM server and storage hardware in its datacentres. For each of the principal server types—mainframe, UNIX, mid-range and Microsoft® Windows®—the bank has a single physical machine in the production datacentre, with a duplicate machine for each in the backup datacentre.

Mainframe-based core banking systems now run on a single IBM @**server** zSeries in the production environment, while Windows-based systems—including Web serving and file and print servers—run on IBM @ server BladeCenter servers. The bank has a BladeCenter chassis with twelve blade servers in each datacentre, which boot from the SAN.

"By consolidating to IBM, we have dramatically simplified our datacentre operations," comments Massarotti. "As we move from physical servers to logical partitions or virtual servers on the IBM hardware, we expect to make significant long-term cost savings in management and maintenance. "Scalability will also be improved: for each type of system, we can upgrade capacity or processors in a single server, and share the new power across all the applications running on that server. With the option to boost capacity on demand on some systems, we can even increase power to manage temporary peaks in demand, then switch off the additional resources when the peak demand is over."

Always-on business

The production datacentre now hosts some 80 applications, used by private banking employees and customers all over the world. As ABN AMRO increases the scope of its international private banking operations, the importance of the Swiss datacentres will grow. Equally, the bank's continuing efforts to consolidate its business-critical systems will place growing demands on the Swiss operations to ensure continual availability.

"Business continuity is a key concern in the banking sector," comments Massarotti. "If our systems were to fail even for a short time, the damage to our business would be very great. Our new datacentre architecture is designed to enable systems to keep running even if one whole centre is knocked out by a power failure.

"With the new IBM infrastructure, we are confident that we have taken all the right steps to ensure that our employees and customers always have access to the data and systems they need."

IBM products and services that were used in this case study.

Hardware:	BladeCenter, Storage: DS6000, Storage: Enterprise Storage Server, System i: System i5 595, System i: i5 Server, System p: eServer p5 570, System i, System p, System z
Operating System:	AIX 5L, i5/OS

DISCUSSION QUESTIONS

1. Explain the main differences among the terms: availability, reliability and scalability.
2. Define the concept of "computing" and "continuous computing."
3. What are the main factors affecting the levels of availability?
4. What are the business continuity drivers?
5. Why do we need the systems approach while defining and investigating the business continuity framework?
6. Identify the main server hardwarebased continuous computing technologies.
7. Redundant devices and units are used in assuring higher levels of availability. List some of them.
8. What are advanced server technologies for business continuity?
9. How does the networking and security affect the business continuity?
10. How might the "onion" model help in defining the architecture of the high availability infrastructure?

Discussion Questions: Lessons Learned from Cases

1. How these three real cases differ in terms of business goals, business continuity solutions, implementation methods and hardware platforms?
2. Visit the Web sites of these three vendors (Sun, HP and IBM) and make a comparison of their business continuity solutions.
3. Try to create a TCO model (framework) for your company's integrated business continuity solution.

Chapter IV
Information Architectures
for Business Continuity

CHAPTER OVERVIEW

Based on the framework defined in Chapter III, the fourth chapter discusses the models of information architectures that are used in implementing business computing solutions. In addition to the traditional mainframe-based architecture and most widely used client-server architecture, some recently developed architectures are briefly explained. This chapter aims at locating server configurations within these architectures critical points for ensuring continuous computing and business continuity.

INFORMATION ARCHITECTURE

Most widely used information architectures such as mainframe-based and client-server are explained and the critical points from business continuity perspective are identified. Specific business continuity-related layers of the client-server architecture are identified: client layer, networking layer, server operating platform layer and data storage layer.

Information technologies are implemented in business in several forms of business information systems or enterprise information systems. These systems are designed, developed and implemented by using several approaches and methodologies. No matter which information system methodology is used, business information system is consisted of several information technologies such as: servers, desktop computers, portable/mobile computing devices, systems software, application software, data communication technologies, computer networks. Information systems employ several types of IT specialists while end-users can be considered as part of information system as well.

All these technologies are used for organizing, processing and managing data, hence, data management subsystem is crucial component as well. Business information systems are implemented today within several forms of enterprise information systems (see Figure 4.1) such as:

- Enterprise resource planning systems (ERP)
- Messaging systems
- Document management systems (DCM)
- Customer relationships management systems (CRM)
- Supply chain management systems (SCM)
- Business intelligence systems (BI)
- Legacy systems, and so forth.

Turban, Rainer, and Potter (2005) defined the notion of "information technology architecture" as "…a high-level map or plan of the information assets in an orga-

Figure 4.1. Contemporary enterprise information system and its subsystems

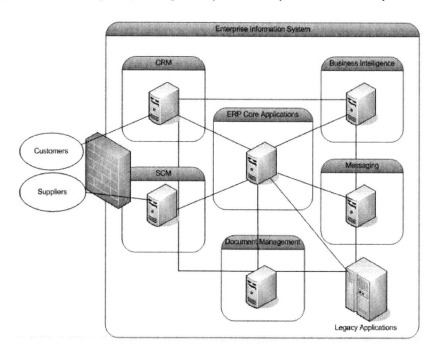

nization, which guides current operations and is a blueprint for future directions." In preparing the IT architecture, the designer needs similar information, which can be divided into two parts:

- The business needs for information
- The existing and planned IT infrastructure and applications of the organization

Such a computing environment is defined as a way in which an organization's information technologies (hardware, software, and communications technology) are organized and integrated for optimal efficiency and effectiveness.

Jonkers, Lankhorst, Doest, Arbab, Bosma, and Wieringa (2006) define architecture as "structure with a vision" which provides an integrated view of the system being designed and studied. They build their definition on top of a commonly used definition by the IEEE Standard 1471-2000 (IEEE Computer Society, 2000): "Architecture is the fundamental organisation of a system embodied in its components, their relationships to each other, and to the environment, and the principle guiding its design and evolution." Kim et al. (2002) proposed new architectural metrics that consist of six dimensions: internal stability, external security, information gathering, order processing, system interface, and communication interface. The six measures were found to be relevant to important technical and managerial aspects of Internet business. Versteeg and Bouwman (2006) define the main elements of a business architecture as business domains within the new paradigm of relations between business strategy and information technologies. Goethals, Snoeck, Lemahieu, and Vandenbulcke (2006) argue that enterprises are living things, they constantly need to be (re-)architected in order to achieve the necessary agility, alignment and integration. Balabko and Wegmann (2006) applied the concepts of system inquiry (systems philosophy, systems theory, systems methodology and systems application) in the context of an enterprise architecture.

From information architecture perspective, businesses mainly use two major types of information system architectures:

a. an old-style mainframe environment, and
b. several models of client-server architectures.

Access to corporate data has always been determined by type of information architecture, which an information system is built on.

In the traditional, but now obsolete, **mainframe environment**, the processing was done by a mainframe computer, while the users used to work with "dumb" terminals (Figure 4.2). The terminals were used to enter or change data and ac-

Figure 4.2. Mainframe-based operating platform

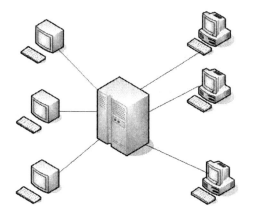

cess information from the mainframe. This was the dominant architecture until the late 1980s. A version of this computing environment is an architecture where PCs are used to connect to host machines through so-called PC-terminal emulation programs.

In this kind of mainframe-operating environment, a mainframe computer does the whole processing; dumb terminals and/or emulation programs on PCs are used just to enter/get data.

However, contemporary business computing is mainly based on **a client-server architecture** or one of its several modifications such as:

- "Thin" or "Thick" client-server
- Two tier client-server
- Three tier client-server
- n - tier client-server,

although several types of old-style mainframe-based architectures can still be found as well.

Client-server architectures consist of servers and clients (desktop computers) with applications being installed and running on server computers. There are also specific types of servers still named mainframe computers (e.g., IBM's mainframes, Hitachi's mainframes, Amdal's mainframes), but they are installed, implemented and used within client-server architecture and without dumb terminals.

A client-server-based information architecture divides processing into two major categories: clients and servers. A client is a computer such as a PC or a workstation attached to a computer network consisting of several dozens (hundreds or thousands) clients and one or more servers.

A server is a machine that provides clients with services. Examples of servers are the database server that stores a database and the SMTP server that provides e-mail services. Traditional client/server applications have their own client programs that need to be installed on all client machines (see Figure 4.3).

Server's side of such architecture is called "Business Server" or "Enterprise Server" or in a broader sense: "Operating Environment Infrastructure." It consists of standard server-based and additional continuous computing technologies that are used to enhance key server platform features such as reliability, availability, and scalability.

A Hybrid architecture is used as well: a combination of mainframe (legacy) platform with newly implemented "thick" and "thin" client-server applications installed on enterprise servers (Figure 4.4).

From e-business perspective, server configurations and server operating systems (SOS) are expected to provide an operating environment that must meet much more rigorous requirements than a standard desktop operating system can provide. System uptime is one of the most critical requirements. Particularly in modern e-business applications, system downtime is unforgivable. Financial institutions that perform ATM transactions, electronic funds transfers, internet-based banking, airline reservation systems, point-of-sale systems, computer-aided dispatching systems, online shops, and so forth, cannot afford "our system is down" excuses. Therefore,

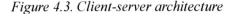

Figure 4.3. Client-server architecture

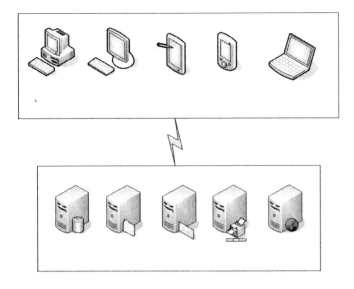

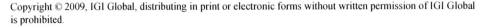

Figure 4.4. A hybrid architecture (Mainframe and Client-server); legacy systems and new client-server applications

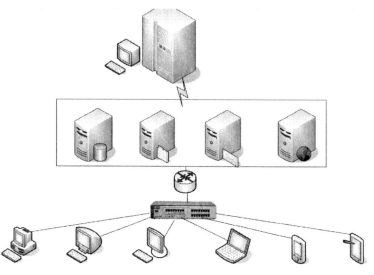

server operating systems that provide zero-downtime or 100% uptime or a solution "near it" are of extreme importance for such businesses. For example, typical reboot operation that all computer users are accustomed with while working with desktops is an operation, which is not desirable on server systems.

All e-business requirements with regard to server operating systems depend on the type and complexity of the business, therefore, a contingency or similar approach should be applied when selecting appropriate platform.

The following requirements are most common:

- SOS must be reliable and available such that server-based software (application servers, data servers, e-mail servers, Web servers, etc.) run on reliable machines with high availability ratio.
- SOS must be scalable enough, because as time goes on, business can be extended with new users and necessary applications.
- SOS have to support open hardware-software communication protocols in order to be able to exchange data.
- They are expected to provide several types of networking services: Internet-Web technology services, directory services, security services, remote access capabilities including support for mobile computing.

Within the evolution of the client/server architecture the following models have been identified:

a. File-oriented architecture
b. Shared databases
c. Traditional client/server: data processing is split between client and server; client software is needed
d. Advanced client/server; multi-tiered c/s architecture with two or more servers (data server, application server, file server, shared database, etc.)
e. Web-enabled client/server architecture, with Web server(s), application servers, data servers, and without a "thick-client" software—a "thin-client" (Web browser is used instead).

No matter which of these models is implemented, some most commonly used layers of the client-server architecture can be identified as follows (see Fig. 4.5):

•   **Client layer**—client application (can be „thick" or „thin," depending on the type of client-server architecture that is implemented). Each user, from any business unit, department or business process, uses an appropriate application by using this client layer.

Figure 4.5. Client-server infrastructure layers and components

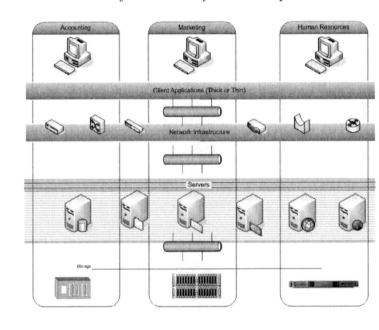

- **Networking layer**—a layer that includes a number of different data communication devices, media, hardware and software communication protocols and softwares.
- **Server operating platform layer**—a layer that is consisted of one or more servers (data, application, Web, messaging, firewall, etc.) accompanied with server operatin systems and integrated serverware solutions.
- **Data storage layer**—a layer that contains several data storage, data backup and recovery solutions intended to be used for primary and secondary data storage.

When one of these servers running mission-critical applications is not reachable, for any reason, this can be considered as system downtime. In addition, whenever end users have no access to the application, again for any reason, it can also be considered as some sort of downtime.

Having in mind such a kind of infrastructure, a number of critical points at which a downtime may occur can be identified with regard to possible downtime problems (see Figure 4.6):

- Hardware conflict or glitche on a client PC
- Problems with desktop operating system

Figure 4.6. Client-server infrastructure components and possible downtime points

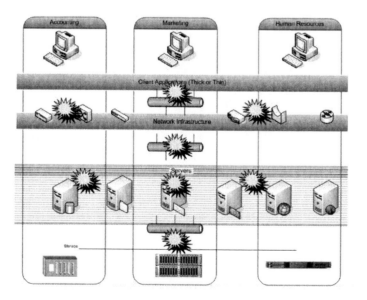

- Problems with client application
- LAN/WAN/Internet—related problem which causes disconnection from servers and other resources
- Server operating platform—related problems (dump on core operating system, application protocol, library, networking protocol, security intrusion, etc.)
- Data storage (hard disk crash, file or file system corruption, magnetic tape broken, etc.).

These downtime points are considered as critical points in creating continuos computing soluitons for enhancing business continuity.

NEW INFORMATION ARCHITECTURES AND COMPUTING PARADIGMS

In addition to standard client-server computing environments, some new computing paradigms and models such as Web-enabled legacy systems, utility or on-demand computing, software-as-a-service (SaaS), Web-based software agents and services, subscription computing, grid computing, clustering, ubiquitous or pervasive computing are explained briefly.

Recently introduced new computing paradigms and models such as Web2, Web-enabled legacy systems, utility or on-demand computing, software-as-a-service or service-oriented architecture, Web-based software agents and services, subscription computing, grid computing, clustering, ubiquitous or pervasive computing, cloud computing, use the combination of the previous configurations and newly developed Internet technologies. According to Hickey and Siegel (2008), providers of highly reliable information technology services have adopted multiple service delivery quality standards and have obtained certificates of registration or certification associated with these standards.

Web2 or Web 2.0 is regarded as a second generation of World Wide Web and was created as a term by Dale Dougherty, O'Reilly Media VP, in 2003. Web2 focuses on improving collaboration, networking, and so forth, by implementing technologies such as hosted services, Web-based communities, Web-based social-networking, creation of wikis, blogs, and so forth.

The new application paradigms such as: **Utility computing, on-demand computing, software-as-a-service, service-oriented architecture, grid computing, cloud computing, green computing,** and so forth, have been introduced in order to lower total costs of ownership of IT infrastructures and improve both efficiency and effectiveness of information processing. **Utility computing** approach uses the logic of providing services which is behind electricity and water services: the service – computing power can be obtained "on demand" and priced on the amount of time it is used. **Grid computing** is an approach of establishing such configurations consisted of several computers on regional or interregional basis, connecting them by using high speed communication lines and using as a single system. In addition, this approach can be extended and used around the globe by connecting unused computer configurations, connect them and integrate into a powerful computing infrastructure. Computer systems are connected with a grid topology. **Ubiquitous (pervasive or embedded)** computing integrate processors and computing power everywhere. **Multi-agent system (MAS)** is a system composed of several software agents, collectively capable of reaching some goals that are difficult o achieve by an individual agent or monolithic system. **Web-based legacy systems** use Web technology in order to integrate legacy applications and systems such as old-style mainframe and minicomputer-based applications with client-server and Web-based applications. A number of middleware tools are used in order to "webify" legacy applications, by keeping their functionality. Several so-called "Web-to-Host" or "Web2Host" tools are used in order to improve the efficiency of reporting capabilities of the "old-style" applications written for instance in Cobol.

CHAPTER SUMMARY

Information technologies are today mainly implemented within several forms of enterprise information systems. These systems are designed, developed and implemented by using several approaches, methodologies, application development tools, implementation strategies and they are dependent on selected model of information architecture. Chapter four presents the most widely used models of information architectures and computing paradigms as well as those that have been recently introduced.

REFERENCES

Balabko, P. & Wegmann, A. (2006). Systemic classification of concern-based design methods in the context of enterprise architecture. *Information Systems Frontiers, 2006*(8), pp. 115-131.

Goethals, F. G., Snoeck, M., Lemahieu, W. & Vandenbulcke, J. (2006). Management and enterprise architecture click: The FAD(E)E framework. *Information Systems Frontiers, 2006*(8), pp. 67–79.

Hickey, J. & Siegel, J. (2008). Improving service delivery through integrated quality initiatives: A case study. *IBM Systems Journal, 47*(1), 2008.

Jonkers, H., Lankhorst, M. M., Doest, H. W. L., Arbab, F., Bosma, H. & Wieringa, R. J. (2006). Enterprise architecture: Management tool and blueprint for the organization. *Information Systems Frontiers*, 8, pp. 63-66.

Kim, J., Lee, J., Han, K. & Lee, M. (2002). Businesses as buildings: Metrics for the architectural quality of Internet businesses. *Information Systems Research, 13*(3), September 2002, pp. 239-254.

Turban, Rainer, & Potter (2005). *Introduction to Information Technology*, Wiley.

Versteeg, G. & Bouwman, H. (2006). Business architecture: A new paradigm to relate business strategy to ICT. *Information Systems Frontiers, 2006*(8), pp. 91-102.

REAL WORLD CASES

Rebuilding the legacy—modernizing mainframe code (Adapted and compiled from: Robert Mitchell, April 24, 2006 (Computerworld) http://www.computerworld. com/hardwaretopics/hardware/mainframes/story/0,10801,110717,00.html)

By some estimates, the total value of the applications residing on mainframes today exceeds $1 trillion. Most of that code was written over the past 40 years in Cobol, with some assembler, PL/1 and 4GL thrown into the mix. Unfortunately, those programs do not play well with today's distributed systems, and the amount of legacy code at companies such as Sabre Holdings Corp. in Southlake, Texas, makes a rewrite a huge undertaking. "We're bound by our software and its lack of portability," Sabre Vice President Alan Walker says of the 40,000 programs still running on IBM Transaction Processing Facility (TPF), Agilent Modular Power System and other mainframe systems.

With a shortage of Cobol programming talent looming in the next decade and a clear need for greater software agility and lower operating costs, IT organizations have begun to make transition plans for mainframe applications. The trick lies in figuring out which applications to modernize, how to do it and where they should reside. Applications fall into one of three groups based on scale, says Dale Vecchio, an analyst at Gartner Inc. Applications under 500 MIPS are migrating to distributed systems. "These guys, they want off," Vecchio says. As organizations begin peeling away smaller applications, they may move to a packaged application; port the application to Unix, Linux or Windows; or, in some cases, rewrite the applications to run in a .Net or Java environment, he says.

In the 1,000-MIPS-and-up arena, the mainframe is still the preferred platform. Applications between 500 and 1,000 MIPS fall into a gray area where the best alternative is less clear. An increasingly common strategy for these applications is to leave the Cobol in place while using a service-oriented architecture (SOA) to expose key interfaces that insulate developers from the code. "If you expose those applications as a Web service, it's irrelevant what that application was written in," says Ian Archbell, vice president of product management at tool vendor Micro Focus International PLC in Rockville, MD. "SOA is just a set of interfaces, an abstraction."

"SOA at least allows you to break the dependency bonds," says Ron Schmelzer, an analyst at ZapThink LLC in Waltham, Mass. Cobol is not going away, but it's also not moving forward. While the Cobol code base on mainframes is projected to increase by 3% to 5% a year, that's mostly a byproduct of maintenance, says Gary Barnett, an analyst at Ovum Ltd. in London. "No one is learning [Cobol] in school anymore, and new applications are not being built in Cobol anymore," says Schmelzer. "Cobol is like Latin."

Vendors such as Micro Focus have abandoned the idea of evolving the Cobol language for distributed application development. "Micro Focus is not about a better Cobol compiler," says Archbell. Instead, its approach is to "embrace and extend," he says. "We expose things like aggregated CICS transactions as JavaBeans, Web services, or .Net or C# code. It's wrappering." But with so much legacy code, that process won't take place overnight. "It could take 20 years," Archbell says.

Sabre still has more than 10,000 MIPS of applications on mainframes, and Walker plans to migrate everything off over the next few years. The company's TPF-based fare- searching application, used by Travel-ocity.com LP and travel agents, has been rewritten to run as a 64-bit Linux program on four-way Opteron servers. Sabre migrated the back-end data to 45 servers running MySQL that each contain fully replicated data. The new system is more flexible and "pretty cheap" compared with the mainframe, Walker says. He questions the conventional wisdom that all high-end applications need to stay on mainframes, noting that the search application was in the thousands of MIPS. "It's pretty obvious that you do not need mainframes to do large-scale transactions," he says, pointing to the successes of eBay Inc. and Amazon.com Inc. In Sabre's case, it's worth noting that the application was CPU- and memory-intensive and that competitive pressures would have forced a rewrite anyway. "We solved a larger problem," which was the need to generate hundreds of results instead of the 10 to 20 the TPF system could deliver per search, Walker says.

Simply rewriting millions of lines of code to deliver the same features not only would not cut it financially at The Bank of New York Co., but also would require a lifetime of work, says Edward Mulligan, executive vice president of the technology services division. A gradual transition to packaged applications might help such businesses, says Ovum's Barnett. "Eighty percent of core business processes in banks are the same. In 10 years, it will make little sense to have your own, unique homegrown savings program," he says.

Mulligan has been migrating some smaller applications, freeing up expensive mainframe capacity. The big reason: cost. When the vendor of his problem management software refused to bring licensing in line with equivalent packages in the Windows arena, he migrated to a cheaper Windows version. The total operating costs of running applications on the mainframe can be "easily" 10 times that of a Unix or Windows architecture, says Sabre's Walker. While IBM has begun offering sub-capacity, usage-based pricing, few third-party vendors of mainframe software have followed suit. "Vendors who do not embrace flexible pricing are accelerating the decline in their business," says Barnett. At Sabre, Walker plans to continue to migrate off the mainframe, which he says is simply too expensive.

What's in a Name: Is 'SaaS' Really New?
November 2, 2007
By Matt Villano
Adapted and compiled from: http://itmanagement.earthweb.com/entdev/article. php/3708731

It was Juliet Capulet in Shakespeare's "Romeo and Juliet" who uttered the famous question "What's in a name?" in her biting commentary on names as meaningless conventions.

If only she were around to comment on IT services: What would fair Juliet say about the evolution of Software as a Service?

That's right, SaaS, that software application delivery model where a software vendor develops a Web-native software application and hosts and operates it for use by customers over the Internet. The moniker (for you grammarians, technically it's a "camelback acronym") came in to widespread use after a conference in 2005.

But some vendors and experts alike say the model has been around for decades under a different name: Application Service Provider, or ASP.

Remember the ASP? The software model coined the notion of delivering computer-based services to customers over a network. It emerged out of service bureaus of the 1970s and 1980s, fuelled the dot-com boom of the 1990s, and largely was blamed for the dot-com bust of Y2K. Now, at least according to some, it's back, only with a different name. What in the name of guerrilla marketing gives?

That depends on whom you ask. Some say SaaS is nothing more than a marketing ploy to repurpose the ASP model under a different, less controversial name.

Others admit that while the SaaS and ASP models once were cut from the same cloth, SaaS is a new-and-improved version, ASP 2.0, if you will.

Oli Thordarson, president and CEO of Alvaka Networks, a managed service provider in Irvine, Calif., is a critic. "We don't call Splenda 'saccharin' after saccharin was found to be cancer-causing," Thordarson says. "People latch on to names, and ASPs got such a bad rap in the 1990s that I don't think anyone would go near it if you brought back the name 'ASP' today."

Mike Masnick, CEO of Techdirt, a technology analyst firm in Sunnyvale, Calif., agrees, going so far as to say that he does not see any "major" differences between the two at all. "Sure, the technology has changed a bit, but when you look at functionality, they're identical," Masnick says. "It's a classic example of marketing a newer version of the same thing to avoid negative reaction from those who might have been turned off previously."

Others have a different perspective. David Sockol, for instance, CEO of Emagined Security, a managed service provider in San Carlos, Calif., says he prefers to think of SaaS as a dramatic evolution of the ASP model, the same idea only better.

"When ASPs were first designed, they were mostly people using the Web to interface with backend software," he says. "By allowing organizations to put software on their machines that interfaced over the Internet with backend processes, SaaS takes this another step."

According to Sockol, the primary differences between SaaS of today and ASP of yesteryear are in where the native business data resides and how much control (in terms of application software licensing, possible system failures and security breaches) the native business has.

Under the ASP model, he says, customers really never really had much code running locally—all of it was running off of a server or other engine at the host. Under the SaaS model, however, customers have the code conveniently sitting on their networks in the form of application programming interface (API), which communicates with a host server remotely.

Greg Olson, CTO of Coghead, an application vendor in Menlo Park, Calif., takes this dichotomy even further, saying that other than the word "service" and monthly payment plans, current SaaS models and the ASP model of the late 1990s share little. According to Olson, the service provider in the ASP model basically offered an IT infrastructure for rent—an inefficient method of delivering services, to say the least. "ASPs didn't provide applications, just the infrastructure, and the deployment and management expertise to run those applications," he says. "Today, with SaaS, customers of all sizes (both businesses and individuals) can procure a very broad array of applications in very fine grained increments by service subscription."

SaaS certainly provides customers with a bevy of individual applications. A quick count indicates that there are more than 1,700 SaaS providers out there currently, including Instill, which offers business intelligence technology for companies in the food service industry, and Convoq, which peddles video conferencing. These and hundreds of other SaaS entities can be found on the SaaS Showplace, a Web site put together by Jeff Kaplan, managing director of THINKstrategies, a consulting firm in Wellesley, Mass.

Kaplan, who has studied SaaS for years, bolsters comments from Sockol and Olson by summarizing that the new iterations differ from ASPs in three important categories:

- Attitude: Why sign up for more applications than you need? SaaS, unlike the ASPs of old, lets customers receive only those applications they'll use.
- Economics: Under the SaaS model, customers pay as they go, instead of paying one price for a monthly subscription service that encompasses stuff they might never use.
- Technology: The one-two punch of broadband networking and Web 2.0 makes SaaS quicker, nimbler and more agile than ASPs ever were with slower, older technologies. "Don't get me wrong, the value proposition of SaaS is the same as it always was with ASPs in that customers need not have to do these things themselves," says Kaplan, who notes that Managed Service Providers (MSPs) fill a different niche entirely. "Is SaaS just a new and improved version ASP? I'm not sure I'd say that at all."

With this in mind, then, perhaps there's more than separates the SaaS and ASP models than marketing or semantics (that's semantic, not Symantec) after all. What's in a name? In the case of SaaS, apparently quite a bit of innovation over its much-maligned predecessor.

Microsoft's SaaS Strategy: A Giant Copes with Change
January 24, 2007
Adapted and compiled from: http://itmanagement.earthweb.com/feedback.php/http:/
itmanagement.earthweb.com/netsys/article.php/3655766
By James Maguire

The entire IT community, it seems, is agog over software-as-a-service (SaaS). The notion of delivering applications over the Internet appears to gain more market steam with every passing quarter.

Research firm Gartner forecasts that by 2011, 25% of new business apps will be delivered via SaaS, a jump from 5% in 2005. So while software-as-a-service is in its infancy—and the biggest bucks still go for traditional on-premise software—this new delivery paradigm is growing up fast. As the software industry moves toward

SaaS, one of its defining questions is: what is Microsoft's approach to this new delivery model? As one of the 800-pound gorillas of the software business, Microsoft's decisions tend to have industry-wide repercussions.

To find that out, *Datamation* spoke with Tim O'Brien, director of Microsoft's Platform Strategy Group. In a wide-ranging discussion, he spoke about the company's early SaaS initiatives, and its emphasis on what he refers to as a "software plus services" approach. O'Brien notes that many industry observers view the movement toward SaaS as an "either/or" proposition: Either businesses will host their software on-premises, or they'll move overwhelmingly to a SaaS model. But he disagrees with this dichotomy. "It's not 'either/or,' it's about 'and,'" he says. This 'and' scenario is where the industry is headed, in his view. Businesses will combine SaaS applications with on-premise applications, choosing between them based on a wide array of variables.

Therefore, he says, Microsoft's strategy does not focus exclusively on either the on-premise or the SaaS model. Instead, the emphasis is on facilitating customer choice. "If the need is keeping that application on-premise and customizing it, and extending it, and doing all the things that you do when you host an application in-house, we'll help them do that," he says. However, "If they just want to move costs or overhead or some commodity outside their business and put it onto the cloud—that is, host it where someone else can worry about it—we want to be able to do that, too."

"What is the goal you're trying to achieve? Is the goal taking a commodity business process and moving it out of your environment so you can focus on things that are more core to your business and value-added?" This goal could call for SaaS. Yet the total costs of SaaS need to be calculated, he says. "Think of renting software. That's what software-as-a-service is in terms is pricing models—you're subscribing to that. So you have the whole lease vs. buy discussion with the car dealer. If you're going to drive this thing until the doors fall off, you should buy it. If you get a new car every three years, you should lease it."

Indeed, the car lease vs. buy analogy calls to mind a key issue with SaaS. "The canonical question is: at what point have you paid enough for your software? So if it's an economic discussion you need to look at, over time, what is the cash outflow stream for service-based procurement going to look like, versus if I buy the perpetual license and pay maintenance?"

To be sure, O'Brien sees the advantages of the on-premise model. "There's a whole bunch of capability in terms of processing power and storage that lives on the edge of the network," he says. "And to just say, 'Software as a service is going to be the be-all, and kind of the endgame here, ignores all that unused storage and processing capacity that lives on the edge." Furthermore, what about those moments—rare, but not gone—when people are not connected to the Net? "Offline capability matters," he says. "Despite what you read about the ubiquity of broadband and wireless access, there are some situations where you just don't have access to a network. There are situations where you need local access. There are situations where you want to take advantage of some of the power you have on your local desktop. And there are some situations where you don't want to put sensitive data up in somebody's cloud. And there are regulatory issues there as well, like HIPAA, which says you can't store patient data in a third party data center."

The leading edge of Microsoft's SaaS initiative is the company's Dynamics CRM application, code-named "Titan." Due for release this summer, Titan will be available three ways: 1) Traditional on-premise deployments, 2) SaaS deployments hosted by numerous hosting partners, and 3) SaaS deployments hosted by Microsoft. Although it offers three deployment choices, Titan consists of a single code base. The point of offering various deployment choices, O'Brien says, is enabling customer choice. "If you're a small or medium-sized company and you only need a dozen or two seats of CRM, consuming it as a service makes a lot of sense, especially if you don't want to bear the IT overhead or you don't have the staff to do that," he says. "But as your company grows...needs change, and the opportunity then exists for that customer to move that service-based application out of the cloud, out of our data center, right into their shop, using the same code base, same data set, same set of functionality, and the same set of customizations."

The Titan release brings up a critical question: Given that Microsoft is making such a complex application available via SaaS, does that mean that other Microsoft apps will at some point be delivered as a service?

"To be determined," O'Brien says. "We're looking at this as: this is a fairly revolutionary approach." At this point the focus is on CRM "because it is, for all intents and purposes—at least today—the canonical application category for a lot of people who think about software as a service." The concept of offering multi-choice deployment goes against the status quo, he says, in a market like CRM, in which vendors are "either 90% or 100% on-premise or, in the case of companies like Salesforce, 100% service based."

"Our view, from a software plus services perspective, is based on the premise that 'software plus services' is a better model than just software alone or just services alone," notes O'Brien. And what exactly is 'software plus services'?

"It's hard to think of an application today that doesn't have at least some sort of service component," he explains. For instance, Microsoft Exchange. "So you have the messaging and collaboration application that lives on the server side and the back end. And you've got a rich client head on that, which is the thing we know of as Microsoft Outlook today. If you're like me, you get a few hundred e-mails a day, and you use the local graphics capabilities of your PC and the local processor to rifle though all that content. "But if you're running through an airport trying to catch a plane and you need to check mail real fast, there's a version of Outlook that runs in the browser called Outlook Web Access. And that touches the same backend, synchronized with the client." The point: "This is browser-based, basically Exchange delivered as a service through a browser," he says. It's an example of an application that can be accessed as a service, but also makes use of the local environment. In other words, it's a hybrid.

Likewise, the future of software consumption will be a hybrid, O'Brien says. It will take many forms. "It's going to be local code, it's going to be server-side code, code consumed through the cloud, and a series of peer-to-peer interactions...you see the platform evolving from client-server, to client-server-services." In addition to its Titan launch, Microsoft is also working to enable software as a service for its ISV partners. In terms of technical enablement for ISVs, "We're doing quite a bit on the architecture side to help them understand how to migrate from a so-called entry-level SaaS deployment into multi-tenancy," O'Brien says, "to help them get the economics of scale from delivering one instance of an application to a broad market of users." On the licensing side, in 2006 Microsoft introduced the Software Provider Licensing Agreement (SPLA). "This is a means by which you can procure server licenses with no upfront costs and no minimum commitment," he says. "It gives you, as the ISV, as the service provider, the ability to build out your infrastructure without having to pay all these upfront capital costs. So in other words, the upfront cost that it takes to get started in SaaS mirrors the revenue that you're receiving from your customers."

DISCUSSION QUESTIONS

1. Explain the major enterprise information system applications.
2. Explore the main features of mainframe information architecture and the reasons why some businesses still rely on it.
3. What are main models of the client-server architecture?
4. Identify main critical points within the mainframe-based and client-server architectures with regard to business continuity.
5. Why some companies are reluctant to give up legacy code?
6. How to connect legacy and Web-based applications, how to make them "communicate" and exchange data?
7. Define the major client-server infrastructure layers and components.
8. Explain the role of server operating systems and desktop operating systems within the client-server architecture.
9. Define the Utility Computing.
10. What is the difference between the standard ASP model and SaaS model?

Discussion Questions: Lessons Learned from Cases

1. What IT architecture is already in place in your organization?
2. Explore the main differences between the ASP (Application Service Provider) model and the SaaS model of application outsourcing platforms.
3. Does the modernizing the legacy code can be cost-effective?
4. Why Microsoft decided to cope with SaaS model as well?

Chapter V
Server Operating Environment and Business Continuity Drivers

CHAPTER OVERVIEW

After identifying major downtime points within a client-server architecture in Chapter IV, Chapter V discusses in more details enterprise servers and server operating environments from continuous computing and business continuity perspective. The main features of enterprise servers are identified and a framework for selection of the server operating environment is presented.

ENTERPRISE SERVERS

Server operating environments consisting of enterprise servers, server operating systems and serverware applications are introduced. The role of these components in enhancing continuous computing levels is explained. Examples of most widely used server platforms are provided.

From historical perspective, the following categories of computer systems can be identified as most common: supercomputers, mainframes, minicomputers, workstations, and personal computers.

Today, the old-style mainframes and minicomputers are mainly replaced by "enterprise servers" or simply "servers" although some companies still have in use the "big-iron" mainframes or minicomputers. Today's high-end servers already possess the supercomputing power, while new supercomputer systems are implemented in either single-node or multi-node configurations. In addition, the term "computer" has been renamed into "computing device" with newly designed portable and mobile computer devices. Several computer configurations have been added to the previous list such as: portable computers, mobile computers, mobile-portable devices, personal digital assistants, tablet PCs, smart-phones, and so forth.

Modern business computing is dominantly based on the two main types of information system architectures:

- an old-style mainframe environment and
- several models of client-server architectures.

In a **mainframe**-operating environment, mainframe computer does the whole data processing; dumb terminals, terminal emulation programs and client software on PCs are used to enter/get data.

Client-server architecture consists of one or more servers and a number of clients with applications running on server computers. From business perspective, server configurations and server operating systems (SOS) are expected to provide an operating environment that must meet much more rigorous requirements than a standard desktop operating system can provide.

Figure 5.1 shows the old-style IBM mainframe from the 1960s, while figure 5.2 shows Digital VAX minicomputer from the 1970s.

Figure 5.1. IBM mainframe S360 (Source: Wikipedia, http://en.wikipedia.org/wiki/IBM_System/360)

Figure 5.2. Digital VAX (Source: Wikipedia, http://en.wikipedia.org/wiki/VAX)

All computers that are in use in business computing today can be classified into the following classes:

- Enterprise Servers or simply "servers"
- Workstations
- Personal Computers
- Portable computing devices
- Mobile computing devices.

The following three figures (Figures 5.3, 5.4, and 5.5) show three main categories of computer systems that are in use in business computing: a) servers, b) desktop/portable computers, c) mobile computing devices.

Figure 5.3. Contemporary servers

Figure 5.4. Desktop and portable computers

Figure 5.5. Mobile computing devices

Server platforms or enterprise servers play crucial role in modern computing environments especially from business continuity and business agility perspectives. Servers comprise several components such as server hardware, server operating system (SOS), application servers, and server-based applications called ServerWare. They are expected to provide such an operating environment that must meet much more rigorous requirements than a standard desktop operating system can provide (e.g., Windows XP). Such platforms are of special interest for businesses that require "always-on" or "online-all-the-time" computing environments. Therefore, server operating systems that provide zero-downtime or 100% uptime or some solution, which is "near it" are of extreme importance for such businesses.

Figure 5.6 shows an example of the server configuration.

Server platforms must be reliable, available and scalable such that server-based applications (application servers, data servers, e-mail servers, Web servers) run with high reliability/availability/scalability ratios. In addition, they are expected to provide several types of services: Internet-Web technology services, Directory services, Security services, and remote access capabilities including support for mobile computing.

How is Server Configuration Different From a Standard PC?

Both computers are designed to store and process data. PC does that in two different ways: a) as a stand-alone (desktop or portable) machine and b) as a client within a client-server architecture. PCs and portable-mobile computers are used

Figure 5.6. Examples of today's servers—IBM System z (Source: http://en.wikipedia.org/wiki/IBM_System_z)

by a single user, they run desktop applications such as Microsoft Office and other personal productivity tools. Enterprise servers run server-based applications that need to be accessed from several dozens, hundreds, even thousands users. From business continuity perspective, on PC (desktop) side, when a desktop PC's mouse pointer "gets frozen" on the screen, end-user can simply reboot the system and, in most cases, the problem is resolved.

However, server configurations are expected to do much more, much faster and, what is more important, they have to be much more available, reliable, and scalable than personal computers. In short, servers are expected to be:

- Multi user computer configurations (running multi user server operating system), with capabilities of supporting multi-user application environment.
- Faster with regard to data processing speed
- More reliable than PC
- More scalable than PC
- More secure than PC
- Able to run business—critical applications.

In addition, servers should have the following features:

- Fully integrated and high-availability oriented system architecture: 32-bit or 64-bit processor, symetrical multiprocesing and shared-memory architecture, very large memory, support for non-uniform memory access (NUMA architecture), built-in resilience to failures, interconnect architecture, networking architecture, increased levels of L1, L2, L3 cache memory, support for ECC (error-correcting code) that can repair errors resulting from a corrupted bit.

- Server operating system designed for symetrical multiprocessing, hardware and software-based fault tolerance, virtualization and clustering, kernel level cache and application pools, system and operational robustness, workload management, support for online reconfiguration.
- Powerfull system administration, including online management, remote system administration and management, online and remote backup.
- Support for database management system that includes VLDB capabilities (very large database support).
- Support for middleware products and enterprise application integration.

An **enterprise server**, by definition, is a computer system that runs core IT operations of the whole enterprise or its subsystem within a client-server platform, providing processing capabilities for business-critical applications. Most widely used enterprise servers in contemporary computing are:

a. Mainframe servers,
b. UNIX-based servers,
c. Proprietary servers,
d. Linux-based servers
e. Intel/AMD processors-based servers,
f. Apple Macintosh servers.

Enterprise Servers can be configured, implemented and used as:

- Application aervers
- Data servers
- File servers
- Print servers
- E-mail servers
- Web servers
- E-commerce servers
- Firewall servers, and so forth.

As Internet and Web technologies mature, new servers are introduced and implemented. For instance, the BlackBerry Enterprise Server consists of services and components that are designed to provide mobile users an efficient access to a number of standard office tools and applications such as Internet applications and personal productivity tools (email, instant messaging, personal information management) and provide data access to enterprise applications.

All business applications can be classified according to business "criticality:"

a. Front-end server applications, such as: application servers, e-commerce servers, firewall servers, portal servers.
b. Mid-tier servers: ERP, SCM, CRM applications.
c. Data-tier servers: large database servers, enterprise-wide ERP systems, enterprise-wide business intelligence solutions, and so forth.

Accordingly, specific server processor configurations are used. For instance, Intel's Xeon-x86-based platforms are used for those business applications on the front-end servers and middle-tier servers, while Intel Itanium 2 processor-based platforms are used for data-intensive, business critical applications, on the data-tier servers in which the highest levels of availability, reliability and scalability are required.

Most frequently used enterprise servers are the following configurations:

*   Mainframe servers such as IBM S/390-zSeries 900 models based on IBM's 64-bit z/Architecture.
*   UNIX-based servers - various RISC-based platforms running commercial versions of UNIX operating system.
*   Linux-based servers—various processor platforms running Linux distributions (ReadHat, SuSE Linux, Debian, Mandrake, FreeBSD, etc.).
*   Servers that run so-called proprietary operating systems, usually based on proprietary processors (e.g., Digital/Compaq/HP Alpha-based servers).
*   Intel/AMD processors-based servers using either 32-bit or 64-bit processor architectures (several IT-vendors' server configurations based on Intel or AMD processors).
*   Apple Macintosh servers (Apple's server configuration running MacOS X Server OS).

Business requirements towards a specific server configuration are mainly bound to overall performances of the server configuration.

Typical server configurations include several dozens or hundreds of gigabytes of RAM, several hundreds of TB in external memory space, while the processing speed ranges from 500 to +10.000 MIPS. Depending on the desired configuration, the price can be in the range from $5.000 to $5-10 million. Within this class, three subclasses can be identified:

- High-end servers (prices range from $200,000 to $1-10 million) such as S/390 mainframe systems from IBM, Hitachi and Amdahl, some models of UNIX-based servers such as Sun Enterprise servers, HP SuperDome, NonStop-Himalaya and Integrity servers and other high-end Alpha or Itanium 2 servers running OpenVMS or HP-UX operating systems.
- Mid-range servers ($50-200,000) such as IBM AS/400 systems, mid-range UNIX or proprietary servers from Sun, HP, IBM, SG, Dell.
- Entry-level, Workgroup, Departmental or Small Business servers ($1,000 - 50,000). These are mainly entry-level UNIX/Linux and Windows Server Intel/AMD-based servers.

In the IT world, there are other approaches as well, with regard to the classification to high-end, mid-range and entry-level. Some IT professionals argue that small business servers or entry-level servers should be those that are priced at less than $25,000, midrange servers are priced from $25,000 to $500,000, and high-end enterprise servers are priced at $500,000 or more.

High-end servers (mainframe servers, some proprietary systems and UNIX-based servers) are characterized by:

- Very high processing speed
- Very high levels of the reliability, scalability and availability
- Support for several thousands concurrent users
- VLM and VLDB support (very large memory, very large data base)
- Multi processor and multi node support
- Powerful "fault-tolerance" capabilities.

Robb (2007) pointed out that while some machines are clearly mainframes, the line is blurring between the high end of the midrange - such as IBM's System i (iSeries, AS/400) servers or HP's Superdome (with 128 64-bit processor cores, 2TB of RAM and 192 I/O slots) — and the bottom of the mainframe product ranges. As the Hutchinson Dictionary of Computing, Multimedia and the Internet explains in its mainframe definition, "Because of the general increase in computing power, the differences between the mainframe, supercomputer, minicomputer and microcomputer (personal computer) are becoming less marked." Many of today's powerful midrange servers, even those running x86 processors, can now outperform the mainframes of a few years ago.

In addition, servers can be classified according to a number of processors installed:

(a)   single-processor
(b)   multi-processor/single-node
(c)   multi-processor and multi-node.

However, servers can be made as multi-node, cabinet and multi-cabinet configurations.

Blade servers or server blades are new server configurations designed couple of years ago with a concept of sharing some hardware resources (devices). Blade servers include more computer power into a smaller space than traditional server configurations. This feature has made blade servers a more attractive option when trying to integrate server applications, consolidate servers, balancing data processing workload and its optimization, cutting costs, and so forth.

IDC (2005) defines a server blade as "an inclusive computing system that includes processors and memory on a single board. Most notably, power, network access, and storage services are not contained on the server blade. These necessary resources, which can be shared among a collection of blades, are accessed through the backplane pf the chassis, that is, the power and network interconnect bus connections are a part of the cabinet that houses a collection of the blades. Blades are easily installed and removed.

Figure 5.7. HP Proliant blade enclosure (full of blades), with two 3U UPS units below (Source: Wikipedia, http://en.wikipedia.org/wiki/Blade_server)

SERVER CONFIGURATIONS OF MAJOR SERVER VENDORS

The section provides a snapshoot of server offerings by major server vendors such as IBM, SUN, HP, Dell. Server configurations are presented according to business requirements, operating system platform and processor technology.

Major server vendors such as IBM, Sun, HP, Dell, Silicon Graphics offer several models of server configurations according to business requirements.

Models are classified according to:

a. business requirements (high-end, mid-range, entry-level)
b. operating system platform (proprietary OS, Windows, UNIX, Linux)
c. processor technology (proprietary—RISC based, Intel/AMD based, 32/64 bit technology, single-core—multi-core).

In many ways, the choice of a specific processor platform reflects the choice of an operating system.

For instance, **IBM** (www.ibm.com) has a number of server configurations with regard to:

a. Business needs (high-end, mid-range, entry-level servers)
b. Processor (proprietary POWER5 and POWER6, Intel processors, AMD processors)
c. Operating systems (z/OS, AIX, Linux, Windows Server).

Today, IBM offers the following server configurations with regard to operating system that they use:

a. System z
b. System p
c. System i
d. System x

System z servers are most powerful high-end mainframe computers running z/OS or Linux OS. System p servers run AIX or Linux operating system, can be used as high-end or midsize server configurations. The third group of IBM servers belong to "system i" servers and are based on OS/400 or i5/OS platform. OS/400-based servers are also midsize server configurations. System x servers use Intel/AMD x86 architecture.

Sun Microsystems (www.sun.com) has several server configurations that operate Sun SPARC and UltraSPARC processors and run Solaris operating system.

Dell (www.dell.com) has its own line of servers, including several models such as: rack servers, blade servers, tower servers and rack infrastructure-based servers.

Hewlett-Packard (www.hp.com) offers several possibilities for choosing server configuration. After the acquisition of Digital in January 1998, Compaq decided to continue with Digital platforms such as Alpha-processor, True64UNIX and Open-VMS operating systems. HP-Compaq acquisition (merge) in 2003 followed and HP decided to port Alpha processors—based platforms to Intel's Itanium 2.

Today, HP has a wide choice of servers that are based on several processors such as:

a. x86
b. Intel Itanium 2
c. PA-RISC
d. MIPS
e. Alpha

and server operating platforms including:

a. HP-UX 11i
b. OpenVMS
c. NonStop
d. Tru64 UNIX
e. Windows Server
f. Linux

IDC (2007) pointed out that these three vendors: HP, Sun and IBM are the top 3 vendors in the UNIX server market worldwide, comprising more than 85% of worldwide market share for all UNIX servers, by revenue.

PC-LIKE INTEL/AMD PROCESSORS-BASED SERVERS

The section provides a summary of server configurations that use Intel's and/or AMD's server processors such as Xeon, Itanium 2, and Opteron.

In addition to their proprietary processors, almost all server vendors offer the servers based on Intel and/or AMD processors such as Xeon or Itanium 2 and Opteron. These servers in most cases run Windows Server or Linux operating system, however, some other operating systems can be installed as well (e.g., Novell NetWare, Sun Solaris). IBM had its own proprietary server operating system OS/2 Warp Server, however, they decided to stop this server product line. HP decided the same for its MPE/x operating platform.

PC-like servers from Intel and AMD can also be configured with regard to the following classification:

- Enterprise servers
- Small Business servers
- Workgroup servers
- Departmental servers
- Entry Level

All these servers can be configured in a way that they include one, two or more processors. Intel and AMD are two main players on this market with their Xeon, Itanium 2 (Intel) and Opteron (AMD) server product lines.

Intel offers its 32-bit Xeon processor (IA32) and Itanium 2 (64-bit processor—IA64), while AMD has two product lines: Athlon MP (32-bit) and Opteron (64-bit).

Intel Itanium 2-based solutions are designed for data-intensive, business-critical applications, in which the highest levels of scalability, availability and security are required. These applications include large database—based and high-level transaction processing applications, OLAP and data mining and other business intelligence applications that require large shared memory and/or fast floating point performance. As workloads grow, these types of applications can typically be scaled most effectively on large, multi-processor server platforms.

Intel x86-based solutions are suited for mainstream applications in the front-end and middle-tier of the enterprise infrastructure; and for workloads that can be distributed easily across multiple, smaller servers. This can include very demanding technical and analytical applications, as long as they can be broken down into relatively small, independent sub-processes that do not share substantial amounts of data

AMD's server platform is based on the AMD 64-bit Opteron processor. The AMD64 family of processors consists of the following products (www.amd.com):

- AMD Opteron processors—for servers and workstations
- AMD Athlon 64 processors—for desktops and notebooks
- AMD Turion 64 mobile technology—for notebooks

The Third-generation AMD Opteron (AMD64) with AMD's Direct Connect architecture enhances system performances and efficiency of data processing by directly connecting the processors, the memory controllers, and the I/O to the CPU. The platform is designed to:

- enable simultaneous 32- and 64-bit computing
- dedicated L1 and L2 cache per core and large L3 cache shares between cores
- reduce memory latency time
- allow processors and cores to operate at various voltages and frequencies
- reduce processor energy consumption by turning off unused parts of processor
- better scaling of memory bandwidth
- reduce I/O bottlenecks
- improve the efficiency of virtualized environments.

APPLE MACINTOSH SERVERS

Apple server configurations are briefly introduced. While not being the major server vendor, Apple has also included server platforms into its hardware program.

Apple decided to enter server market as well. After leaving Motorola and PowerPC processors and making transition to Intel-based processors, Apple today offers Intel Xeon-based servers called Xserve. These processors use two Dual-Core Intel Xeon "Woodcrest" processors running up to 3.0 GHz.

Xserve server configurations come with Apple's native server operating system "Mac OS X Server," the UNIX-based server operating system. In addition to standard UNIX-based features and services, Mac OS X Server provides cross-platform management, collaboration features, imaging and security, and so forth, with all these features integrated with Apple's desktop and mobile environments based on the newest versions of Apple iMac desktops, Mac Pro Xeon-based workstations, Mac Mini configuration for digital-video world, Apple Mac Book notebooks.

Figure 5.8. A small Xserve cluster with an Xserve RAID (Source: Wikipedia, http:// en.wikipedia.org/wiki/Xserve)

According to the IAPS Report (2007) on server hardware and operating system deployments and usage:

- Users are gradually moving to more powerful processors. In the 2005 survey an overwhelming 93% majority of businesses' servers was either a single CPU or two processor machine. The use of four-processor machines has more than doubled in the past 18 months, from 6% in the summer of 2005 to 13% today run four processors. However, users are still slow to migrate to the more powerful eight- and 16-processor machines. Only 1% of respondents said they currently use eight- and 16-way servers.
- Application server configurations are a bit more powerful: 56% of companies have two processors compared with only 26% that have a single CPU application server; 15% have four-processor machines; 2% have eight-processors and 1% have a 16-processor CPU application server.
- Web server configurations are equally split with 45% of firms having a server with a single CPU and 46% who have two-processor CPU configurations.
- Windows usage remains high: 55% of the respondents noted that 80% to 100% of their servers are running Windows. Only 3% of respondents said they had no Windows installed.
- Linux deployments also remain healthy: 38% of the respondents reported that up to 20% of their servers were running Linux, while only 28% said they did not have any Linux installed.

CHOOSING A SERVER FOR BUSINESS CONTINUANCE

Purchasing a server is not a simple task, even when it is done for small business and even in case when a high availability is not critical requirement. It happens to be a strategic decision having in mind all kinds of the factors including: processor type and vendor, operating system, total costs of ownership, commercial versus open-source dilema, and so forth.

The selection of a server or server configuration is an activity which has to provide answers to a number of questions. These questions are listed here having in mind server's business continuity perspective (availability, reliability and scalability).

- What is the planned application portfolio?
- What is the number of users; how many users, both named and concurrent users?
- Which server operating system will be used?
- How fast data processing do we need?

- How many servers do we need?
- What are the Input/Output Considerations?
- What kind of backup technology will be used?
- What kind of networking do we need?
- What kind of system administration and system management?
- What is industry support for operating systems? What is the viability of OS vendors?

In the section that follows, these quesstions are briefly explained.

1. **Application server portfolio.** What kind of data processing will this server be used for? What kind of application software will be installed on that server (file server, print server, database server, comunication server, application server, etc.)? Is this application a mission-critical application?

The starting point in the process of providing details on server configurations is an answer to a question as defined previsously. Are we going to purchase, configure and later use a database server, application server, messaging server, Web server, print server, file server, and so forth? Depending on the type and size of business, all these servers could be installed on a single machine, however, there can be several server configurations: each machine for a specified server. Server virtuallization approach can be applied as well: a single machine with several OS-layers and belonging applications running within their virtual spaces. In case of business-critical application, the issues of availability, reliability and scalability should be carefully addresses.

In case of planning and purchasing a server for mission-critical applications, the selected server should have most of high-availability oriented features such as:

- Multi-core processor technology
- Dedicated L1 and L2 cache per core
- Large L3 cache shares among cores
- Reduced memory latency time
- Recovering from data bus errorr
- Ability to turn off unused parts of processor
- ECC memory (error correcting code)
- Cache ECC coverage
- Cache reliability
- Lockstep support
- Better scaling of memory bandwidth
- Bad data containment

- Memory error correct
- Double-bit error detect
- Memory spares
- Hot swappable components
- Hardware partitioning

2. **Number of users.** How many users, both named and concurrent users will be "on server?" How many employees are in the company? How many clients must be supported on concurrent basis (simultaneously)? How many users we can expect from outside, the users who will be provided with user accounts (customers, suppliers)? What are expectations with regard to growing of these numbers over time? How to address potential scalability problems?

Both numbers are important: named users and concurrent users. Theoretically, all named users (all employees) can become concurrent users, a situation which may cause a problem with internal system scalability. This issue should be addressed for external system scalability as well. For example, in case of planning a CRM application where a number of customers willing to access that application can increase inexpectedly overnight. Only a scalable system can handle an increased number of concurrent users on a system.

A typical scalability problem occured recently (in October 2007) when the Beijing 2008 Olympic Committee decided to start the proces of online ticket reservation. The server (servers) went down immediately after activating online reservations and sales. It was because of the fact that during the first hour of server operation, the Web site for online ticket sales received couple of million page views with an average of 200,000 ticket requests filed every minute. The system (server and application) was designed to handle maximum of one million visits per hour and a maximum of 150,000 ticket requests per minute. However, due to a huge number of requests, much more than predicted and designed, the system could not handle as many as eight times bigger number of requests. The organizers attempted later on October 30 to reconfigure the system in order to make it handle heavier traffic load. However, their efforts did not help, and organizers decided to suspend online tisket sales.

3. **Which server operating system** will be installed on server: proprietary server operating system (e.g., IBM z/OS, IBM OS/400, HP OpenVMS), commercial UNIX and which UNIX: AIX, Solaris, HP-UX, IRIX, various Linux versions—which Linux, Windows Server, and so forth?

The decision on which server operating system will be used on server platform depends on several factors and should be considered together with decision on which server platform will be selected. Several options and decision points exist: proprietary system—the system that works on a specific processor platform (e.g., z/OS, OpenVMS), commercial UNIX version from a variety of UNIX versions (IBM's AIX, HP's HP-UX, HP's Tru64UNIX, Sun's Solaris, Silicon Graphics' IRIX), free-open source UNIX such as FreeBSD UNIX, several Linux versions (RedHat, SuSE, Debian), Windows Server, Novell NetWare, and so forth.

4. **How fast data processing do we need?** Which processor will be used for server configuration? How many processors, do we need symetrical (multi-processing) processing system? Are we going to have a 32-bit processor server or 64-bit processor based server? How much RAM? How much disk space, what kind of disk controller (SCSI or Serial ATA).

The answer to this question determines the number of processors needed (2, 4, 8, 16, 32, etc.), processor type (32-bit versus 64-bit, CISV vs. RISC), the size of RAM, and so forth. A server should support symetrical multiprocessing such that additional processors can be added if needed.

5. **How many servers do we need**; one for each application or all applications are to be installed on a single server? How to address potential problems with server consolidation and server sprawl? Do we plan virtualization and on which level; consolidation, partitioning? What kind of server configuration is more appropriate: a tower or a rack mount server (dilema: taking less space or having more room for later expansions)?

Small business can run all its applications on a single server that hosts several server-based applications such as: database management system, messaging server, Web server, e-commerce server, and so forth. Mid-size businesses and large companies employ several dozens, hundreds and even thousands of servers. For instance, Siemens company has 8,900 servers and almost 400,000 desktop PCs. Server consolidation and server sprawling are two issues that might occur while configuring multiple servers. Another alternative is server virtualization, a solution that can place several server operating environments on a single hardware platfom.

6. **Input/Output Considerations:** internal and external network connectivities (PCI, SCSI, ATA, SATA, USB, FireWire, Gigabit Ethernet, Fibre Channel)?

Most of the server configurations include by default all up-to-date data communication and networking protocols. The decision to include some of them, that is, Fibre Channel depends on the planned activities of the server configuration (clustering, grid, etc.).

7. **What kind of backup technology will be used**? Is it enough to have only standard tape-based backup system, do we need RAID technology?

Backup strategy and policy on organizational level determines some server-related decisions. Are we going to have a separate backup server, what kind of backup technology will be used (only tape, or combination of tapes with other technologies), is RAID needed, and so forth.

8. **Networking** infrastructure (LAN, WAN, wireless), what network protocols (Fiber Optic, Gigabt Ethernet, etc.), how many network cards per server? What kind of remote data access will be needed?

The type of business in terms of single or multi location, number and character of remote sites and users, availability of VAN services, determines the structuring of local and wide area network infrastructures.

9. **Do we need an integrated system management** (server management) software? Do we have appropriate human resources (specialists, system administratos) for the servers we plan to purchase?

Are we going to use only system administration module of the server operating system that comes preinstalled, or do we need additional comprehensive system management tool? An integrated system management suite provides a brader set of system management tools that are needed in fixing and resolving problems of system downtime. In addition, all server configurations need one or more system administrators, how to find an experienced system administrator. Experienced system administrators can resolve system problems more efficiently and reduce the downtime. On the other side, lack of necessary skills and less experienced system administrators can cause more hours in order to fix the problem of downtime.

10. **Industry support for operating systems? Viability of OS vendors?**

Commercial operating system costs more that an open source operating system in terms of initial - license and servicing costs. However, other dimensions should be considered as well, such as support and viability of OS vendors. The following dilemas are present when this question is considered:

a. Linux versus commercial UNIX
b. If Linux, which Linux?
c. Windows Server versus Linux
d. Free—open source UNIX (e.g., FreeBSD) versus commercial UNIX
e. Free—open source UNIX versus Linux.

Just to give an example of how complex the decision on which operating system to select could be, we give a short explanation on what hapenned this year after the final decision on SCO's case.

The SCO's (www.sco.com) battle began in 2003 when SCO filed a suite against IBM claiming that it had violated SCO's rigths by providing UNIX code to Linux. Many organizations decided to migrate to Linux in late '90s and beginning of 2000s, even their mission critical applications. However, when SCO filed a suite against IBM, Novell, Sun, Red Hat, and other vendors in 2003, including Linux-using businesses, it created a very real threat to the Linux users - the newly created Linux community who opted for Linux and open-source to run their enterprise-wide applications. SCO had even started sending invoices to Linux users to buy licenses from SCO. Many organizations who decided to migrate to Linux operating platform, after SCO's suite in 2003, decided to halt their plans, at least for some time.

When a U.S. district court judge ruled on August 12, 2007 that Novell, not SCO owns UNIX's IP rights, the decision finally eliminated SCO's threat to the Linux community based upon allegations of copyright infringement of UNIX operating system code.

This ruling decision from August 12, 2007 was a good news for businesses and other organizations that decided to use Linux or migrate to Linux from UNIX, Windows and other OS platforms.

CHAPTER SUMMARY

Server operating environments consisting of enterprise servers, server operating systems and serverware applications are introduced. The role of these components of an operating environment in enhancing continuous computing levels is explained. Examples of most widely used server platforms from server vendors are given. Most widely used enterprise servers in contemporary computing are briefly explained as well as server configurations of major server vendors such as IBM, HP, Sun, Dell, are presented. Server configurations are explored according to business requirements, operating system platform and processor technology. The framework for choosing a server for business continuance and selecting a server configuration is presented.

REFERENCES

IAPS Report (2007). 2007 Server hardware and OS deployment and usage survey. Institute for Advanced Professional Studies, 2007.

IDC Report (2005). Worldwide systems integration services market finally takes a turn for better, Retrieved on July 28, 2006 from http://www.integrationconsortium. org/page.php?news_id=136&parentId=59.

IDC Report (2007). Business process agility: The next ERP imperative. *March 2007.*

IDC Report (2003). Retrieved on August 5, 2006 from http://www.hp.com/hps/news/news_072303.html.

IDC Report (2006). True high availability: Business advantage through continuous user productivity.

REAL WORD CASES

Are Mainframes Making a Comeback?
October 30, 2007
By Drew Robb
Adapted from: http://itmanagement.earthweb.com/cnews/article.php/3707936

Mainframes have always been known for their stability.

"Anyone who has dealt with servers and their associated software and operating systems know they take a lot of care to keep up and running," said Dennis Carter, ERP systems manager for electronics manufacturer LaBarge in St. Louis. "With our mainframe, one IPL [Initial Program Load—a formal term for booting a computer] a week keeps us going on a 99.9% service level."

Not only do mainframes keep users free from blue screens of death, but they also have survived the predicted demise of the entire platform. Instead of giving way to client/server and Web applications, in many cases, mainframes are now driving the applications.

"What has transpired with the adoption of SOA and Web services is the ability to more fully exploit the robust nature of the mainframe platform to handle multiple, parallel workloads," said Gregg Willhoit, chief software architect for DataDirect Technologies, a mainframe integration software firm in Bedford, MA. "The net result is the mainframe is now more of an equal participant in the overall IT infrastructure."

Although x86-based servers continue to be the largest area of server growth, mainframes are making a comeback after years of decline.

"RISC-Itanium Unix servers were weak for the year on a global basis, falling 1.6% in shipments and 0.8% in revenue," said Gartner Research Vice President Jeffrey Hewitt. "Mainframes had the strongest revenue growth of any segment for the year, pushing ahead 3.9% over 2005."

For years, million-dollar IBM zSeries mainframes have dominated the mainframe market, but there are an increasing number of alternatives. Last year, Big Blue rolled out its z9 Business Class servers which, starting at around $100,000, are affordable for midsize businesses. Fujitsu's GlobalServer line of Unix mainframes use a compact design that fits up to 16 CPUs and 64B main memory on a single board. The Fujitsu GS21 600 delivers up to 3000 MIPS. Unisys has its ClearPath Dorado and Libra Servers, which can scale up to 32 processors and allow partitions to run in Unisys OS 2200, Windows and Linux.

"The zSeries is a primary comparison point because ClearPath and zSeries are both mainframes with mature operating environments that are consistently ranked by leading analysts as having 'best in class' feature/functionality," said Rod Sapp, director of marketing for ClearPath systems and solutions at Unisys.

While some machines are clearly mainframes, the line is blurring between the high end of the midrange—such as IBM's System i (iSeries, AS/400) servers or HP's Superdome (with 128 64-bit processor cores, 2TB of RAM and 192 I/O slots)—and the bottom of the mainframe product ranges. As the Hutchinson Dictionary of Computing, Multimedia and the Internet explains in its mainframe definition, "Because of the general increase in computing power, the differences between the mainframe, supercomputer, minicomputer and microcomputer (personal computer) are becoming less marked."

Many of today's powerful midrange servers, even those running x86 processors, can now outperform the mainframes of a few years ago.

For example, United Pipe and Supply, a wholesaler with 33 locations in the Pacific Northwest, uses an AS/400 to house its primary database and ERP system. "It may not technically classify as a mainframe, but it is the primary computing platform in the company," explained CIO Mike Green. "We have a portfolio of applications that surround it, that are integrated with it, that talk to it and that use it as a primary source. Our data marts, our secondary systems, our Web applications, all look to that AS/400 and pull information from it, either in real-time or overnight in a batch operation."

As mainframe capabilities have expanded, however, they have left some users behind. Atlantic Cape Community College (ACCC) in southern New Jersey, for example, started running its enterprise applications on an 11 MIPS IBM 9221 191 mainframe in 1994. That was enough processing power to meet the college's needs, but IBM has since stopped producing mainframes in that performance range.

"When IBM started putting the pressure on us to go forward with the new zSeries mainframes, the costs were prohibitive, and the jump in MIPS [from 11 to 80] was too extreme for what we needed," said Patrick Sweeney, ACCC's director of administrative computing.

This resulted in a search for a less-expensive alternative. ACCC eventually settled on an 18 MIPS tServer from T3 Technologies of Tampa, Fla. The tServers, which now scale up to 200 MIPS, use x86 processors but have middleware that enables them to emulate 32-bit IBM mainframes. The company also sells 64-bit systems that scale to 350 MIPS. This way, the school was able to continue running its familiar enterprise software but was able to partake in the advantages associated with more modern architectures.

"It does everything that the mainframe does but offers so much more flexibility in terms of things like backup capabilities, connecting laster printers and direct attached storage," said Sweeney. "It opened a whole new world to me to take advantage of things I never could afford on a mainframe."

Better interfaces are also letting mainframes integrate with client/server and Web applications. ACCC still uses terminal emulation software on its PCs to let time interact with the mainframe, but other companies are putting GUIs on mainframe applications.

"Users of corporate systems have come to expect the jazz of rich user interfaces and the experiences promised and delivered though Web 2.0 technologies, such as blogs and RSS," said Murray Laatsch, enterprise architect for Online Business Systems in Calgary, Alberta.

LaBarge wanted to keep its OS/390 enterprise software and add additional functionality. "Implementing a new ERP system is expensive, risky, and sometimes you have to shut down parts of the business for a while," said George Hayward, Director of Information Systems at LaBarge, an electronics and electromechanical equipment manufacturer headquartered in St. Louis. "We didn't really need new guts, I just wanted to find a better way for people to get at the data." To improve the interface, and the access to the data, he installed Information Builders' WebFOCUS business intelligence software along with IBM's WebSphere portal software. This offered employees an easy way to run their own queries and analysis, without having to wait for the IT organization to print out a report.

"It has completely changed the way we handle the data," says Hayward. "Before we just reported on things after the fact; now we can do real-time analysis and see what is going on in our factories as it is happening."

SABRE BIDS MAINFRAME ADIEU WITH UNIX MOVE

Four-year program to migrate applications from IBM to Unix servers begins
By Larry Greenemeier
Adapted and compiled from: InformationWeek
October 7, 2002 12:00 AM (From the October 7, 2002 issue)
http://www.informationweek.com/story/IWK20021004S0035

Sabre Holdings Corp. last week revealed it has begun to migrate its well-known airfare-pricing application from its home on IBM mainframes to Hewlett-Packard NonStop servers. The application migration is the first part of a four-year program to switch Sabre's entire pricing, scheduling, and seating system from IBM's proprietary transaction-processing technology to Unix systems using relational-database technology.

The Sabre airfare-pricing application continuously updates about 20 million fares and 1.5 million schedules to provide travelers and travel agents with real-time data. The app evaluates billions of potential fare combinations for each requested origin, destination, and nearby airports that may offer lower fares.

Sabre's pricing application is critical for it to compete with Expedia.com and Galileo International. NonStop servers will cut the cost of running Sabre's airfare-pricing application by about 40%, says Craig Murphy, Sabre's chief technology officer, though he wouldn't provide specific figures.

IBM's mainframe system has been reliable over the past 25 years, but NonStop will let his company better plan for the future, Murphy says. It's easier for him to hire programmers proficient in languages such as C++ and Java than to maintain aging code written in assembler language and C. Availability is key. If Sabre's system goes down and an airline's pricing changes, it's still responsible for selling the tickets at the price a customer has agreed to pay. "We have to pay the difference if we mess up," Murphy says. Service provider EDS will maintain the NonStop servers, but Sabre will own them. Sabre outsourced its IT operations to EDS in March as part of a 10-year, $2.2 billion contract.

DISCUSSION QUESTIONS

1. Describe the main differences between mainframe-based and client-server architecture.
2. Think about the company you know very well. What would be a model of client-server architecture for that company?
3. What server architecture do you have in your company?
4. Is your company planning to replace the existing legacy system?
5. How does the server platforms affect the choice of the IT architecture?
6. What, in your opinion, is the main difference between the old-style mainframes and modern servers?
7. Why people should be carefull while selecting an open source server platform?
8. How will the recent decision on SCO-IBM case affect the server market?
9. Explain the concept of server scalability; provide some examples of the situations when a system failed because of not being scalable.
10. Explain the magic triangle: 64-bit processors—64-bit operating systems—64-bit applications.

Discussion Questions: Lessons Learned from Cases

1. Why some companies still use the-old style mainframes, dumb terminals and character—base application interface?
2. Why Sabre decided to give up IBM mainframe platform and migrate to UNIX servers?
3. Which server platforms are known of having "blue screen of death?"
4. Is it possible to integrate the old-style mainframe-based Cobol applications with newly developed c/s applications. What kind of applications are used?

Chapter VI
Server Operating Systems

CHAPTER OVERVIEW

Server configurations described in Chapter V are operated by server operating systems. Server-based application software and business-critical applications are installed on these platforms. Taken together, they form what is called "server operating environment," the hardware-operating system platform responsible for running business applications and keeping "business in business." Chapter VI explains in more details server operating systems and their role in ensuring continuous computing and hence business continuity.

THE BASICS OF SERVER OPERATING SYSTEMS

Server operating systems are described according to several attributes. One of the most widely used approaches is the one that makes classification according to the processor that is used by a server configuration.

Servers are operated by server operating systems. By definition, an operating system is a collection of programs that manage the computer's activities. The main function of the operating system is to control the computer system's operations including monitoring activities and the assignment of system tasks. The operating system supervises the overall operation of a computer, including such tasks as monitoring the computer's status, handling executable program interruptions, and scheduling of operations, and controlling of input and output processes. Operating system provides not only an interface between the user and the hardware itself but also an operating platform on top of which other programs—application software, can run.

Every operating system should include the basic functions such as: process management, memory management, file management, secondary storage management, I/O management, network management, security and protection management, user management, and so forth.

Computers with single processor never really do more than one job at a time, but since they are fast enough in processing data, from user's perspective it looks like doing many things at once. Multitasking is basically the ability to run multiple programs or tasks "at the same time."

As almost all contemporary operating systems support multitasking capabilities, but not all of them are multi-user operating systems, we will adopt the approach, which divides all operating systems into two main groups:

- desktop operating systems (supporting multitasking, but not multi-user features, they are single user operating systems), and
- server operating systems (supporting both multitasking and multi-user capabilities).

Actually, having in mind portable and mobile computing devices, we can say that today's computers use three types of operating systems:

a. desktop operating systems (DOS)
b. server operating systems (SOS)
c. mobile operating systems (MOS).

Desktop OSs are single-user and multi-tasking operating systems, while server OSs are multi-user and multi-tasking operating systems. Unlike server OS that are aimed at running mission-critical applications, desktop OSs run on desktop platforms and provide both local processing capabilities and client access to server systems. Mobile computing devices run mobile (portable) operating systems and have similar features as desktop operating systems.

Server operating systems can be classified in different ways. One of the most widely used approaches is the one that makes classification according to the processor that server configuration is based on. We are going to respect this approach as well. While most people consider Windows Server, UNIX and Linux as being current mainstream server operating systems, most widely used server operating systems today are:

1. **Intel/AMD-based commercial server operating systems** such as the following commercial operating systems: Windows NT Server/Windows 2000/Windows

2003 Server family, Novell NetWare, UNIXWare, Sun Solaris, OS/2 Warp Server.

2. **Windows NT** was the first version of Microsoft's server operating system, developed between 1988-1993. It was named as "New Technology" in the operating systems area. This project was launched in 1988 when Microsoft hired David Cutler from Digital, the developer of Digital's VMS operating system. The first version of NT Server (3.1) was released in 1993 when Microsoft positioned Windows NT as the operating system for business environment. Since then, this operating system underwent several versions (Windows NT 3.5, Windows NT 4.0, Windows 2000 Server, Windows 2003 Server). Today's version is Windows Server. All these versions are in use today, even Windows NT Server 4.0, the version that was released in 1996. After introducing Windows NT server 4.0, Microsoft introduced the first version of its BackOffice as an integrated set of server-based applications such as: SQL Server, Exchange Server, Web Server (IIS), Proxy Server, and so forths.

3. **Novell's server operating system NetWare** was originally developed as a network operating system. Some 10–15 years ago it was dominant OS platform for LAN-based environments. In late '80s and the beginning of '90s Novell NetWare was the "king" of network operating systems. It used Microsoft's DOS and Windows 3.x as client systems. However, Novell lost its dominance over Microsoft Windows Server operating environment. Today, Novell seeks new ways of competing with Microsoft by offering NetWare in a combination with SuSE Linux.

4. **OS/2 Warp Server** is IBM's network operating system, which rivalled Windows NT Server and Novell NetWare some 10–15 years ago. However, couple of years ago, IBM decided to stop offering this operating system.

5. **Linux operating system running on both proprietary RISC-based and Intel/AMD-based server configurations**. In addition to the previous operating systems listed, various Linux versions such as Red Hat, SuSE, Debian, Mandrake, and so forth, are also used for establishing server configurations on Intel and AMD server processor platforms.

6. **RISC-based commercial server operating systems** mainly different **UNIX versions** such as: IBM's AIX, HP's HP-UX, HP's Tru64UNIX (formerly Digital, Compaq), Sun's Solaris, SGI's IRIX. UNIX operating system is a multi-user, multi-tasking operating system that runs on most minicomputers, workstations and contemporary enterprise servers. Even though UNIX is said to be standardized, every IT-vendor provides its own version of UNIX (HP-UX, IRIX, AIX, Solaris, etc).

7. **Intel/AMD-based servers running UNIX operating system.** The two major configurations that run on Intel/AMD processors are Sun Solaris UNIX and "free-UNIX" configurations such as FreeBSD.

8. **Single-vendor or proprietary server operating systems**are such operating systems that are developed for specific processor platforms. IBM OS/390 (formerly MVS) and its upgraded 64-bit version called z/OS, IBM OS/400, OpenVMS, HP MPE are just some examples of proprietary server operating systems. IBM's MVS (Multiple Virtual Storage) was the first mainframe-based operating system from IBM (www.ibm.com) that was installed on most of IBM mainframes. It was first renamed to OS/390, today it is called z/OS. OS/400 is an IBM proprietary server operating system that runs on the IBM AS/400 midrange server configurations. OpenVMS (www.hp.com) is an operating system originally developed some 30 years ago by Digital Equipment Corporation (DEC) that used to run on Digital's VAX (CISC) and Alpha (RISC) computers. OpenVMS evolved from VMS, which originated as the operating system for the VAX in 1979. OpenVMS server operating system is still offered by HP and is known as one of the most reliable server operating environments. There was another HP's proprietary operating system called HP MPE (HP MPE/iX), but it is no longer offered by HP.

9. **Apple server-based server operating systemMacOS X Server** is Apple's server operating system—a product that is installed mainly within Apple Macintosh client-server operating environments. Apple's Mac OS X Server and Mac OS X as a desktop operating server are also based on UNIX core operating system platform.

SERVERWARE

The concept of ServerWare is introduced as a set of server-based utilities aimed at enhancing capabilities of a server. A conceptual model to illustrate the role of server operating system and ServerWare in the design of an information system for continuous computing infrastructure is provided.

All contemporary server operating systems come pre-installed on server configurations. They are usually accompanied by some additional server software that is also in most cases delivered in bundled form. These software packages aim at enhancing the capabilities of core server operating platforms.

In addition to standard, core operating system features that come within the core server operating system, a new approach in developing server operating environments for running business critical applications brings several enhancements called "ServerWare." As a result, both IT-vendors and IT-specialists introduced a new, broader term called "server operating environment" or "server operating platform."

A conceptual model to illustrate the role of server operating system and server operating platforms in the design of an information system for continuous computing infrastructure is given in Figure 6.2.

This additional set of server-based software includes the following features:

- Bundled servers such as: Messaging server, Web server, e-mail server, e-commerce server, file-print server, terminal server, DNS, DHCP-WINS servers, Remote access server.
- Built-in support for: Automatic failover, system recovery, fault-tolerance, reloadable kernel, online upgrade, 64-bit computing, crash-handling techniques, memory mirroring, workload management, high-availability clustering, TCP/IP failover, storage scalability, and so forth.
- Server extensions for: Application development tools (e.g., JRE), TCP/IP extensions, HTML/XML, Web-based presentations, Windows/UNIX integration, dynamic page caching, bandwidth allocation, VLM and VLDB support, transaction prioritization, encryption acceleration.

All these ServerWare solutions aim at improving the server operating system's continuous computing attributes such as: uptime, scalability, reliability, availability, recovery time objective, recovery point objective. They are presented here within Churchman's systemic model defined in Chapter III (see Figure 6.1).

Figure 6.1. Server operating environment for business continuance

Modern server operating systems are expected to provide a set of features and functions that are crucial in achieving business continuance. These features and functions usually come bundled (pre-installed) together with core operating system. This "built-in support" includes the following major functions or business continuity drivers (see Figures 6.2 and 6.3).

For instance, Microsoft offers a number of server applications (servers), as many as 32 servers, on its Microsoft Windows Server operating platform (www.microsoft.com):

1. Antigen
2. Application Center
3. BizTalk Server
4. Client Security
5. Commerce Server
6. Content Management Server

Figure 6.2. Server operating platform: Built-in functions

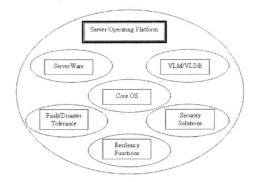

Figure 6.3. Server operating platform—continuous computing drivers

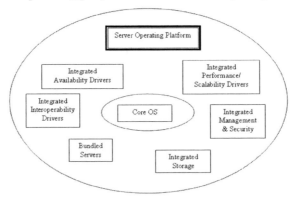

7. Data Protection Manager
8. Edge Security
9. Exchange Server
10. Expression
11. Forefront
12. Forms Server
13. Groove Server
14. Host Integration Server
15. Identity Integration Server
16. ISA Server
17. Live Communications Server
18. Operations Manager
19. Project Server
20. Server Security
21. SharePoint Server
22. Speech Server
23. SQL Server
24. System Center
25. Systems Management Server
26. Virtual Server
27. Visual Studio
28. Windows Compute Cluster Server
29. Windows Server
30. Windows Server Update Services
31. Windows Small Business Server
32. Windows Storage Server

As can be seen from the list, as many as 32 server applications can be installed in order to support standard and specific requirements of contemporary business. This is just an example, similar server application portfolio can be found on other server operating platforms as well.

The rapid advances in Internet technologies have resulted with changes in traditional server operating system structures. Therefore, in addition to core server operating system capabilities that are necessary to run a typical server configuration, an increasing number of both application and networking-oriented features, so-called "ServerWare" applications, are required on server systems to fully support contemporary Internet-based computing. Some of these applications come in the form of pre-installed or pre-integrated software "bundles" while some others are operating system - independent but very closed to that specific SOS platform.

These features, so-called "ServerWare applications" represent additional set of continuous computing drivers, hence, critical success factors needed in implementing an efficient business continuity platform.

The most important features in successfully accomplishing both continuous computing and business continuance are the following server and server operating systems' technologies and accompanying ServerWare solutions:

- **Support for online reconfiguration, online upgrade and reloadable kernel**features that allow making changes (reconfiguration, updates, upgrades) on hardware components, kernel and the whole operating system while keeping the system on. These technologies include functions such as: online CPU and memory reconfiguration, online I/O reconfiguration, alternate root installation, dynamic loadable kernel, dynamic kernel patching and dynamic partitioning. These features reduce both planned and unplanned downtime.
- **Fault-tolerance support** a set of hardware and/or software facilities that provide "resiliency functions"—functions that allow SOS to adapt to outages by hardware components: failure detection and recovery, failover configuration, disaster recovery. This support includes failure recovery functions, planned downtime reduction functions, partitioning functions. All these functions and features may significantly improve "time-to-recovery" operation.
- **Kernel-based "crash-handling" features such as** kernel dump facilities, dump analysis tools, dynamic core file generation, multimode boots, automatic hang detection, and so forth.
- **Support for storage scalability**, including support for RAID systems and scalability clustering options.
- **SMP (Symmetric Multiprocessing) support** for higher levels of availability and scalability. Symmetric multiprocessing system gives an ability to make use of multiple processors in a single machine. These technologies include SMP range, storage scalability (maximum memory supported, maximum supported file system size), clustering capabilities.
- **Support for system virtualization and system partitioning**. The technologies such as Sun's "N1 Grid Container" allow creating up to 8,000 software partitions (containers) per single instance of the SOS. Each instance has its own IP address, memory space, hostname, root password, and so forth.
- **Support for 64-bit computing** the ability to utilize processor, RAM and storage beyond the 4GB limitation on 32-bit machines. It includes support of several "large" options such as: large files, large file systems, VLM and VLDB. VLM concept gives the ability to address large amounts of RAM on the order of several dozens and hundreds of gigabytes, while VLDB represents the possibility of addressing multi-gigabyte databases stored in RAM. This feature speeds up data

access because it eliminates the need to go out to disk for frequently queried data within large data warehousing and other data-intensive applications.

- **Support for workload management** in terms of partition fault isolation and dynamic partition reconfiguration.
- **Bundled Servers**. Contemporary server operating systems usually come preinstalled and accompanied with a set of server-based applications, which is aimed at enhancing its core capabilities. Mail server and Web server are just two examples of such server software. Among other server-based applications that may come bundled (integrated) with a SOS, the most important are the following ones: Proxy servers and/or firewalls, E-commerce servers, Chat server, News server, List server, and so forth. Moreover, most SOS vendors include parts or even the whole application servers to their OS platforms. For instance, Sun's decision to bundle Java 2 Enterprise Edition application server and Sun ONE directory server with its Solaris 9 server operating system transformed the operating system environment into a fully-integrated platform for implementing Web services and Java-based applications.
- **Support for TCP/IP Extensions and/or protocols** such as: Mobile/Wireless TCP/IP, IPv6, IntServ, DiffServ, SLP, BGP and RIP, including support for TCP connection failover.
- **Support for HTML/XML development tools and Web services**. This kind of bundled software enhances capabilities of the server in order to support Web-based applications (cgi-bin, Perl and PHP support, FrontPage extensions, e-mail services such as listing, filtering, support for different e-mail formats: MIME, uuencode and Bin/Hex, Active Server Pages support, software for stabilizing Web server performances under heavy loads, bots or intelligent agents, e.g., Data Mining Bots, shopping bots, e-mail bots, search bots, news bots, etc.).
- **Extensions for application development tools and DBMS**. These extensions include support for Windows, UNIX and Linux APIs, object-oriented middleware solutions such as CORBA, COM/DCOM, Java/JavaBeans, support for Java Runtime environment, J2EE, server database extensions (Oracle, MS SQL Server, MySQL), indexing & search engines, ODBC support, Web-to-DBMS features, and so forth. Support for these application development tools, DBMS extensions, data exchange and integration, Web-to-Host solutions, make the process of application development easier and improves both efficiency and effectiveness of application platforms.
- **Support for Web-based presentations**: MStreaming media (ASX, ASF, MPEG, Real Audio, Real Video), Net-based road shows (using online PowerPoint, streaming media, chat), RealAudio/Video support are some examples of such a software.

- **Support for Windows/UNIX integration.** In today's dominant information architecture, client/server computing, unlike desktop systems which are in most cases WIntel-based, enterprise servers run on different processor types and vendor-specific OS platforms, hence there is a need for an efficient integration capabilities. Dominantly multi-platform e-commerce infrastructures, models such as B2B, B2C, usually employ several types of server configurations. Therefore, solutions such as SMB/CIFS (Common Internet File System) which is a middleware for UNIX-to-Windows integration), PC-NFS and WebNFS are extremely important from data integration point of view.
- **Enhancements for e-commerce** solutions that support and enhance e-commerce applications such as:
  - Dynamic page cachingutility which allows the system to dynamically cache frequently accessed pages in memory.
  - Bandwidth allocationallows I/O bandwidth to be reserved or prioritized according to the type of Internet protocol, or location of the page.
  - Transaction prioritizationa feature which gives priority to transactions or high volume customers.
  - Encryption accelerator supportaimed at improving performance and scalability of e-commerce sites.
- **Other Web page supplements** such as: Web statistics, site performance, data traffic reports, Guest books, Online polls and counters, auto-responders, aliasing and forwarding.

To give an example on the server operating system level, for instance, HP offers a range of server operating features and bundled solutions for its UNIX-based server operating system—HP-UX 11i (www.hp.com):

- **HP-UX 11i Foundation Operating Environment**HP-UX core – UNIX – foundation.
- **HP-UX 11i Enterprise Operating Environment**—for enterprise-class performance and stability, with the added value of resource management, monitoring, scalability, and online data management.
- **HP-UX 11i Mission Critical Operating Environment**—for top levels of availability, workload management, and security.
- **HP Virtual Server Environment Suite for HP-UX 11i**—providing very broad mission-critical virtualization capabilities coupled with high availability.
- **HP Serviceguard Storage Management Suite for HP-UX 11i**—enabling improved manageability and performance for Oracle and Oracle RAC databases.

The latest release of HP's UNIX operating system, HP-UX 11i v3, puts an emphasize on the following features:

- enhanced virtualization
- workload management
- high availability
- security features.

HP has defined a platform for the next generation of integrated enterprise-wide IT operations, called "Adaptive Enterprise" which aims at linking business processes with information technologies in order to break down the barriers between so-called "islands of automation."

IDC (2007) reported that HP-UX 11i v3 provides an integrated computing environment with a number of features that fulfill key requirements for running mission-critical applications. Some of these features include:

- **Support for faster performance.** Changes to the operating system kernel improve cache locality and optimize communication between the modules within the kernel.
- **Support for scalability.** HP-UX 11i v3 supports an extensible range of systems, scaling up from volume servers (servers that are priced less then $25,000 to 64-socket, 128 core Superdome systems at the high-end enterprise range (servers priced more than $500,000).
- **Support for reliability and availability.** With the HP-UX 11i v3 release, the Serviceguard high-availability (HA) software is now shipping as an integrated part of the mission-critical version of the HP-UX 11i v3 release. In addition, there are pre-tested and supported extensions for Serviceguard such as Serviceguard for SAP and Serviceguard for RAC, supporting rapid deployment of Serviceguard-enabled application solutions.
- **Support for next-generation mass storage software stack.** HP-UX 11i v3 now supports zettabytes of data, as the compliance requirements are boosting demand for ever-increasing amounts of storage.
- **Support for advanced automation.** As more servers are installed in scale-out deployments, and as virtualization of workloads on each server increases, the ability to manage all of these objects becomes a critical element to controlling operational costs.
- **Support for enhanced security features.** Several security enhancements have been added such as: automatic encryption of data, now offered directly within the operating-system kernel, speed performance of the encryption process and HP protection systems, which support data isolation in HP-UX 11i-defined

compartments and different security settings, as needed. In addition, HP is providing the option of an embedded chip for its Integrity servers that includes digital keys to support decryption of the data that has been protected.

- **Support for high availability. IDC underscores the fact that** the high-availability software drives down the amount and the cost of both planned and unplanned downtime. HP-UX 11i v3, along with HP Serviceguard, addresses this business requirement by minimizing unplanned downtime. Online patching of HP-UX 11i software, via the Dynamic Root Disk feature, addresses planned downtime by allowing updates to be added to the system first.
- **Deployment.** HP-UX 11i v3 has been tested together with other key HP software products, to ensure that customer deployments will support high levels of availability.

With regard to processor architecture, HP is giving up on its proprietary RISC processor called PA-RISC, which was used for more than 15 years as a major processor platform for HP servers and workstations. HP replaced mainly PA-RISC processor platform by Intel's Itanium 2 processor.

After acquiring (merging with) Compaq four years ago, HP acquired all former Digital's platforms (Alpha processor, Digital's proprietary operating system Open-VMS and Digital's Tru64UNIX). However, HP decided to continue with HP-UX and is reiterating its commitment to HP-UX as the high-end operating system for mission-critical applications.

In case of application-related ServerWare, the server can provide a number of pre-installed (bundled) programming utilities, libraries, tools, and so forth, that can be used in application development.

INTEGRATED APPLICATION DEVELOPMENT AND WEB PROGRAMMING TOOLS

An example of an integrated set of Web programming tools for UNIX and Linux platforms is given in this section. It contains the following tools: Perl, PHP, CGI and FastCGI, and several Apache server utilities.

Server operating environments include several sets of application development and Web application development tools. In the section that follows, we give an example of these tools[1].

Perl (Practical Extraction and Report Language) is one of the most popular languages for Web programming. Perl was initially designed as a language for efficient text processing for UNIX platforms. As time passed, however, Perl acquired numerous additional features. At the end Perl had grown into a very powerful general-purpose programming language. During late nineties, when CGI was a dominant, language-independent method of dynamic Web page creation, Perl became the leading programming language for dynamic Web content creation. Creation of CGI.pm led to such popularization of Perl as web-technology of choice, that CGI programming almost became a synonym for Perl/CGI and Perl/FastCGI programming. Perl's extensibility and modularity allowed it to become one of the most flexible and rich languages. This gives freedom of creation to Perl programmers, but in turn also requires a steeper learning curve. Perl's designer, Larry Wall, made the decision to direct Perl towards experienced programmers even if this meant introduction of additional complexities that made learning this language more difficult. As pointed out in official Perl documentation: "The language is intended to be practical (easy to use, efficient, complete) rather than beautiful (tiny, elegant, minimal)."

PHP (PHP: Hypertext Preprocessor) is the most popular open-source programming language for the web. It was created some 7-8 years after Perl. As opposed to Perl, PHP was designed specifically for the web. It is primarily used for server-side programming. PHP was designed to eliminate unnecessary details not essential for the web. Although PHP code can be executed on most major web servers, PHP was designed to be especially effective when used in combination with Apache (*mod_php* module). Compared with Perl, PHP is a relatively straightforward language. PHP syntax is relatively simple and does not contain much complexity. This simplicity enables novice programmers to learn and use PHP more easily than the Perl language. Usually, PHP code gets embedded into HTML markup, but, as with Perl HTML markup can be embedded inside scripts themselves. Despite the fact that it is easy to learn and use, PHP grew into a powerful language oriented toward integration of Web and server-based databases.

CGI and FastCGI are not classical web technologies as are PHP and Perl. CGI and FastCGI are language-independent protocols for communication between web server and external (independent) processes—processes that are in charge of creation of dynamic web content. Both CGI and FastCGI are in practice usually programmed with Perl.

CGI was the first widely used technique for creating dynamic web content. Apache web server processes CGI scripts by using *mod_cgi* module. The module is by default the part of Apache core server. CGI interface defines the way in which web servers communicate with clients. When a web server recognises a CGI request, the server starts a new process which will execute CGI script. For every single request, the server creates a new CGI process which then exits after it services that request. This was not a problem some 5–6 years ago, but in today's world where system performances and business continuity are increasingly important this can lead to problems. The following main reasons for the performance weakness of the CGI technique are identified as follows:

1. Necessity of forking (creation of new CGI processes) for every new request. Creation of a new processes is time-expensive and introduces a relatively large overhead for the operating system.
2. Necessity of loading Perl interpreter for every new request.
3. Necessity of loading scripts' source code and its modules into memory and compiling them, for every new request

These factors are inherited into CGI technique because every single request results in the creation of a new process which dies immediately after it serves the request. Previously mentioned factors lead to additional shortages:

1. Inability to use persistent variablesinability of persistent database connections (creation of DB connections are very costly operations).
2. Inability of memory-sharingwhich could otherwise be set up by loading-in program modules during server start up.

FastCGI seeks to solve CGI's inherent problems. It is a technique that enables FastCGI processes to function like server processes (daemons). FastCGI processes do not die after processing individual requests but, rather are waiting for other possible incoming requests. As a result, the previously mentioned overheads of CGI are eliminated. Furthermore, it is possible to write scripts so that initialization parts of code identical to all users are executed only once. FastCGI applications can be single-threaded and multi-threaded. For single-threaded applications web server can be configured to start multiple copies of FastCGI applications by starting multiple FastCGI processes that can then concurrently execute multiple requests. The web server communicates with FastCGI applications via TCP or UNIX sockets. This allows for distributed architecture of FastCGI applications, which can reside on the same machine as the web server or on some other networked machine. As a result, is possible to set up:

• dedicated application servers and
• dedicated web servers.

This, in turn, allows for better optimization. Web servers can be freed from script-executions and therefore better tuned up for efficient serving of client's request. On the other hand this also allows for better optimization of FastCGI application server(s).

Apache module methods (*mod_perl* and *mod_php*) of creating dynamic content incorporate perl/php interpreters inside Apache processes. This allows Apache to directly execute scripts. Performance issues associated with CGI are eliminated because there is no need for:

- forking
- loading interpreters
- loading script's source code and its modules into memory and compiling them

However, incorporating interpreters inside Apache can introduce potential problems.

First, *httpd* processes become much larger with perl/php interpreters incorporated. Apache processes therefore require more memory for their execution. This can influence availability of a system, especially when memory of a server is scarce.

Second, there is a potential problem because potentially buggy modules (*mod_php* & *mod_perl*) execute inside Apache, have access to Apache internals and therefore have potential to crash Apache web server.

A third problems can arise because of the persistent environment which is created by *Apache::Registry mod_perl* module. This frequently used module allows standard CGI scripts to execute as *mod_perl* scripts. It cashes scripts, which results in better performance. If scripts are not written well, however, problems such as memory leaking or problems with un-initialized variables can arise. Such problems can compromise security and cause continuity problems.

Another frequently used module for converting CGI scripts to *mod_perl* scripts is Apache::PerlRun module. This module does not do cashing, and should therefore be used for scripts that are not thoroughly tested for bugs/un-initialized variables.

A very common misconception that arises when choosing the most appropriate programming language for implementation of a specific Web-related project, is that ease and speed of coding are the most important factors. Among software engineering cycles it is a known fact that maintainance costs for more complex applications account for up to 80–90% of total life-cycle costs for a given application. As it is case with most of other applications, today's e-business applications are larger and more complex then ever before. It is likely that in the foreseeable future these applications will tend to become even larger. It is clear that (for complex applications) code maintainability should be one of the most important factors when considering the implementation language for a project. This relates to business continuity, since software availability is frequently dependent on its ability to be effectively maintained.

Perl is one of the most flexible programming languages. With Perl it is possible to implement one functionality in many different ways. The well-known Perl's motto says "There's more than one way to do it." It is precisely this flexibility that allows Perl programmers to write Perl code in many unorthodox ways. This often leads to specific "dialects" of programming that many programmers adopt. These "dialects" can become unreadable when viewed by other programmers. If it happens (and it often does) that other programmers need to maintain an application written by programmers who have developed a specific way of writing Perl code, it could lead to a chain reaction: bad readability means bad maintainability, bad maintainability can lead to bad and buggy application code which in turn can easily cause continuity troubles down the road. Perl does provide certain methods for development of readable Perl code. Some of these are *strict* and *warning* pragmas. Using *strict* and *warning* pragmas together with disciplined syntax can help create readable Perl scripts. However, the reality is that large number of Perl applications are very unreadable and thus hard to maintain.

PHP receives its share of criticism for its maintainability as well, although perhaps not as loudly as it is case with Perl. One problem is that simplicity and ease of coding that PHP allows often leads to leaving out the design phase of software development since programmers are often inclined to start right away with implementation. Secondly, insertion of PHP code inside HTML markup leads to mixing presentation (HTML markup) with logic (PHP code). This often negatively influences readability and maintainability of the code since it can complicate creation of dynamic documents. This is especially true when designers and programmers collaborate to create an application. Because of intermixed HTML markup and PHP code, they may have to work on same files. Errors can occur when designers "accidentally" interfere with the programmer's code while working on HTML markup. Again, problems can be reduced by using the right software engineering principles, using *include* functions, and using template engines. In practice, however, these principles are often not followed.

The programming language stability, for example, the stability of both Perl and PHP languages, represents an important factor while selecting an appropriate application development platform within a specific ServerWare integrated suite. Through analyzing documentation for both programming languages, it can be found that PHP stable releases come out more then twice as often as was the case with Perl stable releases. Also, a good number of PHP releases come out primarily to remove bugs previously introduced. An additional disadvantage of PHP is that its versions are not always 100% backward compatible. One of the reasons for Perl's higher stability is that that it was created before PHP. PHP is still a developing language, whereas Perl is relatively mature.

Support for most widely used database management systems is another feature of these programming languages. If, for any reason, a company decides (or it is forced) to "move" its application or application portfolio from one database platform to another database management system, portability can become a critical factor for the continuity of business. Both Perl and PHP come with excellent database support.

Perl comes with DBI (DataBase Interface) module for connecting to databases. DBI API provides a uniform API interface to programmers by hiding the specifics of individual databases. DBI level provides a uniform interface for all databases. Below this layer is the DBD (DataBase Driver) layer. With the help of database-specific drivers, DBD is able to support specific databases. This architecture allows programmers to create dynamic applications using uniform calls for database manipulation. In most cases, the only part of code, which is database-specific happens when connecting to the database since at this point it is necessary to specify the driver for a particular database.

PHP also comes with a universal module for database manipulation known as PEAR DB. This module is a part of PEAR (PHP Extension and Database Repository)—a collection of modules and libraries for PHP. The PEAR DB module operates in a way similar to Perl DBI, providing an uniform abstract interface for various supported databases. As with Perl DBI, database-dependent code occurs when connecting to a database. PHP comes with database-specific functions for various databases. For different supported databases, PHP provides different application programming interfaces. These are often used by developers rather then PEAR DB.

Database portability for Perl and PHP are at approximately same level when abstract modules (DBI, PEAR DB) are utilized. However, many PHP applications are written using native PHP functions for specific databases instead of using PEAR DB. When one such application needs to access a different type of database, problems can arise.

The most popular way of using Perl and PHP as dynamic technologies for Apache is with Apache modules (*mod_perl* and *mod_php*). In this utilization Perl/PHP interpreters execute as parts of Apache processes. Although they execute similarly, there are some significant differences between the two modules.

One difference is that *mod_perl* takes up more memory then does *mod_php*. In another words, Apache processes become larger with *mod_perl* then with *mod_php*. Because *mod_perl* processes take more computer memory, web servers are able to support lesser number of Apache processes then with *mod_php*. This makes a difference when memory-resources of a web server are strained or scarce. An additional advantage of *mod_php* is that it is easier to install. *Mod_perl* is relatively poorly documented, especially when it comes to native *mod_perl* scripting.

Mod_perl was created to enable writing of handlers for each of HTTP request phases. The capability of writing efficient handlers is one significant advantage that *mod_perl* posses over *mod_php*. An additional advantage of *mod_perl* derives from a PHP's weakness: certain number of PHP modules are not thread-safe. As a result, it is often not possible to use threading capabilities of Apache 2.x server.

FastCGI protocol is supported by Apache via *mod_fastcgi* module. FastCGI has some significant advantages over *mod_perl* and *mod_php*. Some of the most important of these advantages are:

- Possibility of process isolation. FastCGI scripts are executed from separate, non-Apache processes. This isolation reduces the possibility of Apache crashing, since access to Apache internals is now restricted. This feature enhances the availability of a Web server and Installed Web-dependent applications.
- Natural support for distributed computing. FastCGI applications can use TCP or UNIX sockets to communicate with web servers. Because of this it is possible to set up dedicated application servers and thus reduce the load on web servers.

One of the main disadvantages of FastCGI is its poor documentation. Despite the extensive literature search we were not able to find a single book dedicated solely to this protocol. Online documentation is also very poor. Company that created FastCGI is out of the market for long time already. A small group of volunteers are casually maintaining *mod_fastcgi* module. Week support for FastCGI is probably one of the main reasons why this method never achieved popularity of Apache-module techniques. As opposed to *mod_perl*, FastCGI does not have access to Apache internals. This is good from the security perspective, as we already noted. However, this prevents FastCGI to interact with HTTP request processing phases.

LAMP is an example of an integrated Web-based application development open-source platform on Linux machines. The term LAMP was coined from the first letters of the four components of that platform: Linux as an operating system, Apache as the most-widely used Web server, MySQL as a relational database management system (RDBMS), and PHP as the most popular scripting language (sometimes "P" is substituted with Perl or Python).

There is a also **WAMP** acronym which describes the platform that combines Apache, MySQL and PHP on Windows operating platform.

INTEGRATED DRIVERS: AVAILABILITY, RELIABILITY, SCALABILITY, AND HIGH-PERFORMANCE DRIVERS

Integrating availability, reliability and scalability drivers comprises including several technologies such as: resiliency drivers, solutions that minimize planned downtime such as online CPU and memory reconfiguration, online I/O reconfiguration, alternate root installation, dynamic kernel patching, crash-handling techniques (kernel dump facilities, dump analysis tools, dynamic core file generation, multimode boots, automatic hang detection, etc.), workload management solutions and high-availability clustering features.

Creating a highly available and resilient system represents a major effort when trying to improve the levels of availability and reliability of server operating platforms. Resiliency of the systems means their ability to return to their original state sooner or later after encountering some sort of problem, which causes system shutdown. In that sense, a highly resilient system is a system, which returns back to its function as soon as possible, if possible in a matter of seconds. Making a system resilient requires a lot of planning activities having in mind numerous possibilities that may occur and cause system shutdown (hardware and software crashes, cutting power for several hours, exhausting UPSs, etc.).

Reliability, availability, and serviceability (RAS) basically include the following drivers:

- Resiliency driverstechnologies that allow SOS to adapt to outages by hardware components (online failure recovery functions).
- Solutions that minimize planned downtime such as online CPU and memory reconfiguration, online I/O reconfiguration, alternate root installation, dynamic kernel patching.
- Crash-handling techniques (kernel dump facilities, dump analysis tools, dynamic core file generation, multimode boots, automatic hang detection, etc.).
- Workload management solutions such as: partition fault isolation, dynamic partition reconfiguration, and so forth.
- High-availability clustering features including: fault tolerance, failover capabilities, disaster recovery/disaster tolerance, cluster file system, work with partitions, TCP connection failover, high-availability storage support.

This set of built-in drivers includes the following features: support for memory and processor-scaling, dynamic memory page sizing, support for large file and file systems, support for very large memory (VLM) and very large databases (VLDB), support for high-availability clustering. It includes support for 64-bit computing as well which means support of several "large" options such as: large files, large file systems, large-very large memory, large-very large databases, and so forth. VLM concept gives the ability to address large amounts of RAM on the order of several dozen gigabytes, while VLDB represents the possibility of addressing multi-gigabyte databases stored in RAM.

For instance, SAP AG recommends migrating to 64-bit platforms for running SAP enterprise suites (Fritz, 2006). According to SAP, 64-bit servers are currently prerequisite for running SAP on HP-UX, AIX, Solaris, IBM OS/400 and z/Linux operating platforms. In adition, starting from 2007 on, new releases of SAP NetWeaver and applications based on this platform will no longer be supported on servers running 32-bit Windows and Linux operating systems.

SMP (Symmetric Multiprocessing) support is intended for higher levels of availability and scalability. Symmetric multiprocessing system gives an ability to make use of multiple processors in a single machine. These technologies include: SMP range, storage scalability (maximum memory supported, maximum supported file system size), clustering capabilities. Support for workload management consists of partition fault isolation, dynamic partition reconfiguration, and so forth.

INTEGRATED COMPATIBILITY, CONNECTIVITY, AND INTEROPERABILITY DRIVERS

Server operating systems in their extended versions include a number of application development, networking, middleware, interoperability tools and protocols that enhance their performances. They are presented here as business continuity drivers.

This set of drivers consists of several protocols, extensions, bundles and supports that are intended to be used for resolving compatibility, connectivity and interoperability problems. The integrated operating environment has to provide availability, reliability, compatibility, manageability, and interoperability required to control today's distributed, heterogeneous IT environments. In addition, it must be based on an infrastructure that enables systems integrators to manage every IT resource, from desktops to mainframes and UNIX machines, from LANs to WANs, from standard data to knowledge, from databases to applications. To achieve true integration, it must contain integrated functions, built upon common objects and services, which are open and available to all applications.

The integrated operating environment should provide support of the following drivers:

- Extensions for application development tools and DBMS such as: Windows/ UNIX/Linux-GNU compatibility, application binary interface (ABI), support for Microsoft .NET platform, HTML/XML protocol, SOAP and WSDL protocols, data and source code compatibility, binary compatibility.
- Support for HTML/VRML/XML development tools and Web services. This kind of bundled software enhances capabilities of the server in order to support Web-based applications, such as: cgi-bin, Java, ActiveX, Perl and PHP support, FrontPage extensions, e-mail services, Active Server Pages, software

for stabilizing Web server performances under heavy loads, bots or intelligent agents: Data Mining Bots, shopping bots, e-mail bots, search bots, news bots, and so forth. This support should also include integration languages such as: industry-specific XML vocabularies (FinXML-data interchange format for financial management, eBIS-XML for procurement management, HR-XML for HRM, etc).

• Support for TCP/IP Extensions and/or protocols such as: Mobile/Wireless TCP/IP, IntServ, DiffServ, SLP, BGP and RIP, including support for TCP connection failover, TCP/IP, IPv.4, IPv.6, Mobile IPv.4., DHCP, DNS, BIND, WINS protocols.

• Support for Windows/UNIX/Linux integration, NFS/NIS, CIFS, SAMBA protocols. Solutions such as SMB/CIFS, which represent a middleware for UNIX-to-Windows integration, PC-NFS, WebNFS, are extremely important from data integration point of view.

INTEGRATED MANAGEMENT AND SECURITY DRIVERS

Integrated management and security comprises several server-based drivers that are aimed at enhancing manageability and security of the server operating platforms.

The solutions that belong to this set of drivers include the following features:

• Centralized, online, and GUI-based systems administration
• Online and GUI-based dynamic kernel configuration
• Reloadable kernel
• Online upgrade
• Crash-handling techniques
• Memory mirroring
• Centralized management of remote computers
• Automatic OS-related and application software updates
• Partitioning and virtualization
• Workload management
• Centralized cluster management
• TCP/IP failover
• Integrated authentication services, Active Directory, NIS, PKI, IPsec
• Host Intrusion Detection System
• Built-in encryption-decryption
• Secure Socket Layers
• Transaction prioritization
• Encryption acceleration.

INTEGRATED BUNDLED SERVERS AND DBMS-BASED SERVERWARE FEATURES

Several application servers are included in a bundled form into server operating systems. In addition, DBMS-based ServerWare features are briefly explored and examples of buisness continuityoriented solutions of most widely used DBMS platforms (Oracle, DB2, SQL Server) are given.

Contemporary server operating systems are today usually accompanied with a set of server-based applications, which is aimed at enhancing its core capabilities. Mail server and Web server are just two examples of such server software. Moreover, SOS vendors include parts or even the whole application servers to their SOS platforms.

Vendors of commercial operating systems such as HP, Sun, IBM, Microsoft, in addition to standard messaging servers, Web servers, file and print servers, remote access servers, security servers, and so forth, provide in bundled form solutions that support and enhance e-commerce applications such as:

- Dynamic page cachingutility which allows the system to dynamically cache frequently accessed pages in memory.
- Bandwidth allocationllows I/O bandwidth to be reserved or prioritized according to the type of Internet protocol, or location of the page.
- Transaction prioritizationa feature which gives priority to transactions or high volume customers.
- Encryption accelerator supportaimed at improving performance and scalability of e-commerce sites.

Data base management system is a typical server operating environmnet that provides a powerful platform for efficient data management and application development. Examples of this sofware and the most frequently used DBMS environmnts include Oracle data base management system, IBM DB2 data base management system, Microsoft SQL Server data base management system. All these DBMS suites are commercial products and have to be purchaed on a specific license scheme in order to be used. An alternative that appeared couple of years ago is an opensource product called MySQL, a data base management system that can be installed on several server platforms: Windows Server, Sun Solaris, HP's HP-UX, IBM AIX, Red Hat Linux, Novell SuSE Linux, Debian Linux, Apple MacOS X Server.

Here are some examples of business continuity-oriented ServerWare solutions based on DBMS level:

- Microsoft SQL Server's component called "**SQL Server 2005 Always On Technologies**" provides a full range of options to minimize system downtime and maintain appropriate levels of application availability. This set of DBMS-based features include: database mirroring, failover clustering, database snapshots, snapshot isolation, peer-to-peer replication, log shipping, and online operations. In addition, Microsoft SQL Server has been supporting integrated archive log shipping since the introduction of SQL Server 2000.
- **Oracle's Maximum Availability Architecture (MAA)** is a feature of the Oracle DBMS for achieving a highly available database management system. In addition, Oracle supports log shipping method of data replication as a replication method of disaster recovery. So-called the Log Writer Facility (LGWR) transfers the logs immediately to the disaster recovery site.
- **IBM DB2 Universal Database has a high-availability disaster-recovery Product called (HADR)** with the primary aim of recovering from physical disasters.
- **MySQL** data base management system environment provides several solutions in order to achieve a highly available database operating environments. Some of them are:

1. **MySQL Master/Slave Replication,** the set of utilities that is used by several world's most trafficked Web sites such as: YouTube, Yahoo, Wikipedia, and so forth.
2. **MySQL Distributed Block device (DRBD)** for propagating data in an active/passive configuration.
3. **MySQL Cluster** as an in-memory storage engine that can synchronously replicate data to all data nodes in the cluster.

One of the most commonly availability-related problems on database management platforms is the problem of database upgrade or database migration. Moving a DBMS platform across different operating platforms or upgrading a DBMS, is a common requirement in today's dominant DBMS-based IT environments. An approach which is based on so-called "rolling upgrade" refers to the process of upgrading a database without stopping the database. The opposite approach is called "in-place upgrade," the technique that requires stopping the database and making it inaccessible for applications and end-users during the process of DBMS upgrade.

CHAPTER SUMMARY

Server operating systems are described according to several attributes. Most widely used server operating systems today are presented. The concept of ServerWare is introduced as a set of server-based utilities aimed at enhancing capabilities of a server. A conceptual model to illustrate the role of server operating system and ServerWare in the design of an information system for continuous computing infrastructure is presented. As an example of a server operating system, HP's UNIX-based server operating system - HP-UX 11i is elaborated in more details. In addition, as a typical part of ServerWare component, an example of integrated set of Web programming tools for UNIX and Linux platforms is given in this section. It contains the following tools: Perl, PHP, CGI and FastCGI, and several Apache server utilities.

REFERENCES

IDC Report (2007). HP-UX: A Foundation for Enterprise Workloads, May 2007.

Fritz, F. J. (2006). 64-bit servers—No longer just an option, but a necessity, for enterprises running SAP. *SAP Insider*, July–August 2006, pp. 75–77.

REAL WORLD CASES

New HP-UX platform makes SAP fly for leading aerospace company
Compiled from the HP Success Story, 2001 www.hp.com

Thirty years ago a consortium of plane makers was formed with the brave aim of taking on the world's established airline manufacturers. They called themselves Airbus Industrie, and such has been their success that the name Airbus is now synonymous with setting the standard for short, medium and long-range jet airliners.

With over 40,000 employees based in four countries, Airbus has grown into a multi million dollar business with a family of 14 aircraft. Its orders have surpassed the 4,000 mark and there are more than 2,300 aircraft in service with 187 operators. The consortium includes four companies that employ 37,000 people and is served by more than 1,500 component suppliers with 100,000 employees in 30 countries.

Challenge

- Needed to migrate its SAP/3 to a new hardware base to support its upgrade path
- Wanted the scope to implement an improved strategic storage solution
- Required an 'always-on' infrastructure to cut downtime cause by on-line and off-line backup

Solution

- Migrated SAP/3 to hp-ux platform supporting 1,000 users
- Consultancy and hardware installation provided by hp partner CSC
- Data migration assisted by SAP UK
- For 'always-on' availability, new service run from CSC Managed Datacentre

Results

- hp XP256 disk technology and CSC UNIX backup design have cut off-line backup downtime from 12 hours to 10 minutes
- Batch suite processing speeds have dropped from nine hours to less than 40 minutes
- The solution has provided 11TB of storage to cope with huge amounts of data

VMS Operating System Is 30 Years Old; Customers Believe It Can Last Forever
Compiled and adapted from: InformationWeek
November 2, 2007 10:00 AM
http://www.informationweek.com/news/showArticle.jhtml?articleID=202801418
By Charles Babcock

Created by DEC, now sold as HP's OpenVMS, it's used by the Deutsche Borse in Germany, the Australian Stock Exchange, and Amazon.

The venerable VMS operating system from Digital Equipment Corp. turned 30 years old last week. Hardly anyone noticed.

Nevertheless, in an industry where change is a constant, VMS has few peers in its age bracket. The hoary software of the IBM (NYSE: IBM) mainframe also is over 30 years old, but that's mainly because it's embedded in a kind of castle that will not fall.

VMS never had a castle. It succeeded at first as the prime operating system of the DEC VAX minicomputer. As Data General, Wang, IBM, and others moved into minis, DEC stayed ahead with its VAX architecture powered by the VMS. VMS could run a VAX efficiently; for that matter, it could run whole clumps of VAXes, known as VAX clusters.

But the VAX was no castle. When competition intensified, VMS had to move on. It powered the Alpha line of servers brought out first by DEC, then Compaq Computer. When Compaq was bought by Hewlett Packard (NYSE: HP), VMS—now known as OpenVMS—moved on again, this time to Intel (NSDQ: INTC) Itanium architecture servers. VMS was never royalty in a castle; it was more like a resourceful, gypsy worker.

VMS was designed by Dave "eat your own dog food" Cutler when he was one of the top programmers at DEC. Cutler would move on also, putting his development talents to work at Microsoft (NSDQ: MSFT), where his experience led to leadership of the Windows NT project. NT's security gains over earlier forms of Windows flowed directly out of his VMS experience.

VMS was designed to be secure from the ground up, not as an afterthought, and it had multiple barriers for would-be intruders. It would check the role of someone giving it commands to see whether they were authorized to do what they were trying to do. If your password was X, and an intruder starting trying to guess passwords using L, M, N, and so forth, by the time he got to X, VMS would have spotted the pattern and locked his account, even when he got to the right letter.

"We've never had a virus on OpenVMS. It's never been hacked into for the life of the product," says Ann McQuaid, general manager of OpenVMS at HP.

Gareth Williams, associate director of the Smithsonian Astrophysical Observatory Minor Planet Center, knows about VMS' security and other virtues. Williams is a self-taught programmer trained in astronomy. When he arrived at the observatory on the Harvard campus in Cambridge, Mass., it became his job to track the 400,000 orbits of known asteroids and comets in the solar system. His computing resources for the job were two MicroVaxes running VMS. The system was gradually expanded with several larger Vaxes until the center had a cluster of 12.

The center shares space with the university's observatory, and when the pinch was put on office space, it was decided by building authorities that 12 Vaxes in an office were a waste of white collar space. Seven were wheeled off to a remote corner of the building known as the "gobs of gear" room, says Williams. But the Vaxcluster still performs, he says.

Not to worry, adds McQuaid. The Vaxcluster can run whether the computers are right next to each other or separated by up to 500 miles.

The Deutsche Borse stock exchange in Frankfurt runs on VMS. The Australian Stock Exchange runs on it. The Amsterdam police department in the Netherlands runs on it. The train system in Ireland, Irish Rail, runs on it. And Amazon (NSDQ: AMZN) uses OpenVMS as the OS for the system which controls the shipment of 112,000 customer packages of books, CDs, and DVDs every day. The operating system "has a very loyal installed base of customers," McQuaid says, and they show no signs of wanting to give it up.

After 30 years, can this operating system go on forever? When Compaq decided to kill off the Alpha chip, "that did not sit too well around here," says Williams, who's still tracking asteroids on his Alpha servers. HP says it's willing to continue to support OpenVMS as part of its Itanium server lines. Williams can't be sure when he'll be able to migrate to Itanium or whether HP's commitment is concrete enough to warrant the conversion. So he's stuck with an old dilemma. "We always said we would move away from VMS when something better came along. There isn't anything better," he says.

Continental Lower Costs, Improves Security, and Achieves 99.9 Percent Server Reliability
Compiled and adapted from: http://download.microsoft.com/download/9/a/2/9a2fb399-4991-4f36-bba1-9d23efe083b9/Continental_WinServ_Final.doc

Customer Profile

With headquarters in Hanover, Germany, and sites in more than 27 countries, Continental AG is one of the world's leading suppliers to the automobile industry. It has 81,000 employees.

Business Situation

Continental AG had out-of-date and disparate client-server infrastructure that needed groupwide standardization. This involved providing more than 80 sites worldwide with a total of 24,000 new workstations and portable computers, installing new server computers, and setting up modern operating systems and applications. Continental first tested a Linux solution, but the company decided instead on a platform based on Microsoft® Windows Server™ 2003 Enterprise Edition and Windows® XP Professional because of the opportunity to lower costs and improve security. The new system architecture has considerably reduced IT costs at Continental AG. With Active Directory as a groupwide directory service, the corporate network can now be centrally administered.

Solution

Continental chose a uniform client-server infrastructure based on the Microsoft Windows Server™ 2003 operating system (for its server computers) and the Windows XP Professional operating system (for workstations and portable computers).

The company decided to equip each client computer with Microsoft Office Professional Edition 2003.

Continental is migrating its server computers to Microsoft Windows Server™ 2003 and its 24,000 client computers to Windows XP Professional. The computers will also be equipped with Microsoft Office Professional Edition 2003.

Benefits

- Infrastructure Reliability of 99.9%
- Considerable cost savings
- Centralized IT administration
- Easier conversion and specialized support
- Automated client management

DISCUSSION QUESTIONS

1. Describe the major continuous computing drivers of the server operating platform.
2. How can server operating platforms be used strategically?
3. Do you think that "free Linux" as a server platform must always be prefered toward "commercial UNIX?"
4. What is the strategic advantage (if any) of those companies who opted for open source platfrom?
5. What kind of bundled severs should be delivered by server operating system vendor?
6. Why is 64-bit technology important from business continuity perspective?
7. Briefly explain the components of the HP-UX 11i v3 server operating environment?
8. Make an assessment of DBMS-based business continuity—oriented solutions of major DBMS vendors.
9. What are server-based high-availability clustering features?
10. Briefly explain Microsoft's server applications (servers) on its Microsoft Windows Server operating platform (www.microsoft.com).

ENDNOTE

[1]   Compiled from Memic, H., Bajgoric, N., ServerWare Dynamic Web Technologies for Business Continuity, IT Conference 2006, Faculty of Information Technologies, Mostar, September 2006

Chapter VII
Advanced Server Technologies for Business Continuity

CHAPTER OVERVIEW

Server operating systems described in Chapter VI usually come preinstalled. Additional components can be installed "on-demand" in the form of ServerWare components and modules, as explained in previous chapter. However, there exist more advanced technologies, both hardware and software, aimed at further enhancing the levels of continuous computing and business continuity. These technologies are introduced and briefly explained in this chapter.

FAULT TOLERANCE AND DISASTER TOLERANCE TECHNOLOGIES

Fault tolerance and disaster tolerance technologies are presented, including fault-tolerant servers. In addition, server virtualization technology is briefly explained. Server management software and its components are presented as to business continuity perspective.

Servers may include several types of additional hardware and software features that support so-called "high-availability" technologies such as: SMP/Clustering, support for 64-bit computing, support for Storage Scalability, RAID Technology, Fault Tolerance, Online Reconfiguration, N1 Grid Containers, Dynamic System

Domains, Virtual Machine Managers, and so forth. In addition, server platforms-based ServerWare suites include: bundled servers, reloadable kernel and online upgrade features, crash-handling technologies, workload management, Windows/UNIX integration, and so forth.

Further details on these continuous computing technologies are presented in the section that follows.

Fault tolerance is a term describing the ability of a server to continue operating despite the hardware and/or software failures. Fault tolerance typically refers to hardware failures and hardware fault tolerance, even though, software failures such as operating system crashes or network protocols' crashes are considered as parts of an integrated fault tolerance solution as well. Technologies include redundant hardware devices and components and special hardware with error-checking and hot-swap support. By default, fault tolerance solutions are onsite solutions, the solutions that are installed within the datacenter. They provide the highest level of availability on onsite basis. Fault-tolerant technologies in broader sense contain redundant units-based features as well (e.g., power supply, fan, disks-RAID, network cards, routers and other communication devices, UPS, etc.).

In addition to fault-tolerant technologies, contemporary business is forced to cope with demands for more efficient and effective computing and storage solutions as part of its efforts to recover from any type of failure and/or disaster.

Disaster tolerance is the ability of a server to continue with performing operations despite a disaster.

Disaster Recovery refers to an ability of computer system/operating system to resume operations after some sort of disaster that occurred in data processing unit. In most cases, disaster recovery operation takes some time and almost always there is a delay before data processing can continue. Disaster Recovery methods include: standard tape backups and advanced methods such as: hot sites, data vaulting, disaster recovery sites, and so forth.

There exist several levels (layers) of fault tolerance:

a. Hardware fault tolerance—including redundant components, replicated processors, additional—redundant memory, redundant networking devices (routers, switches, modems, network cards, etc.), redundant power supplies, and so forth.
b. System software fault tolerance. This is the second level of fault tolerance that operates on the system software (operating system) level.
c. Application fault tolerance relates to the application software and ability of the software to be tolerant to a specific code–related problem.

In broader sense, fault-tolerant and disaster-tolerant capabilities include three main technologies:

- Fault-Tolerance Technologies
- Disaster Recovery Technologies
- Disaster Tolerance Technologies.

Fault-tolerant and Disaster-tolerant systems in broader sense include the following technologies: Redundant Units, Data Replication, Hot Sites, Data Vaulting, Disaster Recovery Sites. Some of these technologies overlap with Data Storage Systems, which comprise: standard tape backup technology, Storage Area Networks (SAN), Network Attached Storage (NAS), Off-site Data Protection. SAN and NAS technologies are mainly based either on Fibre Channel as a mature storage backbone technology and/or newly developed Internet SCSI (iSCSI) and Serial ATA technologies.

Fault-tolerant servers are such servers that are able to continue to operate properly even when one or more faults within their hardware components occur. The logic behind this model is very simple: if a primary hardware device fails, its twin component takes over the process of running an application. This feature helps in achieving higher levels of application availability. Such configurations called fault-tolerant servers differ from traditional clustering systems in which a specific failure (hardware failure, communication failure, system software failure, application software failure) on one server causes moving (transferring) the partial or the whole application processing to a second server within a cluster configuration.

Standard server configurations usually include redundant components such as: hot-swappable power supplies, ECC (Error-Correcting Code) memory units, hot-swappable disk units. However, these servers still are not full fault-tolerant servers if they do not include processor-based redundant components. A truly fault-tolerant server includes the redundant processor components perform the processing instructions in lockstep, while self-checking technology can detect and isolate errors at the component level.

Examples of fault tolerant servers include IBM's mainframes based on z/OS architecture and HP's NonStop Himalaya servers.

An alternative to a pure hardware component-based fault – tolerant servers is a standard server architecture with a fault-tolerant software. An example of such software is the "Marathon **everRun HA**," a product of Marathon Technologies (www.marathontechnologies.com).

Marathon **everRun HA** can increase the level of application availability by protecting applications, data, networks and operating systems from faults, failures, and dropped network connections. Running on standard Windows servers, **everRun**

HA provides a significantly greater level of protection than clusters and rudimentary failover solutions, but at a lower cost and with far greater simplicity. **everRun HA** software synchronizes two standard Windows servers to create a virtual application environment that is inherently protected from downtime due to faults and failures. Data integrity is guaranteed by keeping an exact copy on the secondary server to ensure zero data loss in the event of a failure.

SERVER VIRTUALIZATION

This section introduces briefly the server virtualization technology that is used today for reducing downtime, sharing applications on several virtual servers, distributing workloads among servers, and implementing disaster recovery solutions.

New technology introduced recently—**server virtualization** brings the possibilites of running multiple servers on a single server computer. Each virtual server is assigned its own operating system, processor power, memory, applications, virtual network infrastructure, and so forth. An example of such a system is IBM x445 (www.ibm.com), a system which supports up to 64 virtual servers on a single 16-processor server.

Server virtualization is enabled by additional software called "hypervisor." This software is placed between server's hardware and its operating system. Its role is to provide a platform or "a container" that behaves as a logical hardware interface to server operating system. Newly created operating environment is called a virtual machine (VM) which consists of a "guest OS" which is running applications and/or other software. Similar technologies that are based on abstracting the interface of a resource from its physical implementation have been in use for many years in IT, for example, logical volumes in operating systems' file systems, RAID systems, virtual LANs, and so forth.

A single physical server may now host many virtual operating environments that host applications separately (see Figure 7.1 and Figure 7.2). Graphical user interface on a VM infrastructure is shown on Figure 7.3 and Figure 7.4. The VM environment shown on these two figures show two server operating platforms: Windows Server 2003 Enterprise Edition and SuSE Linux.

Among other approaches, server virtualization is also used as a way for resolving an issue called "server sprawl." **Server sprawl** is a problem that may occur in any kind of server configuration (DBMS server, e-mail server, application server, etc.). It is defined as a widespread, unplanned, uncontrolled, and/or uncoordinated server deployments in the form of many individual servers. As a result, this may put a business into an ever-growing number of servers.

Server virtualization technology has several advantages when compared with traditional systems:

Figure 7.1. A Non-virtualized environment: three physical servers, three different operating systems, and three applications running on separate machines

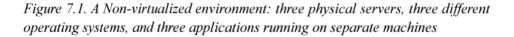

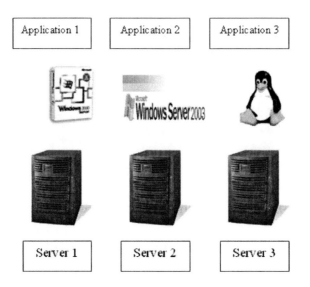

Figure 7.2. Server Virtualization in action: a single physical server, three different operating systems running on a single machine creating three virtual machines for three different applications

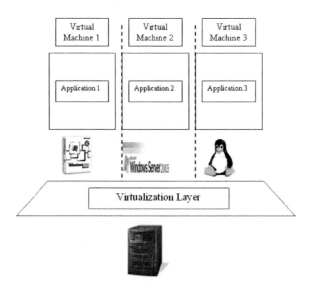

Figure 7.3. VMWare Platform: Windows 2003 Server and SuSE Linux

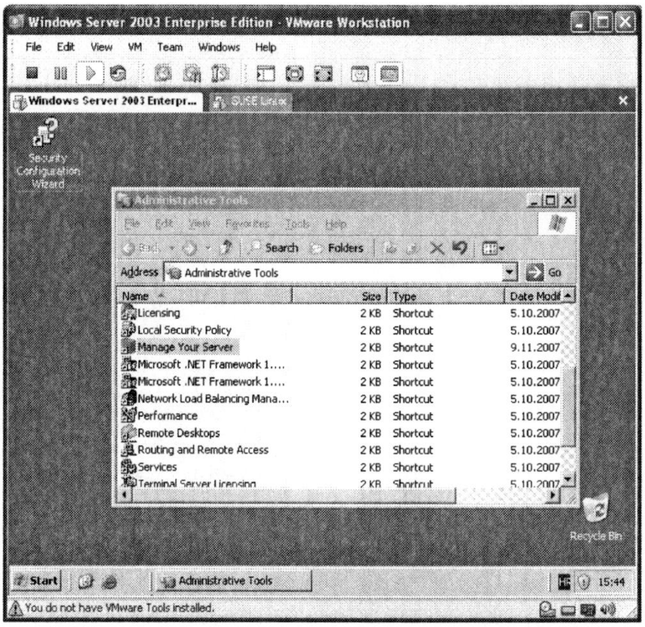

Figure 7.4. SuSE Linux on VMWare virtual infrastructure

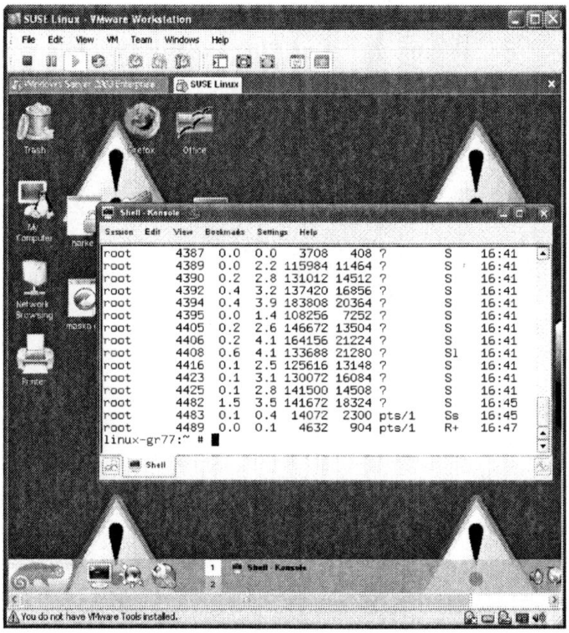

a. Lower server costs (less server configurations needed)
b. Lower infrastructure costs
c. Lower costs due to less space needed for traditional servers
d. Lower costs of system administration (less administration personal needed).

Virtualization helps improve uptime by:

- Reducing or even eliminating downtime needed for hardware upgrades and software upgrades/updates.
- Sharing applications on several virtual servers, if one virtual server fails, the other from the pool can take over.
- Ability to distribute workloads among servers.
- Implementing disaster recovery solutions by restoring lost operations regardless of the target physical platforms.

Server virtualization helps also in:

- Achieving higher hardware utilization rates
- Ensuring better alignment of IT and business processes
- Reducing the problems of "server sprawling".

However, virtual configurations require specific server software that has to be installed. Most widely used server virtualization packages are:

- VMWare (www.vmware.com, www.emc.com),
- Microsoft Virtual Server
- Xen (www.xensource.com)
- Sun's Solaris Containers
- HP VSE (Virtual Server Environment)
- IBM z/VM.

The three main virtualization technologies are as follows:

- Hardware virtualization
- Para-virtualization
- OS virtualization.

VMware and Microsoft's Virtual Server are based on the hardware virtualization technology. Xen open source project is based on so-called "para-virtualization," while the third approach—OS virtualization is used and implemented by Virtuozzo (SWsoft) and Sun's product called Solaris Containers.

Strom (2007) provides a comparison of the main virtual server products: EMC's VMware, Microsoft's Virtual Server and Xen OpenSource (Xen was acquired by Cytrix in July 2007).

Xen is a free virtual machine software for IA-32, x86-64, IA-64, and PowerPC processor configurations. It is software that runs on a host operating system and allows one to run several guest operating systems on top of the host on the same computer hardware at the same time

Strom (2007) suggests a list of questions to be answered while considering buying VM environment:

1. What host hardware and operating system will you want to run?
2. What guest operating systems do you plan on using?
3. How many VM hosts do you plan on operating and how will you manage them?
4. How familiar are you with VM concepts and how important is support?
5. What is the difference between free and paid products?

Figure 7.5. Virtual Server product comparison (adapted from Strom, 2007)

	VMware/EMC	**Microsoft**	**Xen**
URL	Vmware.com	Microsoft.com/virtual server	Xensource.com
Free server product	VMware Server	Virtual Server 2005 R2	XenExpress
Paid server products	Infrstructure v3 (Starter, Standard, and Enterprise)	None	XenServer and Enterprise
Pricing range paid product	$1000–$5750 (two CPU versions)	Free	Server: $99/yr. Enterprise: $750
Host OS (if any)	**Server:**Windows Server 2003, various Linux**Infra v3:**bare metal	Windows Server 2003 SP1, XP Pro SP2 (for testing purposes only)	Bare metal
Management tools	Virtual Center VMotion migration tool	System Center VM Manager (beta)	Administrator Console
Support resources	High	Medium	Medium
Advantages	• Widest selection of pre-built appliances • Widest selection of guest OS support • Wizards galore for install aids	• Can run on any IE browser with Internet access • Less expensive option • Easy cloning of VM images	Open source solution that does not require any host OS
Disadvantages	Confusing array of pricing and configuration options	Only four "virtual hard disk" pre-built appliances of MS server products	• Limited hardware support • Limited Windows guest OS support

IDC (2007) predicts that the global virtualization services market will grow in a way of reaching more that $10 billion by 2011.

SERVER MANAGEMENT SOFTWARE

Integrated server management software suites are presented in this section. These suites are used for efficient, centralized and advanced system administration. The more efficient system management is, the higher levels of availability can be achieved.

In addition to standard system administration tools that are available in bundled form on any server operating system, more comprehensive integrated system management tools such as IBM Tivoli, CA Unicenter, HP OpenVIew are used for centralized and advanced system administration—system management activities such as:

- Data Management
- Desktop Management
- Backup and archiving
- User Management
- Storage Management
- Print Management
- Process Management
- Performance Management
- Data Recovery
- Fault Tolerance Support
- Disaster Recovery
- Application Deployment and Management
- Configuration and Change Management
- License Management
- Network Administration
- Web Management
- Patch, Update and Upgrade Management
- Cluster Management.

In order to provide an example of such an integrated platform, the Windows Server System and Microsoft System Center (System management Server, Operation Manager) are briefly explained here (www.microsoft.com).

Microsoft's server products line consists of +30 different servers classified into the following categories of servers:

- Operating Systems
- IT Operations
- Application Platform
- Business Productivity
- Security

Servers under operating system category include:

a. Windows Server and its modification for specific types of business such as Windows Small Business Server
b. Windows Cluster Server
c. Windows Storage Server

IT Operations platforms comprise:

- Microsoft System Center
- Microsoft Systems Management Server,
- Microsoft Operations Manager,
- Microsoft Application Center
- Microsoft Visual Studio Team System

The Microsoft's set of application servers provides a platform for business solutions such as:

- Windows Server
- Internet Information Server (Internet Information Services)
- SQL Server
- Exchange Server
- Application Server
- Windows Small Business Server
- Windows Storage Server
- Windows Compute Cluster Server
- System Management Server
- Virtual Server
- Host Integration Server
- Identity Integration Server
- SharePoint Server
- Content Management Server
- BizTalk Server
- Speech Server

- Project Server
- Commerce Server
- Live Communications Server
- ISA Server
- Security Server

A version for small business is called Windows Server 2003 for Small Business server (up to 75 users). Depending of the version (Standard or Premium) Small Business Server contains server-based applications such as: Exchange Server, SQL Server, ISA Server (Internet, Security, and Acceleration Server), front Page 2003, Outlook 2003, Share Point Services.

System management tools such as Windows System Resource Manager (WSRM) and the Group Policy Management Console (GPMC) on Microsoft's Windows Server platform allow rapid configuration changes and necessary updates across multiple deployments. In addition, Windows Server 2003 Enterprise Edition also provides additional utilities, including some GUI-based tools and wizards (e.g., Microsoft Baseline Security Analyser), to help system administrators in achieving efficient and effective system management. Windows Server 2003 set of administration utilities and tools eases system administration by providing a set of tools and utilities to automate routine tasks. The automation of several system administration tasks eliminates tedious and time-consuming manual activities, such as backup, task scheduling, and so forth.

CHAPTER SUMMARY

Server operating environments may include several types of additional hardware and software that are described as "high-availability" technologies. These include the following technologies and features: SMP/Clustering, support for 64-bit computing, support for Storage Scalability, RAID Technology, Fault Tolerance, Online Reconfiguration, N1 Grid Containers, Dynamic System Domains, Virtual Machine Managers, and so forth. In addition, server platforms-based ServerWare suites may include the features such as bundled servers, reloadable kernel and online upgrade features, crash-handling technologies, workload management, Windows/UNIX integration, and so forth. Some details on these continuous computing technologies are presented in this chapter.

REFERENCES

Strom, D. 2007. Virtualization: Xen vs. Microsoft vs. VMware itmanagement.earthweb.com/netsys/article.php/3659286

IDC (2007). Global virtualization services market, http://itmanagement.earthweb.com/entdev/article.php/3694386

REAL WORLD CASES

The London Stock Exchange
By Microsoft
Adapted from: http://download.microsoft.com/download/3/a/0/3a0b6465-a87c-45c0-92c8-4cfd8b4415b6/LSE_WinServ03_Final.doc

Situation

The London Stock Exchange, established in 1801, is the world's premier international cash equity exchange and a leading provider of services that facilitate the raising of capital and the trading of shares for companies across the globe. The London Stock Exchange is the most international equities exchange in the world, with Europe's largest pool of liquidity.

The Main Market has 1,615 companies listed, and there are 1,579 companies quoted on AIM, the London Stock Exchange's market designed for smaller, growing companies. By the end of 2005, the market capitalisation of United Kingdom (UK) and international companies listed on the London Stock Exchange's markets amounted to £4.1 trillion (US$9 trillion), with £5.2 trillion (US$9.8 trillion) of equity business transacted over the year.

The London Stock Exchange needed a scalable, reliable, high-performance, and agile market data dissemination system. The Infolect® project is part of the London Stock Exchange Technology Road Map (TRM), a four-year transition to next-generation trading technology, due for completion in mid 2007.

The London Stock Exchange previously disseminated data through the London Market Information Link (LMIL)—based on an HP NonStop (Tandem) environment and written in COBOL language. HP acquired Tandem when it took over Compaq. Although the architecture is extremely reliable, new developments and capacity increases are complex, time consuming, and costly to implement. The London Stock Exchange needed more flexibility to facilitate new product and service development, reduce latency, and improve scalability. As part of its strategy to win more trading business and new customers, the London Stock Exchange needed a scalable, reliable, high-performance stock exchange ticker plant to replace its earlier system. Roughly 40 per cent of the Exchange's revenues are generated by the sale of real-time information about stock prices. Using the Microsoft .NET Framework in Windows Server 2003 and the Microsoft SQL Server™ 2000 database, the new Infolect system has been built to achieve unprecedented levels of performance, availability, and business agility. Launched in September 2005, it is maintaining the London Stock Exchange's world-leading service reliability record while reducing latency by a factor of 15. Its successful implementation, with support from Microsoft and Accenture, shows the London Stock Exchange's leadership in developing next-generation trading systems.

No Production Outages for Six Years

Reliability is fundamental to the London Stock Exchange value proposition for the market and continues to give its senior managers peace of mind about system uptime. There are approximately 300 customers who connect directly to the live Infolect system to receive real-time market data directly from the London Stock Exchange. The data disseminated from Infolect is then displayed on more than 107,000 terminals in more than 100 countries. In the past six years, there have been no production outages at the London Stock Exchange, and the new systems running on Microsoft technologies are critical to maintaining this 100 per cent reliability record. The London Stock Exchange has a mission critical program in place with Microsoft, which covers ongoing support. Lester says: "Our testing regime makes us very sure Infolect will meet its targets. The level of technical failure testing was very high, and the scenarios from which we have proven resilience are extensive."

One Hundred Per Cent Reliability for Traders on High-Volume Trading Days

Infolect has three times more capacity than LMIL and has proven its resilience on some of the highest-volume trading days in London Stock Exchange history. Infolect currently has the capacity for message dissemination of 3,500 messages a second, with an ability to scale to more than 100,000 messages per second. This capacity and latency reduction has underpinned significant volume growth on the London Stock Exchange. Of the Exchange's 50 highest-volume trading days, 49 have happened since Infolect went live in 2005. Additionally, high-speed, real-time price dissemination leads to greater order execution certainty, which, in turn, generates increased transaction volumes. The "virtuous circle" concept is core to the vision driving the implementation of the TRM.

Software and services:

- Microsoft Server Product Portfolio
- Windows Server 2003
- Microsoft Operations Manager
- Microsoft SQL Server 2000
- Microsoft SQL Server 2005

Microsoft Visual Studio
Microsoft .NET Framework

Minimizing Planned Downtime of SAP Systems
by Sun Microsystems, Inc.
01 November, 2007
Adapted from: http://research.pcpro.co.uk/detail/RES/1196082108_36.html

When business-critical systems are down for any reason—from hardware or software failures or planned downtime for maintenance or upgrades—the costs can be astronomical. This is especially true for SAP infrastructures where hundreds of users work concurrently on systems, such as materials management, supply chain management, and customer resource management (CRM), that interact with each other. In this environment, almost every component requires high availability—a call center without access to the CRM application is as unproductive as a shipping company without a logistics tracking system.

The majority of annual service downtime in datacenters is not a result of unplanned downtime caused by failures and outages of server or software components. Most downtime (80% or more) is due to maintenance and similar planned tasks. Pre-defined maintenance windows are assigned for these tasks, usually at night or on weekends so as to affect a minimum number of users. Planned downtime is calculable for all users and thus tolerable to a certain extent. However, the global economy is generating a demand for more round-the-clock services and as a consequence, maintenance windows are becoming smaller and smaller. Thus it is imperative for IT managers to limit or eliminate maintenance windows.

To help address this difficult task, Sun has developed a best practice procedure using Solaris™ Containers and Solaris ZFS, innovative virtualization technologies that are included in the Solaris 10 Operating System (OS). This procedure is designed to dramatically reduce downtime of the overall SAP environment and enhance the efficiency of IT operations. Minimizing maintenance windows for SAP Portal infrastructures

The availability of SAP Enterprise Portal is especially critical in SAP environments:

-
- It is the central access point for all employees of a company
- It serves as the central communication point between several applications and users
- Many SAP features are currently only available through the portal
- As well as the central internal access point, it is an access point for suppliers, customers, and partners, as a result, downtime can tarnish the reputation of the company
- The portal creates an open environment that must be as secure as possible, requiring immediate action when security updates are released

Upgrading an SAP Portal to a new version of software typically requires multiple hours of downtime. Using Solaris Containers and ZFS and the following steps, this downtime can be minimized to a few seconds, from the users' point of view.

- Using Solaris ZFS, create a clone of the portal environment. This step does not impact the operational process.
- Perform the software upgrade on the clone. During this process, the production system is still available.
- Test and QA the newly upgraded clone.
- After successfully testing, switch all users to the cloned, upgraded system—without interrupting operations.

SAP Portal environments—in contrast to other SAP systems—do not store dynamic data so there is no loss of data when switching from the primary environment to the clone environment. Therefore, the switch form one system to the other is completely transparent to the users.

Solution

An integral part of the Solaris 10 Operating System, Solaris Containers isolate software applications and services using flexible, software-defined boundaries and allows many private execution environments to be created within a single instance of the Solaris 10 OS. Each environment has its own identity, separate from the underlying hardware, so it behaves as if it's running on its own system making consolidation simple, safe, and secure.

Solaris Containers Can

- Dynamically move or replicate applications to fit the changes of the business
- Lower administrative costs by safely combining multiple applications onto a single system
- Reduce conflicts among applications running on the same system by isolating them from one another
- Support Predictive Self Healing to minimize fault propagation and unplanned downtime
- Enhance security by preventing unauthorized access and unintended intrusions.

Solaris ZFS is a new file system from Sun included in the Solaris 10 OS. It provides very high levels of data integrity and performance, and improves the ease of file system management by eliminating the need for a volume manager. Also, because it is 128-bit based, it opens the door to virtually unlimited data scalability. Solaris ZFS has been integrated with the Solaris Containers technology allowing container administrators to take full advantage of the features of Solaris ZFS. Designed with the administrator in mind, Solaris ZFS is the only self-healing, self-managing general purpose file system.

Solaris ZFS Offers

- Simple administration—automates and consolidates complicated storage administration concepts such as copy-onwrite and snapshots, reducing administrative overhead by 80%.
- Provable data integrity—protects all data with 64-bit checksums that detect and correct silent data corruption.
- Unlimited scalability—offers 16 billion billion times the capacity of 32- or 64-bit systems.
- Blazing performance—based on a transactional object model that removes most of the traditional constraints on the order of issuing I/Os, which results in huge performance gains.

DISCUSSION QUESTIONS

1. Explain the differences between fault tolerance and disaster tolerance.
2. What is the difference between disaster tolerance and disaster recovery technologies?

3. What hardware technologies are mainly used in order to have fault tolerant servers?

4. Explain the main reasons for implementing the server virtualization technology?

5. What are the major models of server virtualization?

6. List the major vendors of server virtualization products.

7. How server management softwaredifferentiate fro the main system administration utilities?

8. List and briefly explain the main questions to be answered while considering buying VM environment.

9. Explain the differences between hardware virtuaization and OS virtualization.

10. What is "para-virtualization?"

Chapter VIII
Choosing the Server Operating Platform for Business Continuity

CHAPTER OVERVIEW

Chapter VIII discusses the server operating systems' main attributes from the selection perspective. Several selection criteria are explained through a model that contains 22 most important features of server operating systems in regard to business continuity perspective. Some empirical studies and results on the performances of most widely used server operating systems are provided.

FRAMEWORK FOR SELECTION

An introductory framework on how to select an appropriate server operating system is presented in this section.

Mission critical applications are installed on enterprise servers that are operated by server operating systems. Therefore, availability of such systems is of extreme importance for organizations that use such applications and implement them within the integrated application suites of enterprise information systems such as enterprise resource planning, customer relationship management, supply chain management, electronic commerce. The same applies even if an organization still uses its legacy system.

As already mentioned in the introductory chapters, when server hardware and server operating system platforms are considered, server operating systems' availability is today expressed in terms of "nines," a number that determines the system's uptime. According to this approach, the "five-nines" is referred to as a system with 99.999% uptime—the availability ratio, which is regarded as the highest number achievable today. HP, for example, claims that its Integrity NonStop servers can provide 99.99999% availability ("seven nines"), uptime level which translates to less than 3 seconds of unplanned downtime a year. The availability of mainframes, some proprietary platforms (e.g., OpenVMS) and some UNIX systems can be as high as 99.999%, which corresponds to a downtime of five minutes per year. "Four-nines" availability (99.99%) corresponds to a downtime of 53 minutes per year, while 99.9% ("three-nines") means 8.8 hours of downtime per year.

HP's OpenVMS, developed by Digital thirty years ago in the form of VMS for VAX machines, and IBM's z/OS (formerly OS/390) are generally regarded today to be the two "world class" operating systems for mission critical applications that require high availability. Many of the applications in the banking sector and other financial services, healthcare, transportation and telecommunications industries require both high system uptime and high scalability.

System downtime requirements can range from almost zero-downtime to five seconds per year or five minutes per year. In addition to high availability ratios, these systems are expected to provide high performance ratios (thousands transactions per second) and huge storage requirements measured in multiple terabytes.

Availability classification, levels of availability and corresponding annual downtime are given in the Figure 8.1.

A more detailed specification of uptime/downtime scenarios is given in Figure 8.2.

However, high availability systems are expensive, complex to maintain and administer and require skilled professionals. The *99.999% uptime is difficult to achieve and sometime may not be worth the cost it requires.* Some businesses would benefit from these expenditures, but some would not. Therefore, a serious return of investment analysis (ROI) is needed in order to justify such a kind of investment.

Figure 8.1. Availability classification (Source: Marchi & Watson, 2002)

Availability Classification	Level of Availability	Annual Downtime
Continuous Processing	100%	0 minutes
Fault Tolerant	99.999%	5 minutes
Fault Resilient	99.99%	53 minutes
High Availability	99.9%	8.8 hours
Normal Commercial Availability	99-99.5%	87.6-43.8 hours

Figure 8.2. Downtime classification (Source: Wikipedia, http://en.wikipedia.org/ wiki/Myth_of_the_nines)

Availability %	Downtime per year	Downtime per month	Downtime per week
90%	36.5 days	72 hours	16.8 hours
95%	18.25 days	36 hours	8.4 hours
98%	7.30 days	14.4 hours	3.36 hours
99%	3.65 days	7.20 hours	1.68 hours
99.5%	1.83 days	3.60 hours	50.4 min
99.8%	17.52 hours	86.23 min	20.16 min
99.9%	8.76 hours	43.2 min	10.1 min
99.95%	4.38 hours	21.56 min	5.04 min
99.99%	52.6 min	4.32 min	1.01 min
99.999%	5.26 min	25.9 s	6.05 s
99.9999%	31.5 s	2.59 s	0.605 s

In a report issued in May 2006, IDC stated that "True high availability refers to applications and services that are continuously operational and accessible by users, irrespective of failure type. True high availability addresses availability of user connectivity to applications in a seamless fashion by proactively monitoring for errors, continually keeping local and remote configurations cloned or consistent, and eliminating manual processes such as scripting and reboots."

The ability of a specific SOS platform to provide high levels of uptime depends on several factors (capabilities), such as:

- Reliability and availability of the server platform's components (processor, memory, server operating system)
- Components' integratibility
- Multi-processor and multi-node support
- Fault-tolerant capabilities
- Clustering options
- Workload management support
- Security solutions.

However, system uptime is not the only dimension of continuous computing. Other dimensions need to be considered as well, therefore, a systemic approach that integrates all factors should be followed.

SERVER OPERATING SYSTEMS' MAIN ATTRIBUTES

Server operating systems' performances are studied according to several attributes. These attributes are used in order to make some benchmarking studies and reports on which platform is the best today. The section identifies as many as 22 main server operating systems' features or dimensions that can be used in assessing them from business continuity perspective.

While assessing server-operating platforms for high availability ratios, in addition to high levels of system uptime, both TCO (Total Costs of Ownerships) and ROI (Return On Investments) approaches for a specific platform should be considered as well. Also, one should keep in mind that there may be businesses that need business continuity only on "8 hours x 5 days" basis.

As already pointed out in the very beginning of the book, unlike desktop operating systems such as Windows XP or Windows Vista, server operating systems must fulfil much more rigorous requirements with regard to expectations from modern business computing. Choosing a desktop operating system platform today appears to be a very simple question of preferring Windows against Linux or vice versa, or hating both of them and staying with your Mac with its MacOS operating system.

However, one should always keep in mind that even on the desktop level, the operating system can be more or less stable, more or less reliable; it can also have higher or lower levels of "availability." The main difference between desktop and server operating systems from the availability perspective is in the fact that the downtime of a desktop computer affects only its user (single user), not the whole enterprise-wide application or application portfolio.

Therefore, the process of selecting appropriate server operating platform is a complex task and requires much more considerations that making decision between Windows XP (or Windows Vista) versus Linux desktop.

What follows is a list of the most important dimensions of contemporary server operating systems from continuous computing perspective. This list represents a set of requirements or preferred features that a server operating system should have in order to be selected as a platform for mission critical applications:

1. The lowest level of Total Cost of Ownership.
2. Multiplatform Supportsupport for different processor platforms (CISC-RISC, single-coremulti-core, 32-bit64-bit, Intel processors, AMD processors, proprietary processors).
3. Multiprocessing Supportsupport for multicore, multiprocessor, multinode systems. This includes several models of SMP (Symmetric Multiprocessing, Clustering, NUMA, etc.)

4. Support for 64-bit processingcomprises supports for a) 64-bit processors, b) 64-bit applications.
5. Support for VLM (Very Large Memory) and VLDB (Very Large Data Base) concepts and technologies.
6. Support for fault-tolerance and disaster tolerance.
7. Support for virtualization.
8. System management features.
9. Patch management.
10. Applications availability and integratibility.
11. Application development tools (integrated suites) availability for a specific server operating system platform.
12. DBMS support. Support of major DBMS vendors, both commercial (Oracle, SQL Server, DB2, INGRESS, INFORMIX, etc.), and open source (MySQL).
13. Availability of ERP suites (SAP, Oracle, Navision, etc.) for a specific SOS platform.
14. Availability of system integration tools (middleware support)
15. Support for file/print services.
16. Support for Internet, communication, networking, security protocols.
17. Support for application-programming protocols.
18. Availability of ServerWare products (messaging servers, Web servers, etc.).
19. PC-client and mobile/portable support (PC-X, CIFS, and PC-NFS support, WAP support).
20. Availability of specialists (system administrators) for a specific platform.
21. GUI and Web-based interface.
22. Viability of OS vendor.

In the section that follows, these requirements are briefly explained.

The lowest level of total cost of ownership. The TCO model (total costs of ownership) comprises numerous costs associated with the process of purchasing, installing, customizing, managing, administering and servicing server systems. It usually includes the following categories: acquisition costs, start-up costs, on-going operational costs, maintenance costs, service agreements, and so forth. Before making decision on which server is to be selected, the benchmarking analysis of TCO on several server platforms, even from the same vendor, should be done.

When discussing the TCO of a server system, several factors should be taken into consideration, not only when selecting a hardware platform, but also when server operating platform and mission-critical application suites are considered. A study by Meta Group (2001) showed, for instance, that the total cost of hardware maintenance and additional annual costs for a Windows-based system are significantly less than the costs of a Solaris UNIX-based system. By replatforming to

Windows, according to this study, an organization can reduce total platform costs by more than 50% with respect to Solaris in the first year alone. Over a three-year period, the Meta Group study shows that UNIX is more than three times the cost of a comparable Windows system for running ERP applications.

Multiplatform Support comprises support for different processor platforms (CISC-RISC, single-coremulti-core, 32-bit64-bit, Intel processors, AMD processors, proprietary processors). Some server operating systems are available only for specific processor platforms. Most widely used processors for desktop platforms today are Intel and AMD processors. These vendors do have processor configurations for server platforms as well. However, vendors such as IBM, HP, Sun have their own processors and offer appropriate server operating systems on them. In addition, they offer server configurations on Intel and AMD processors as well.

Some operating systems have such a capability to run on several processor platforms, for example, Sun Solaris can be installed on both Intel processors and Sun's proprietary SPARC processor. On the other side, HP's HP-UX and IBM's AIX as two UNIX versions can run only HP and IBM proprietary RISC-based servers (HP PA-RISC, IBM Power processor). The reason why multi-platform support of a specific operating system is important is because of more efficient integration of such systems.

Multiprocessing Support includes support for multicore, multiprocessor, and multinode systems. This includes several models of SMP (Symmetric Multiprocessing, Clustering, NUMA, etc.). High-performance processing capabilities enabled by multiprocessor and multinode system configurations should be supported by a specific server-operating platform in case when a business decides to implement such a solution. Several models of SMP systems are available today, including standard symmetrical processing configurations, clustering systems, NUMA systems, including recently introduced multi-core processors. All these configurations, in order to be implemented and used properly, require such server operating systems that support them.

Support for 64-bit processingcomprises supports for a) 64-bit processors and b) 64-bit applications. Transition to 64-bit computing that started with introducing Digital-Alpha processor in the beginning of '90s has now come of age. All major processor vendors introduced their 64-bit processors, operating system vendors recoded their existing products or designed new ones in order to support 64-bit processors. Application vendors as well, have to code their applications and application suites in order to be 64-bit ready or 64-bit native.

Support for VLM (very large memory) and VLDB (very large data base) concepts and technologies. Server operating systems should have the possibility of addressing multi-gigabyte databases stored in RAM (very large data base in very large memory). This speeds data access because it eliminates the need to go out to

disk for frequently queried data. The 64-bit processor technology is a basis for this requirement. VLM concept provides the ability to address large amounts of RAM on the order of several dozens and hundreds of gigabytes, while VLDB represents the possibility of addressing multi-gigabyte databases stored in RAM.

Support for fault-tolerance and disaster tolerance. In broader sense, fault-tolerant technologies comprise several redundant units-based technologies (e.g., power supply, fan, disks-RAID, network cards, routers and other communication devices, UPS, etc.), and special hardware with error-checking and hot-swap support.

Support for virtualization. Server operating systems are expected to support the virtualizationthe technique that enables running more operating systems and their application environments on the same hardware platform.

Integrated system management features that include integrated system management tools that are used for centralized and advanced system and network administration.

Patch management support refers to the inclusion of specific tools for smooth installation of operating system patches and service packs. This feature includes several tools and utilities that help in making updates and upgrades of a specific server operating system.

Applications availability and integratibility. Server operating platform, in order to be used by business community, needs an application portfolio of applications that is available on the market for that specific platform. For instance, one of the major advantages of Windows Server environments is a an efficient integration of Microsoft Office applications and personal productivity tools from Windows desktop environments with server-side applications such as Exchange Server, Internet Information Server, SQL Server, and so forth.

On the other side, this was the main disadvantage of UNIX and Linux operating platforms, although, this gap has been closed significantly with the introduction of OpenOffice and similar products.

When applications availability is considered, in addition to Office tools, a number of business applications developed on a specific platform is important, including personal productivity tools, enterprise information systems such as ERP, CRM, SCM, e-commerce, e-business, e-government suites, etc. Recently introduced "Duet Software" for Microsoft Office and SAP is an example of such an integration. By using Duet Software, users of SAP ERP suites can easily access and more efficiently integrate data and processes from mySAP suite with Microsoft Office desktop applications such as Excel, Access, etc. The Duet Software consists of: the Duet Client, Duet Server and mySAP ERP backend. Several Duet features can be used in order to enhance availability and scalability of these configurations: Duet Server Add-ons, Duet Java Add-ons, Windows Load Balancing, J2EE nodes, MSCS, F5 Networks, etc.

Application development tools (suites) availability for a specific server operating system. In order do make a final decision on which operating system will be used, in important dimension is availability of application development tools and integrated suites for that specific OS platform. This is a dimension that Microsoft Windows Server operating system makes more attractive when compared to Linux due to much larger community of application development suites that come not only from Microsoft, but from independent application development vendors as well.

DBMS support. Server operating platform should have of the major DBMS vendors, both commercial such as Oracle, SQL Server, DB2, INGRESS, INFORMIX, and open source (MySQL). This means that in order to be considered as a server operating platform of choice, that platform should have these data base management system software available on it by some vendors. Now one will buy a server with only server operating system installed on it.

Availability of ERP suites for a specific SOS platform. As more and more businesses give up their legacy platforms and select ERP suites due to their numerous advantages over legacy applications, the planned server platform should be supported by a specific ERP suite (SAP, Oracle, Navision, etc.).

Availability of system integration tools (middleware support). Server operating platform should provide an integrated set of middleware tools and products in order to allow multiple applications on the same or different operating system to exchange data in an efficient and effective manner. These include the tools such as: Windows APIs, object-oriented middleware solutions such as CORBA, COM/DCOM, support for Windows/UNIX integration, etc.

Support for Internet, communication, networking, security protocols: TCP/IP Extensions and/or protocols, Mobile/Wireless TCP/IP, IntServ, DiffServ, SLP, BGP and RIP, including support for TCP connection failover.

Support for application-programming protocols. This includes extensions or support for Windows, UNIX and Linux APIs, Java/JavaBeans, support for Java Runtime environment, J2EE, server database extensions (Oracle, MS SQL Server, MySQL), indexing & search engines, ODBC support, Web-to-DBMS features, etc. This feature includes also support for Web-based applications, cgi-bin, Perl and PHP support, FrontPage extensions, e-mail services such as listing, filtering, support for different e-mail formats: MIME, uuencode and Bin/Hex, Active Server Pages support, software for stabilizing Web server performances under heavy loads, bots or intelligent agents, etc.).

Availability of ServerWare products such as: messaging servers, Web servers, List servers, proxy servers, e-commerce servers, firewall servers, etc).

PC-client and mobile/portable support. Server platform should provide the support for desktop, mobile and portable devices (PC-X, CIFS and PC-NFS support, WAP support).

Availability of specialists (system administrators) for a specific platform. When opting for a specific server operating system, the dimension that reflects the availability of IT-specialists who will be working on that platform is also very important. Do we already have them in a company, if not, how to find them, especially those who are more skilled and more experienced.

GUI and Web-based interface. Starting from the mid of '90s, most server operating system vendors implemented GUI and later Web-based interfaces, leaving the old style command-line interface only to UNIX, OpenVMS, OS/390, and OS/400 professionals who used to work with these OS platforms in the '70s, '80s and the beginning of '90s.

Viability of OS vendor. Here, we refer on what we said in chapter five: the story on SCO's case. This story confirms the fact that when considering, not only operating system platform, but any other IT solution, there is no solution that is risk-free. Let's take another example, again in operating system field:

Ten years ago, in January 1998. Compaq acquired Digital for some $8 billion. One of the first announcement made by Compaq was related to the fate of Digital's OpenVMS operating system. Compaq had decided to give up that operating system in a foresable future. However, this decision resulted in a huge opposition by OpenVMS community since, in the late 90s, OpenVMS was said to be installed on more that 400,000 computers. As a result, Compaq was forced by US government authorities to issue a commitment of not abandoning OpenVMS platform with regard to the support for some specific time.

SELECTION CRITERIA

The section provides a list with the main criteria that have to be considered while deciding on server operating system platform. Some well-defined and widely used frameworks in that sense are presented (e.g., Gartner, DH Brown).

When selecting a server operating system platform, the following decision making criteria should be taken into consideration:

- Availability of a specific server operating system
- Reliability of a specific server operating system
- Scalability (in a situation when the number of concurrent users jumps with the rates of several hundreds of percent)
- Serviceability: solutions such as: efficient core dump facility, efficient kernel dump facility, application/system snap-shooting (checkpoint/restart), advanced resource management, and so forth.

- Manageability, ease of administration, familiarity
- Recovery time
- Integratibility with other OS platforms, legacy systems, etc.
- Application support
- Security: Windows is most frequently used desktop OS. In the same time, more and more companies migrate from UNIX to Windows Server platform. Therefore, Windows platform will continue to be the number-one target for all kinds of hackers. However, in the same time, it is evident that Linux-related hacks are on the rise.
- Vendor support.

In addition, the process of selecting appropriate server platform should include quantitative analyses as well (e.g., total cost of ownership, return-on-investment, benchmarking).

Availability, reliability and scalability are very important in modern business because of the following facts that describe it:

- Globalization
- Customer-oriented business
- Virtual business
- Mobile computing

This is especially emphasized for business-critical applications or, in general, mission-critical applications. These applications require what is called "always-on-computing" or "24x7x365 computing," in other words, these applications are characterized by high availability ratios (high uptime ratios).

In order to minimize system downtime server operating system must provide the solutions such as: fault tolerance, disaster tolerance, disaster recovery, etc.

Gartner (2005) advises midsize businesses to base their server OS choices on total costs of ownerships (TCO) model rather than on one-time savings from a licensing perspective. The results of this Gartner's survey conducted in 2005 among North American midsize businesses identified primary considerations when selecting server OSs. According to this survey, respondents from the lower-end midsize-business market (those with 100 to 499 employees) said that the three most important criteria for selecting an OS are:

- The OS works best with the application we are considering
- Recommendations from our IT staff
- Same as the predominant OS we already have

- Compatibility between applications and the prospective OS is a prime consideration.

D.H. Brown Associates, now part of Ideas International (www.ideasinternational.com), in a series of reports (Operating System Function Review, 1999, 2000, 2002), introduced a comprehensive model—a set of SOS-related attributes that can be used in evaluating performances of server operating systems. This model has been expanded to include 167 functional items across five areas: RAS (Reliability, Availability, Scalability), System management, Internet and Web Application Services, and Directory and Security Services. This model, which served as a framework for assessing capabilities of server operating systems, has been expanded later by D.H.Brown to the "RASSIM" model which stands for Reliability, Availability, Scalability, Serviceability, Integratibility, and Management-Maintenance.

According to this model, the scalability of a system is determined by the following functional areas: 64-bit support, SMP support/SMP range, storage scalability, memory range, scalability clustering options, and low-level performance optimisations.

Reliability, Availability, and Serviceability (RAS) basically include the following functions:

- Resiliency functions, which allow SOS to adapt to outages by hardware components (online failure recovery functions).
- Solutions that minimize planned downtime such as: online CPU and memory reconfiguration, online I/O reconfiguration, alternate root installation, dynamic kernel patching.
- Crash-handling techniques (kernel dump facilities, dump analysis tools, dynamic core file generation, multimode boots, automatic hang detection, etc.).
- Workload management solutions such as: partition fault isolation, dynamic partition reconfiguration, and so forth.
- High-availability clustering functions including: fault tolerance, failover capabilities, disaster recovery/disaster tolerance, cluster file system, work with partitions, TCP connection failover, high-availability storage support.

RAS model refers to a set of features which contemporary business is expecting from IT vendors having in mind business requirements towards a higher level of applications availability, in other words, in achieving "continuous," "always-on" or "24x7x365 uptime" computing. In that sense, businesses seek for solutions such as "automatic failover" and/or "disaster recovery" in case of the failure of a device or the whole system. RAS means that end users can use data and applications and system continues running even when system or application software is being upgraded or backed-up.

SOME EMPIRICAL STUDIES ON THE PERFORMANCES OF SERVER OPERATING SYSTEMS

In the section that follows, we provide some empirical results on server operating systems' usage, during the period of the last 10–15 years. These results are useful in explaining how some server platforms have matured, what happened on UNIX arena, and how Linux revolution influenced this area.

When commercial server operating systems are considered from the previously defined standpoint, it is well known that mainframes, UNIX systems and some proprietary systems (e.g., OpenVMS) have exceptional systems availability and reliability.

According to the report published by Continuity Central (2006), the table in Figure 8.3 summarizes the percentages of the specific server operating system platforms on which the respondents' companies run their business critical applications.

With respect to the overall standings of UNIX server platforms, according to D. H. Brown's report (UNIX Function Review, 2002) HP's HP-UX 11i achieved the highest rates in almost every studied category. HP-UX, Sun Solaris and HP Tru64UNIX shared the lead in the Scalability category. When Internet and Web-applications services are considered, the same report named IBM AIX as leader. Report also revealed that AIX and Solaris are the only studied systems to build http acceleration functions into their kernels, facility which helps to boost Web-server performance.

As for Linux and its performances compared to commercial UNIX platforms, D. H. Brown unveiled a study in which several Linux versions were compared with commercial UNIX versions. According to that study (Linux Function Review, 2003), almost all studied Linux versions were behind the strongest UNIX, but some of them like SuSE and RedHat were better that the weakest UNIX in terms of overall functionality. However, newly developed Linux 2.6 kernel brought some

Figure 8.3. The percentages of the specific server operating systems (Source: adapted from Continuity Central, 2006)

Server Operating System	Response Percent
AIX	21.7%
HP-UX	21.2%
Linux	39.7%
NetWare	6.5%
Solaris	26.1%
Windows	78.8%
Other	21.2%

new features such as: support for 64-bit processors, improved scalability (up to 16 processors or even more), asynchronous I/O for performance improvements, improved file-system performance, enhanced high-bandwidth networking support, etc. Increasing level of maturity of the existing 2.4 Linux kernel and planned new features of Linux 2.6 kernel position Linux as an OS platform not only for so-called "edge-of-network" applications (mail servers, Web servers), but for mission-critical applications as well.

Another operating environment—Windows Server platform, which is using Microsoft Windows NT/Server technology on either Intel or AMD processors, includes the following versions: Windows NT Server 4.0, Windows 2000 Server, Windows 2003 Server. All these versions are still in use, but with different levels of availability. Main advantages of this platform over UNIX are indicated as follows: ease of use and administration, price, support and integration with API/Windows application development environments. Most major application vendors have Windows NT versions of their packages, for example, five years ago more that 45% of the implementations of SAP's R/3 ERP package were on Windows NT.

Giga Group's report (Newman, 2001) revealed that Windows 2000 has been improved in terms of performance and reliability, for example, unnecessary reboots declined by 64% compared to Windows NT 4.0. They reported that "…even though Windows 2000 Server closed the reliability gap with all versions of Novell NetWare, Windows 2000 Server is still not as reliable as UNIX. According to the respondents, Windows 2000 still requires 300% more unnecessary reboots than UNIX."

Current version of Microsoft Windows NT platform—Windows Server 2003 includes a number of functions that are particularly important for scalability, such as: 64-bit support for Itanium 2 processors; improved Shared-Memory Multiprocessing (SMP) scalability, ability to support up to 64 processors, support for NUMA systems, with several improvements to the IIS 6.0 Web server.

Business continuity levels provided by Windows Server 2003 platform are additionally improved by separate server product—Windows Storage Server 2003. D.H. Brown pointed out that Windows Server 2003 has made "considerable progress in addressing vertical scalability and reliability needs of enterprise datacenters" (D. H. Brown Report, 2003).

According to Microsoft (2007), the Windows Server platform is now SAP R/3 certified at 93,000 concurrent users on SQL Server 2005 with an average response time of less than two seconds. This 64-processor benchmark demonstrates the scalability of the Windows Server platform with SQL Server 2005, and is more than three times the number of concurrent users certified with SQL Server 2000.

According to Harvard Research Group (Marathon-WP, 2005), Windows servers will continue to be the fastest growing server market segment in foreseeable future.

HRG estimates the current Windows market at more than $10 billion. Gartner (2005) reported that, for midsize business, Linux presents many challenges, including not fully understanding the OS's benefits, resource constraints and the perceived high switching costs to move from Windows.

One of the major advantages of Windows Server operating system is the availability of some most widely used applications or ServerWare products.

For instance, according to the September 2007 Netcraft survey (2007) that was based on responses received from 135,166,473 sites, Microsoft-IIS came closer to Apache httpd (Microsoft-IIS is Microsoft's Web server while httpd is http daemon—a program on UNIX/Linux servers that runs Web server) with the following market shares: Apache—50.23%, Microsoft-IIS—34.94%.

The table in Figure 8.4 indicates market shares of the major Web server products, according to this Netcraft survey.

Windows Server 2003 supports several virtualization functions such as:

- Windows System Resource Manager (WSRM), a tool that can be used to set allocation policies for applications.

Figure 8.4. Web servers – market share (Source: adapted from Netcraft Survey, 2007)

October 2007 Results		
Server	**No. of Sites**	**Market Share**
Apache	67,898,632	50.23%
Microsoft-IIS	47,226,195	34.94%
GFE	6,616,713	4.90%
Unknown	3,309,447	2.45%
Sun-ONE-Web-Server	1,997,150	1.48%
Oversee	1,601,209	1.18%
lighttpd	1,515,963	1.12%
Zeus	546,634	0.40%
Netscape-Enterprise	213,351	0.16%
Rapidsite	206,785	0.15%
tigershark	196,282	0.15%
AOLServer	90,845	0.07%
Lotus Domino	89,060	0.07%
Zope	49,837	0.04%
WebSTAR	23,195	0.02%
thttpd	22,568	0.02%
Oracle-Application-Server-10g		

- Partition support, a tool that can be used to run multiple instances of this operating system on specified servers. Each instance of the operating system behaves as if it were running on a standalone machine.
- Virtual machine support, a feature which involves creating an entire computer system in software. System administrators can host multiple computers on virtual basis on a single physical server.

Jean Bozman, vice president of IDC, with regard to UNIX/Linux predictions said: "True, the Linux is growing, but the UNIX market is not going away any time soon. We see the UNIX market to be fairly strong through this year (2007). From what we can see the UNIX server market is going to be around a long time" (IDC, 2007).

Microsoft's new version of this platform Longhorn Server/Vista is expected to bring a number of advancements such as: Server Core (server roles), Vista Group Policy, Read-Only Domain Controller, Restartable Active Directory, BitLocker drive encryption, Network Access Protection (NAP), Terminal Services Gateway, Secure Anywhere Access, new TCP/IP stack that supports IPv4 and IPv6 natively and enhanced set UNIX interoperability features (SFU - Service for UNIX).

According to the Yankee Group's annual server reliability survey (Keizer, 2006), only UNIX-based operating systems such as HP-UX and Sun Solaris 10 beat Windows on uptime. Windows 2003 Server led the popular Red Hat Enterprise Linux with nearly 20% more annual uptime. On average, individual enterprise Windows, Linux, and UNIX servers experienced 3 to 5 failures per server per year in 2005, generating 10 to 19.5 hours of annual downtime for each server. Windows Server 2003 offers 20% to 35% better reliability on file/print, e-mail/messaging and database servers when compared with the leading commercial Linux distributions in comparable workload scenarios. Windows Server 2003 trounced the Linux market leader, Red Hat Enterprise Linux, achieving nearly 20% more annual uptime in similar deployment scenarios. Microsoft's Windows Server 2003 recorded an average annual server downtime rate of about 770 minutes or 12.8 hours.

UNISYS in its White Paper (2005) claims that 78% of our UNISYS systems delivered 100% non-stop availability with the combination of the Unisys ES7000 server running Windows Datacenter operating systems and achieved an average of 99.996% availability which is less than 22 minutes of downtime a year. Yankee Group report (2006) revealed that UNIX servers spent the least time offline. This report analyzed UNIX Servers versus other major OS server platforms with respect to downtime. In another report, Yankee Group (2005) revealed Windows Server and Linux security levels were nearly equal.

In a report published by Peerstone Research Inc. (Loftus, 2004), it has been stated that "…Linux is making "undeniable inroads" into the core enterprise applications stack, of which the biggest component is the worldwide installed base of 800,000 servers running SAP, Oracle and PeopleSoft applications." This report examined 400 companies running SAP, Oracle or Peoplesoft ERP suites, showed roughly two-thirds were using UNIX, 28% Windows Server or a version of NT, and only 2% were running on Linux.

Many businesses considered migration from commercial UNIX platforms and proprietary systems to either Windows or Linux platform. META Group (2005) reported more than a 20% reduction in the number of servers as a result of the migration. Moreover, in an ERP environment in particular, upgrading major ERP versions often requires about one-third more processing power to provide the same functionality, in addition to the processing power needed to support the new modules or functional components themselves. However, IDC (2006) predicts that UNIX servers will retain business-critical and mission-critical workloads for years to come. This research found real potential for UNIX migration both to other UNIX environments and to alternative platforms including Linux and Windows. On a unit basis, Windows was the leading platform for UNIX migration with 45% of the volume. Other versions of UNIX generate the most server migration spending, capturing 48% of the UNIX revenue opportunity.

According to IDC (2006), Windows has captured 45% of UNIX migrations, making it the leading platform for UNIX migration overall. In 2005, IDC reported that worldwide revenues for the Microsoft server product line surpassed UNIX server revenues for the first time ever.

Gartner (2005) reported that "...with more than 90% of midsize businesses running predominantly on a Windows environment, Microsoft is the server operating system leader among small and midsize businesses (SMBs). Microsoft will remain the dominant server operating-system provider for midsize businesses through 2010. According to this Gartner research, Linux presents many challenges for midsize businesses, including not fully understanding the OS's benefits, resource constraints and the perceived high switching costs to move from Windows.

In its White Paper (2007) "Selecting a Platform for Your ERP System" Microsoft introduces the term "Partner Ecosystem" and reminds that with 750,000 Microsoft partners, more than 300,000 Microsoft Certified Support Engineers (MCSE), more than 1.8 million Microsoft Certified Professional (MCP) certification holders, more than 6 million developers, 2,200 user groups, 400 community Web sites, and the largest community of independent software vendors (ISVs) worldwide, Microsoft fosters the largest and most active global ecosystem of partners, community participants, and vendors. ankee Group's survey (October 2005) of 700 SMB and midmarket companies (2 to 1000 employees) in the United States proves this Gartner's opinion. According to this report, respondents indicated that the biggest influencers for the adoption of the Microsoft platform are:

- **Availability of applications:** business applications, collaboration and personal productivity applications, infrastructure management applications, and embedded system applications.
- **Insufficient IT resources:** the available resources are IT generalists that can support Windows, Exchange and Office-type environments. Also, there is a shortage of Linux-skilled resources as they are in high demand by enterprise-class companies.
- **Integration:** Technology challenges related to the need for integration between different applications also plays well to the Windows environment.
- **Increase in employee productivity:** The goal of SMB and mid-market enterprises is to run business and IT's role is to support the mission-critical revenue generation and customer support activities and not application development and support. Integrated applications that are designed to work together and are properly supported lead to much higher employee productivity and overall efficiency enhancement for the company.

According to Microsoft (2007), currently, more than 58,000 SAP installations are running on Windows Server. That number is more than all other platforms combined. Nearly two-thirds of new SAP installations are deployed on Windows Server family and over 40% of all new SAP installations are deployed on Microsoft SQL Server.

CHAPTER SUMMARY

Server operating systems' performances are examined in this chapter according to several attributes. Chapter VIII identified as many as 22 main server operating systems' features that can be used in assessing them from business continuity perspective. This list represents a set of requirements or preferred features that a server operating system should have in order to be selected as a platform for mission critical applications: The chapter provides a list with the main criteria that have to be considered while deciding on server operating system platform. Some well-defined and widely used frameworks in that sense are presented (Gartner, D. H. Brown).

REFERENCES

Continuity Central (2006). http://www.continuitycentral.com/feature0358.htm.

D. H. Brown Report (2000). Operating System Function Review

D. H. Brown Report (2002). UNIX Function Review (2002), Retrieved on August 7, 2006 from http://www.hp.ru/data/offline/category/0086/2002unix_report.pdf.

D. H. Brown Report (2003). Linux Function Retrieved on August 8, 2006 from http://searchopensource.techtarget.com/originalContent/0,289142,sid39_gci901797,00.html?Offer=ik2.

D. H. Brown Report (2003). Windows Server Reaches Maturity, Retrieved on August 8, 2006 from http://www.microsoft.com/presspass/features/2003/apr03/04-16dhbrown.mspx.

Gartner Report (2005). Costs and benefits still favor Windows over Linux among midsize businesses. Retrieved on July 21, 2006 from http://www.microsoft.com/windowsserver/facts/analyses/gartner_Midsize.mspx.

IDC Pres Release (2006). Worldwide server market slows in 4th quarter but grows to $51.3 billion in 2005. February 22, 2006.

IDC Report (2006). True high availability: Business advantage through continuous user productivity, *May 2006.*

IDC Report (2006). Understanding UNIX migration: A demand side view. January 2006.

IDC Report (2007). Business process agility: The next ERP imperative. *March 2007.*

IDC Report (2007). HP-UX: A foundation for enterprise workloads. May 2007.

Keizer, G. (2006). Reliability survey: Windows servers beat Linux servers, Retrieved on July 5, 2006 from http://www.enterpriseserver.techweb.com/windows/showArticle.jhtml?articleID=189600508.

Loftus, J. (2004). Survey: Linux gets hot, Unix gets cold, and Microsoft stalls, Retrieved on August 7, 2006 from http://searchenterpriselinux.techtarget.com/originalContent/0,289142,sid39_gci1029190,00.html.

Marathon White Paper (2005). At your own risk: A risk-based approach to Windows business continuity, Marathon Technologies Corporation, Inc., Retrieved on July 5, 2006 from http://www.repton.co.uk/library/Enterprise%20Systems/marathon_business_continuity_for_windows.pdf.

Marchi, M. J. & Watson, A. (2002). The network appliance enterprise storage architecture: System and data availability, Retrieved on August 7, 2006 from http://www.netapp.com/library/tr/3065.pdf.

META Group Report (2005). Migrating UNIX ERP installations to a Windows server environment: A qualitative assessment of business impact, Retrieved on July 5, 2006 from http://unix.ittoolbox.com/white-papers/migrating-unix-erp-installations-to-a-windows-server-environment-a-qualitative-assessment-of-business-impact-3293.

Meta Group (2001). The impact of OS/Platform selection on the cost of ERP implementation. *Use and Management*, 2001.

Microsoft White Paper (2007). Selecting a Platform for Your ERP System, Microsoft Corporation, January 2007.

Microsoft White Paper (2007). Selecting a Platform for Your ERP System, Microsoft Corporation, January 2007.

Netcraft survey (2007). September 2007 Server Stats: Apache Decline Continues, Retrieved on October 16, 2007 from http://itmanagement.earthweb.com/cnews/article.php/3705346.

Newman, A. (2001). Giga study reveals slow Windows 2000 server adoption, Retrieved on August 7, 2006 from http://www.serverwatch.com/news/article.php/1400201.

UNISYS White Paper (2005). Hyperion Reporting and Analysis for SAP Solutions on Unisys ES7000 Servers, http://www.hyperion.com/downloads/partners/Unisys_Hyperion_for_SAP_Solutions.pdf.

Yankee Group report (2005). Sanjeev Aggarwal, December 2005, Microsoft—the Dominant Vendor in the SMB and Mid-Market Applications and Platform Ecosystem.

Yankee Group report (2006). Laura DiDio. Unix, Windows and Custom Linux Score Well on Yankee Group 2006 Global Server Reliability Survey.

YankeeGroup/Sunbelt 2006 Server Reliability Survey. (2006). Retrieved on July 24, 2007 from http://download.microsoft.com/download/8/3/8/838E0ACF-6B1B-4C97-9858-AF1B9B82AE93/Unix_Windows_and_Custom.pdf.

REAL WORLD CASES

Reliability Survey: Windows Servers Beat Linux Boxes; UNIX-based systems, including HP-UX and Solaris 10 beat both systems in total uptime
By Gregg Keizer, June 2006
http://www.enterpriseserver.techweb.com/windows/showArticle.jhtml?articleID=
189600508

According to the Yankee Group's annual server reliability survey, only UNIX-based operating systems such as HP-UX and Sun Solaris 10 beat Windows on uptime. Windows 2003 Server, in fact, led the popular Red Hat Enterprise Linux with nearly 20% more annual uptime. On a broader note, said Yankee analyst Laura DiDio, the major server operating systems all have a "high degree of reliability," and have showed marked improvement in the last 3 to 5 years. On average, individual enterprise Windows, Linux, and UNIX servers experienced 3 to 5 failures per server per year in 2005, generating 10 to 19.5 hours of annual downtime for each server. But standard Red Hat Enterprise Linux, and Linux distributions from "niche" open source vendors, are offline more and longer than either Windows or UNIX competitors, the survey said. The reason: the scarcity of Linux and open source documentation. The Yankee Group made a point of stressing that the survey was not sponsored or supported by any server OS maker.

The Yankee Group *2006 Global Server Reliability Survey* polled nearly 400 global businesses ranging from small and medium businesses (SMBs) to large enterprises with more than 100,000 employees. The intent was to quantify the reliability of 10 different server operating system platforms to identify the most reliable platforms, highlight user management trends and assist businesses in deciding which server OS or heterogeneous combination is most suitable for their respective environments.

The Yankee Group survey asked corporate IT managers and executives to detail the number of Tier 1, Tier 2 and Tier 3 outages each server experiences annually. We polled corporate executives and IT administrators on reliability, outage time and the amount of time they spent applying patches across 10 different server operating system platforms, including a variety of niche market Linux and open source distributions:

- Windows 2000 Server
- Windows Server 2003
- Sun Solaris, HP UX and IBM AIX
- Red Hat Enterprise Linux standard distribution
- Red Hat Enterprise Linux with customization
- Novell SUSE Linux standard distribution

- Novell SUSE Linux with customization
- Debian open source Linux
- Other Linux distributions (i.e., Turbolinux, Mandriva)
- Open source Linux distributions with customization

Survey highlights include the following:

- UNIX-based servers, which constitute 10% of the installed base of server operating systems, achieved the highest reliability ratings among mainstream distributions. Corporate users reported UNIX-based operating systems, which typically are deployed in high-end data centers, experienced the least amount of annual downtime: slightly less than 600 minutes or roughly 10 hours per year for each server.
- Windows 2000 Server installations recorded 970 minutes of downtime per server per year. This 6-year-old Microsoft server OS recorded slightly more outage time—about 20 minutes—per server per year than Red Hat Enterprise Linux standard distribution and about 10 minutes more per server than some of the other niche market Linux distributions.
- Organizations that customized their Red Hat Enterprise Linux servers fared much better than the standard Red Hat Enterprise Linux distributions: They reported approximately 750 minutes of outages associated with individual servers each year, or 12.5 hours of downtime.
- Among niche market Linux and open source server distributions, Debian had the dubious distinction of recording the highest outage time: 1,170 minutes per server per year, which equals 19.5 hours. Other niche market Linux distributions such as Turbolinux and Mandriva fared better: They each experienced approximately 960 minutes of outages, equating to 16 hours of per annum downtime for each server.
- Among the niche market server operating system platforms that have less than 5% market share, Novell's SUSE Linux standard distribution and its SUSE Linux custom platforms were the clear winners in terms of the number of Tier 1, Tier 2 and Tier 3 outages per server per year. Corporations using a customized implementation of Novell's SUSE Linux server operating system experienced the least amount of actual server outage time—roughly 430 minutes per year, per server or 7.1 hours. However, because only 14 of the nearly 400 respondents (approximately 3.5%) have a SUSE Linux custom deployment, it is not statistically valid—though it is noteworthy.
- Finally, administrators servicing all of the major server operating system environments (Linux, Windows, and UNIX) reported that the number of aggregate annual outages for each server was in the single digits.

2002 UNIX Function Review
Systems Software, May 2002
D.H. Brown Associates, Inc. 3
Adapted from www.dhbrown.com

METHODOLOGY

This study ranks four leading UNIX operating systems. IBM AIX 5L 5.1, Hewlett-Packard HP-UX 11i, Sun Solaris 8, and Compaq Tru64 UNIX 5.1-based on their functional capabilities as of January 1, 2002. Each operating system receives a rating for its support of 167 functional items across five areas: scalability, RAS, system management, Internet and Web application services, and directory, and security services.

This study primarily notes functional items for their presence or non-presence on a given platform, although it judges some according to the quality and breadth of their implementation. Systems receive maximum credit only for functions that are bundled and integrated. They take a penalty if the function requires a separately priced option, and suffer a greater penalty if the function is not available directly from the operating system's supplier (i.e., if it requires involvement of a third party supplier). They receive a maximum penalty if a function is unavailable for the platform, or if it can be implemented only through an awkward workaround.

Clearly reflecting HP's increased investment in its UNIX product line, HP-UX moves to the head of the class for UNIX operating system functions. HP-UX occupies the top spot in every studied category, with a particularly strong lead in Internet and Web Application Services, and an impressive surge forward in the intensely competitive RAS (reliability, availability, and serviceability) category.

Solaris continues its strong showing overall, sharing the top spot in Scalability with HP-UX and Tru64 UNIX, and also coming up strong in directory and security services. AIX holds its own in system management, Internet and Web application services, and directory and security services, but falls behind in the Scalability and RAS areas. Tru64 UNIX does extremely well in scalability and system management, sharing the top spot in both categories, but falls behind in Internet and Web application services, and directory and security services.

Note: Overall rankings are based on five criteria. scalability; RAS; system management; Internet and Web application services; directory and security services. Please see .Methodology. for additional information.

HP-UX, Solaris, and Tru64 UNIX share the lead in the Scalability category. HPUX has proven very strong SMP (Shared Memory Multiprocessing) capabilities, thanks to its impressive TPC-C performance on HP's 64-processor Superdome server. HP-UX also supports competitive storage ranges, and has implemented many low-level optimizations that can help to boost the performance of key applications. Further, HP-UX dramatically improved its presence on the most recent list of the world's 500 fastest supercomputers maintained by TOP500.Org, substantially boosting the credibility of its technical computing cluster capabilities.

Tru64 UNIX benefits from the enormous storage ranges enabled by its mature 64-bit design. Compaq tests and supports Tru64 UNIX file systems up to 16 TB, while the remaining vendors support at most 1 or 2 TB on their standard file systems.

Solaris offers the strongest proven SMP capabilities, thanks to its industry-leading TPC-C performance on a 128-processor Fujitsu server, but offers only average storage scalability with its 1 TB standard file system. However, Solaris supports the largest overall amount of memory, allowing use of 576 GB on the Sun Fire 15K server. AIX stands out for its strong clustering scalability, pushing IBM's DB2 Database Clusters up to 32 nodes on the TPC-H benchmark, and enjoys strong representation as well as the number one performance slot on the TOP500. Org list of supercomputers. However, AIX trails the other systems in SMP performance on the TPC-C benchmark, and also offers only average storage scalability with a 1 TB file system.

HP-UX earns the lead in the Reliability, Availability, and Serviceability (RAS) category, benefiting mainly from its extraordinary advantage in the area of workload management. With HP.s shipment of its vPartitions and nPartitions, HP-UX now offers the most complete set of server partitioning tools of all studied systems. HP-UX has also pushed resource management functions further than any of its competitors, and resides at the head of the class for online component failure recovery. Solaris follows, leading in the area of server resiliency enhancements, with particularly strong functions for avoiding planned downtime. Solaris also does well in workload management, thanks to its mature and flexible hardware partitioning capabilities with Dynamic Domains.

Tru64 UNIX and AIX follow. Both possess very strong HA (High Availability) clustering capabilities, with AIX supporting particularly strong disaster recovery options, and Tru64 UNIX benefiting from strong cluster management and shared storage capabilities. Tru64 UNIX also does reasonably well in server resiliency enhancements, with surprisingly strong capabilities to handle component failure online. However, both fall behind in the workload management area. AIX is still clearly catching up with competitors with its partitioning capabilities, while Tru64 UNIX trails substantially in the area of resource management.

Differentiation continues to shrink in the System Management category. All of the studied UNIX systems fall squarely into the .Very Good. range, offering comprehensive, Graphical User Interface (GUI)-driven system management frameworks that meet most of the tactical requirements of modern IT environments. HP-UX and Tru64 UNIX share the overall lead, supporting virtually every function included in this assessment. AIX and Solaris fall behind only slightly because of nits associated with remote manageability over the web, i.e., their requirement that clients be configured with a Java Virtual Machine (JVM) for complete remote manageability. By contrast, the HP-UX and Tru64 UNIX management consoles have modes in which web browsers can access their management functions without the use of Java. The Logical Volume Manager (LVM) included in Solaris, Solstice DiskSuite, also lacks the ability to perform hot spot management, unlike its competitors.

HP-UX earns a major lead in the Internet and Web Application Services category, benefiting from significant advantages in its support of IP protocols and fileprint-sharing services. HP has pushed its support for IPv6 particularly aggressively, and also offers by far the strongest compatibility with Windows infrastructures, offering unique capabilities such as integration of UNIX and Windows group information, and the ability to mount remote Windows directories. Solaris and AIX follow, offering roughly equivalent capabilities overall. AIX has the strongest proven web server performance, as well as very strong Java performance. Solaris provides the most complete support for Mobile IP extensions, as well as the most complete support for third-party web application servers. Tru64 UNIX has a good standing in IP protocols, with strong support for Mobile IP extensions, and very competitive compatibility with Windows infrastructures, but falls far short of competitors in its support for web application servers.

HP-UX takes the lead in the Directory and Security Services category. HP-UX has particularly strong support for LDAP directory services, primarily in the extent to which it integrates LDAP into basic system operations. HP-UX also includes some unique host-based intrusion detection functions in addition to bundling strong IP filtering tools. Solaris has strong network security capabilities, also bundling strong IP filtering tools, and aggressively undergoing certification for security standards. AIX has extensively integrated LDAP directory functions into its base operating system, and provides a strong set of secure networking tools. Tru64 UNIX also offers a strong set of networking tools, including a unique feature to bridge Secure Shell functions with traditional remote login tools, but falls short in integrating LDAP and Kerberos functions into the base operating system.

DISCUSSION QUESTIONS

1. Explain the concept of total cost of ownership in the field of server operating systems.
2. What is the difference between multiplatform support and multiprocessing support?

3. What technologies is the 64-bit processing based on?
4. Very large memory and very large data base support is of particular interest for _____ applications?
5. What is the difference between standard system administration and integrated system management features?
6. What do we mean by patch management?
7. Explain the requirement related to applications availability and integratibility.
8. Make an assessment (Internet survey) of the following UNIX flavours: AIX, HP-UX and Solaris with regard to their support for most widely used DBMS platforms.
9. Make an assessment (Internet survey) of the following server operating platforms with regard to the availability of major ERP suites (SAP, Oracle): OS/390 (z/OS), OpenVMS and OS/400.
10. Make an assessment (Internet survey) on the availability and salary ranges of UNIX and Windows server system administrators.

Chapter IX
System Administration and System Administrator's Role in Business Continuity

CHAPTER OVERVIEW

Chapter IX focuses on the role of system administration as an IT-profession and system administrator as a person who does the administrative (managerial) activites on servers and server operating systems. If server goes down for any reason or server operating system crashes, in most cases it is up to this person to "recover" the server from the bad situation and make sure that business – critical applications continue to run and provide services to end users. HP-UX as a server operating system platform is selected in order to demonstrate most commonly used techniques and features that may lead to higher levels of system availability.

INTRODUCTION

A short introduction on why system administration and system administrator as an IT profession are important in the light of business continuity.

As already mentioned in the first chapter, a super-user or sys-admin account represents one of the most exploited vulnerabilities on IT platforms because of the unlimited power of system administrator's "super-user" commands. This so-called "root" account or "super-user" (su) on UNIX/Linux servers and System Administrator on Windows server machines posses all permissions and unrestricted access to all the files. Should the root account fall into the wrong hands, the security of the whole server configuration becomes compromised. Some businesses apply an approach, which redefines the role of a superuser into a number of specific superusers with specific roles assigned to different people.

A business can employ several "administrators" for several fields such as: database administrator, network administrator, security administrator, and so forth, with all of them having "all-powerful" capabilities on their specific domain-tasks. However, system administrator on the operating system level has all kinds of file ownerships and privileges, he/she is a kind of "top-level" system administrator, who in most cases supervises all other administrators. Horror story No.3 from the first chapter provides an excellent example of what could happen if such a person applies a wrong command or perform a sys admin – powerful action on user files. That story revealed that British ISP PlusNet lost 700GB of customer e-mails forever because an engineer accidentally deleted the e-mails and then tried an old admin trick to retrieve them. The trick backfired, and instead made the mails irretrievable.

Therefore, system administrator (sysadmin) is a very important person in every information system.

These IT professionals use system administration commands in order to:

- make/change system settings,
- install/upgrade operating systems,
- install/reinstall applications,
- open/close user accounts,
- make fair use of the system, and so forth.

Depending on the operating system platform, they use different commands or OS tools in order to manage not only operating system but the whole IT platform as well.

SYSTEM ADMINISTRATION ON UNIX (HP-UX)[1]

As an example, a short description of main system administration tasks and activities on HP's HP-UX operating system is presented. The most widely used techniques as well as more advanced system administration utilities are explained. In addition, some business continuity-oriented integrated tools on HP-UX such as Ignite-UX, Bastille, HP Serviceguard, are presented.

In order to demonstrate the role of sys-admin in the context of continuous computing and business continuity we are going to use UNIX OS platform. Among several versions of UNIX operating system that are in use (HP-UX, AIX, Solaris, Tru64UNIX, IRIX,…) we will use HP's HP-UX operating system (www.hp.com). The reader should keep in mind that all these UNIX versions are similar, once you learn one of them, it is not so difficult to switch to another one. However, we should also keep in mind that even within the specific UNIX platform, its vendor may have different approaches and solutions within several versions of its UNIX.

UNIX operating system (Linux uses the same approach) uses a specific directory so-called "etc." directory, which contains most of system administration commands.

HP-UX works on several models of HP servers, including data entry servers, mid-size servers and high-end servers.

Basically there are three sets of system administration activities on HP-UX servers:

1. Hardware activities
2. Software activities
3. End-user activities

Hardware activities include several operations that are aimed at:

•   Verifying of the installation of hardware components (CPU, memory, external memory, peripherals, etc.)
•   Monitoring of the performances of hardware components
•   Activities on hardware repair

Figure 9.1. HP-UX file system and /etc directory

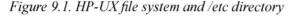
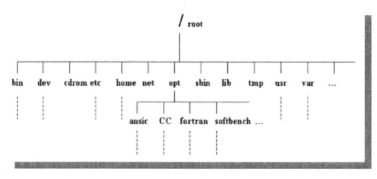

In most cases, hardware vendors deliver the whole system with all necessary components such that system administrator does not have to intervene in that process. However, better understanding of hardware components and their functioning is an advantage for system administrators.

Software activities comprise two major subgroups:

a. activities on systems software
b. activities on application software
c. activities on data (data bases)
d. activities on systems integration

The systems software activities comprise:

- Operating system installation and configuration
- Operating system update and upgrade
- File system creation
- System error detection and fixing
- Monitoring operating system
- Installing several software modules such as communication software, print software
- Design and implementation of backup and recovery routines
- Installing and update of the application software.

HP-UX usually comes preinstalled on the server or it is installed by an authorized system engineer from vendor's side. It comes with a set of CDs or DVDs with several manuals, some of them being intended for system administration operations. Even in that case, if HP-UX comes pre-installed on a server, system administrator has a lot of activities to do on it in order to bring the server into "ready-to-use" state. File system has to be created, network components have to be configured, users have to be added (user account created), application software has to be installed, data base management system has to be installed, and so forth.

HP has decided recently to rename its HP-UX operating platform from "HP-UX Operating System" (up to version HP-UX11.0) into "HP-UX Operating Environment" (HP-UX11v1—HP-UX11v3).

HP-UX 11i version 3 provides the following operating environments:

- HP-UX 11i v3 Foundation Operating Environment
- HP-UX 11i v3 Enterprise Operating Environment
- HP-UX 11i v3 Mission Critical Operating Environment
- HP-UX 11i v3 Technical Computing Operating Environment

User-oriented activities of a HP-UX administrator includes:

- Opening user accounts and providing them access to the server
- Creating user groups
- Implement user policy on company level
- Provide assistance and help in using the system

There are several questions that need to be answered while creating user policy. Some of them include:

- User groups
- Access to specific applications from user groups
- Application and data access policies
- Priority levels of users and programs

For instance, system administrator can allocate higher priority to some users and/or programs, by using a command **nice**.

On HP-UX and all other UNIX versions (Linux as well) system administration activities are performed by using:

a. command line interface
b. GUI (Graphical User Interface) or X-Window-based interface
c. Web-based interface

More experienced HP-UX administrators usually prefer using an old-style command-line interface although GUI-based system administration is easier. HP has developed a System Administration Manager, a GUI-based application that can be used for system administration activities. GUI-based SAM can be used on HP-UX workstations and servers that support X-Window interface. This standard system administration manager (SAM) interface has been replaced in HP-UX11i ver.2 by a Web-based SCM (service control manager) interface. In addition, SCM can be used for managing more systems simultaneously. Even in SCM, a command-line interface can be used.

HP has an additional product called "HP Distributed Systems Administration Utilities—DSAU" which is used for system administration in multi-system and cluster-based configurations.

In the section that follows, we are going to describe most frequently used system administration activities, both in text mode (command-line) and GUI. They are presented within a business continuity perspective in order to demonstrate the importance of system administration and system administrator in the process of ensuring higher levels of availability and business continuity.

1. Changing System Parameters

Several most important system parameters such as hostname, root password, IP address can be changed by using a command **set_parms**. The following screenshot shows using set_parms command:

```
# set_parms
Usage: set_parms <argument>
    Where <argument> can be:
hostname
timezone
date_time
root_passwd
ip_address
addl_netwrk
font_c-s
    or initial (for entire initial boot-time dialog sequence)
#
```

Unauthorized, unintentional or intentional – disruptive changes of some of these parameters will affect the whole system of data processing on that server. For instance, the following problems will occur if some of these parameters are changed:

- hostname changed: the server will become unreachable on the network as all client machines have that information on their networking (TCP/IP) settings
- ip_address changed: again, the server will be unreachable on the network, or there will be "IP number conflict" situation
- root_password changed: the owner or author of new root password becomes the most powerful person when that server is considered: in the worst case, he or she can delete (destroy) all data on server.

set_parms is automatically run during the first boot of the system. Sys admin can later at any time execute this command and by using the **set_parms** dialog screen manually add or modify information.

2. File System Selection and Creation

The notion of file system on UNIX operating system in general can be defined as a system of files: system, application and user files. HP-UX is organized in hierarchical (tree) way as shown in Figure 9.3.

On the very first level there exists a root directory which contains u number of subdirectories and files. Depending on the version of HP-UX the root directory contains a number of standard directories such as: *bin, lib, etc, dev, usr, tmp*

File system contains three different objects (see Figure 9.4).

- Files (ordinary files and special files). Ordinary files can contain data, text or program information.
- Special files – represent input/output devices such as terminal, disk drive or a printer. Special files can be either character special files or block special files.
- Directories. Directory can be defined as a container that can hold files and other directories (sub-directories).
- Links, in the form of pointer to another file. Links can be hard links or soft links.

The actual names, locations and structure of certain directories and system files will differ under different implementations of HP-UX. Here are some examples of typical files and directories under HP-UX operating system:

Figure 9.3. HP-UX file system

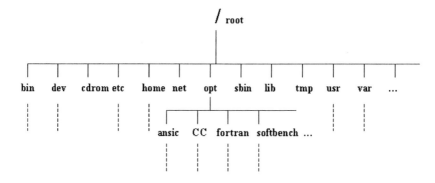

Figure 9.4. UNIX (HP-UX) file system: files, directories, links

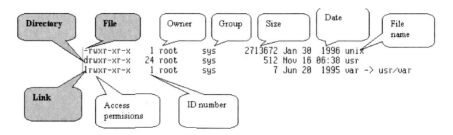

/hp-ux	- The kernel program
/dev	- Device files
/bin	- Executable files and utilities (essential command binary files)
/sbin	- essential system binary files and executables for system admin
/etc	- System configuration and administration files and commands
/lib	- Operating system and programming libraries
/opt	- Directory for application software (add-on applications)
/opt/ansic	- Location of C programming language files and routines
/opt/CC	- Location of C++ programming language files and routines
/usr/lib/	- Additional programming and system call libraries
/usr/bin/	- Additional user commands
/usr/local/	- Directory for local utilities
/usr/man	- The manual pages
/tmp	- Directory for temporary files (all users can use it)
/lost+found	- Location for detached files

HP-UX uses several files systems, most widely used are the following:

1. **HFS (High Performance File System)** – represents HP-UX version of the standard UNIX File System (UFS). It was installed and dominantly used on pre-11 versions of HP-UX. This file system supports files and file system sizes up to 128 GB.
2. **JFS (Journaled File System)** - File system which is installed by default on HP-UX 11, represents HP's implementation of Veritas' VxFS (version 4.1) which supports file sizes up to 16 TB and file system sizes up to 40 TB. From business continuity perspective, this file system provides fast file system recovery in case of system failures and the ability to perform a number of administrative tasks online, that is, online backup.
3. **NFS (Network File System)** is a standard UNIX file system, allows a number of servers to share the same files and programs. In order to do that, file systems need to be mounted from remote systems.
4. **CDFS (CD-ROM File System)** is a file system used for mounting a CD-ROM which allows reading and using compact discs with ISO-9660 format.
5. **UDF file system for reading optical media written in the UDF format.**
6. **MEMFS – memory file system.**
7. **LOFS (Loopback File System)** – allows the same file system to appear in multiple places.

As already mentioned, JFS file system is used as the main file system in HP-UX 11. It is the HP-UX implementation of the VERITAS' Journaled File System (VxFS) which HP introduced for the first time in HP-UX 10.01. As of HP-UX release 10.30, JFS is the default HP-UX file system. JFS is recommended file system for high reliability, fast recovery, and online administrative operations, including backup, resizing and defragmentation. It allows performing backup operations without moving the file system offline.

Compared to HFS, JFS recovers much faster from system failure, due to its mechanism for logging changes to the file-system structure. When the system boots after a crash, the file system synchronizes using its log to speed recovery, in an operation similar to, but much faster than, that performed by **fsck**.

JFS snapshot is a new technique which allows the system administrator to capture the file-system state at a moment in time (without taking it off-line and copying it), mount that file-system image elsewhere, and back it up. System administrator can create a snapshot by using the **lvcreate** command without copying the files and making the file system off-line, mount this newly created file system image to some other location and perform a backup operation from that location.

File system creation is one of the first operations that have to be done after initial booting the operating system in order to make hard disks accessible to users and their programs and files. File system creation consists of the following steps:

- Hard disk installation
- Creation of a device file, by using the **mknod** command
- If necessary, formatting the hard disk (**mediainit**)
- file system creation, by using **newfs** command
- Mounting file system (**mount**)
- Adding the newly created file system into */etc/checklist* file for automatic mounting.

Example:

 # mknod /dev/rdsk/5s0 b 7 0x201400
 # mediainit /dev/rdsk/5s0
 # newfs -b 8192 -f 2048 -m 20 -1 4096 /dev/rdsk/5s0 hp2213A
 # mount /dev/rdsk/5s0 /users

By using the mounting operation, the file system is incorporated into HP-UX root file system.

3. File System Maintenance

HP-UX supports several methods of the file system maintenance, an operation which aims at maintaining the integrity of the file system. These methods are implemented by several sys admin commands that have to be performed on regular basis:

- File system checking **(fsck)**
- Using **sync** routine
- Disk space control
- Using regular backup procedures
- Using the shutdown procedure

- **fsck:** File system checking is performed by using the command fsck: *# fsck -P file_system*
  fsck is the main tool for maintaining the file system on HP-UX. It can be used in bot interactive and non-interactive mode. **fsck** routine places all problematic files into */lost+found* directory.
- **sync:** sync command writes the contents from buffer onto a hard disk. When data is to be stored on a hard disk, it is first stored into a "buffer cache" or "in-memory buffer." This operation is much faster that writing directly to disk, therefore data is first copied into that memory space and when it is full, the system empties the buffer and writes data to disk.
  In case of system crash or unexpected system shutdown, if data is not properly transferred from buffer to hard disk, file system can corrupt.
  In addition to sync routine, system administrator should check from time to time the levels of hard disk space capacity (used versus free space) by using *df* and *bdf* commands:

Figure 9.5. File system usage info on HP-UX

```
# df
/data1            (/dev/vg01/lvol2  ):    767360 blocks    102286 i-nodes
/data2            (/dev/vg01/lvol3  ):   1210000 blocks    161307 i-nodes
/                 (/dev/vg00/lvol1  ):    503472 blocks    252582 i-nodes
#
```

```
# bdf
Filesystem          kbytes    used    avail %used Mounted on
/dev/vg00/lvol1    1775193 1345937   251736   84% /
/dev/vg01/lvol3     647168    1841   605000    0% /data2
/dev/vg01/lvol2     647168  237864   383680   38% /data1
#
```

bdf - reports file system usage statistics
df   - reports on free disk blocks, and i-nodes
du   - reports on disk usage in a specified directory

Sys admin applies quota mechanism in order to limit space for users on the system (hard and soft quotas). The Quota Editor and /etc/quota file are used for this purpose. Quotas allow the system administrator to impose limits on the amount of allocated space to users. Such a limitation can be a soft limit (only a warning is sent to user), or a hard limit, where, if quota is reached, no further operation will be allowed.

4. Network Services and Their Configuration

All UNIX systems, both servers and workstations, provide a set of data communication and networking features that enable the system to communicate and exchange data. Most frequently used are:

* File transfer
* Remote login
* Using e-mail messaging
* Using NFS/NIS services
* Using Internet

File transfer is done by using the command ftp with the following syntax:

$ ftp *host_name*

After a successful login, user is given a prompt (ftp>) which allows him to transfer files between local and remote system, by using commands for data transfer. The two basic commands are: put for uploading the files and get for downloading.

Figure 9.6. FTP

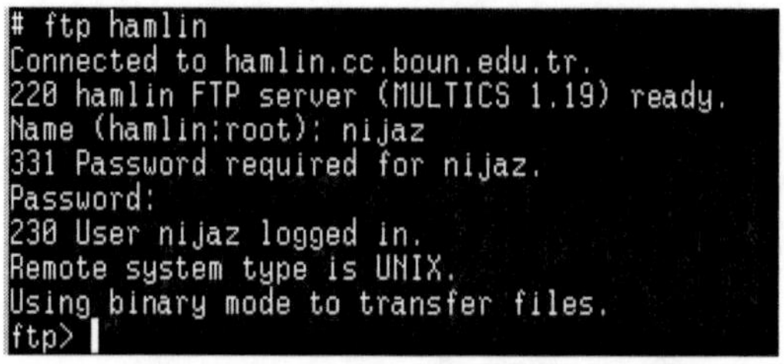

```
# ftp hamlin
Connected to hamlin.cc.boun.edu.tr.
220 hamlin FTP server (MULTICS 1.19) ready.
Name (hamlin:root): nijaz
331 Password required for nijaz.
Password:
230 User nijaz logged in.
Remote system type is UNIX.
Using binary mode to transfer files.
ftp> 
```

Figure 9.7. Telnet

```
# telnet ieiris
Trying...
Connected to ieiris.ef.boun.edu.tr.
Escape character is '^]'.
Local flow control on
Telnet TERMINAL-SPEED option ON


IRIX System V.4 (ieiris)

login: nijaz
Password:
```

Remote login or login to remote computer is done by using **telnet** or **rlogin** command:

telnet *host_name*

Remote login commands are useful for system administrators in order to administer remote computers. Regular users can use these commands as well, if they have user accounts on remote machines.

NETWORK CONFIGURATIONS AND SETTINGS

LAN and WAN services are configured by using several commands. The first step is configuring the MAN adapter or network interface card which is configured by using the following command:

ifconfig *interface address-family address*

Example:

Figure 9.8. Status of the network adapter

```
# ifconfig lan0
lan0: flags=863<UP,BROADCAST,NOTRAILERS,RUNNING,MULTICAST>
        inet 193.140.207.25 netmask ffffff00 broadcast 193.140.207.255
#
```

ifconfig lan0 inet 193.140.207.116 broadcast 193.140.207.255

System admin can get information on the status of network adapter by executing the following command:

ifconfig *device_name*

Information on network card provided by the system is useful for system administrator in order to fix potential problems on the network. For instance, if users on the server get a message "server is unreachable" it might be because of the failure of the network card. The ifconfig command will give information that network card is down. This command is used for several network settings, including IP number, netmask, broadcast, and so forth.

Changes in networking settings should be updated in /etc/netlinkrc or /etc/rc.cnfig.d/netconf files, depending on the version of HP-UX, in order to activate changes during the boot process.

Figure 9.9. Lanscan

```
# lanscan
Hardware Station        Crd Hardware Net-Interface  NM  MAC      HP DLPI Mjr
Path     Address        In# State    NameUnit State  ID  Type     Support Num
10/12/6  0x080009E32A71 0   UP       lan0     UP     4   ETHER    Yes     52
#
```

Figure 9.10. Landiag

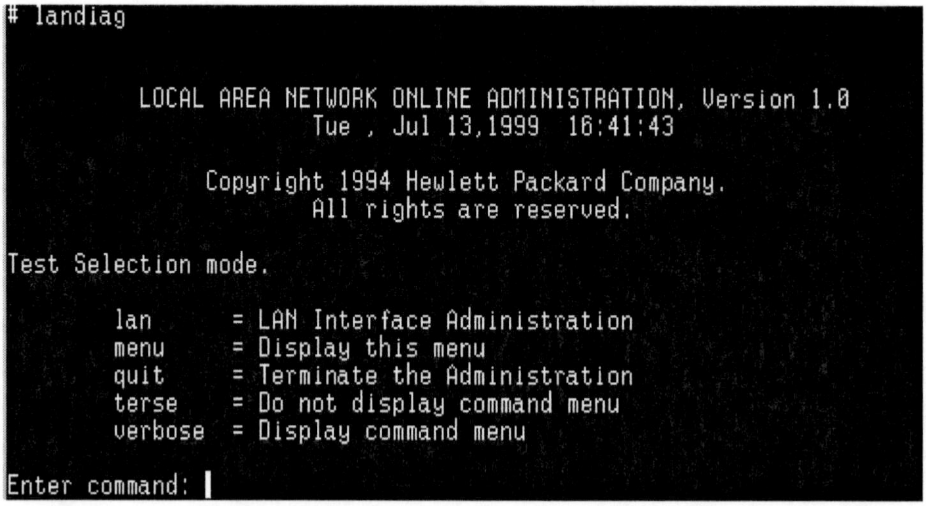

```
# landiag


            LOCAL AREA NETWORK ONLINE ADMINISTRATION, Version 1.0
                    Tue , Jul 13,1999   16:41:43

                Copyright 1994 Hewlett Packard Company.
                      All rights are reserved.

Test Selection mode.

        lan      = LAN Interface Administration
        menu     = Display this menu
        quit     = Terminate the Administration
        terse    = Do not display command menu
        verbose  = Display command menu

Enter command: |
```

The status of the network adapter can be assessed by using the following commands: **lanscan, landiag, netstat, linkloop, ping**.

CONFIGURING THE GATEWAY

Very often, the server can become unreachable because of the fact that information about the gateway is lost or the routing configuration file is corrupted. The gateway is configured (reconfigured) by using the command:

/etc/route add default *hostname metric*

Example:

/etc/route add default router-a 1

Another two /etc files are important in setting the networking parameters:

/etc/hosts
/etc/resolv.conf

These two /etc files contain information on hostnames, their IP addresses and paths to the system which is acting as the main DNS (Domain Name System) server. Here are some excepts from /etc/hosts and /etc/resolv.conf files:

Configured using SAM by root on Mon Aug 25 13:41:35 1997
127.0.0.1 localhost
208.225.57.25 zenne.ef.boun.edu.tr zenne
Host Database
#

Figure 9.11. /etc/hosts file

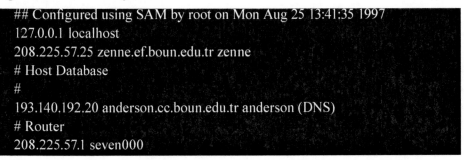

193.140.192.20 anderson.cc.boun.edu.tr anderson (DNS)
Router
208.225.57.1 seven000

search ef.boun.edu.tr cc.boun.edu.tr
nameserver 193.140.192.20
nameserver 193.140.192.21
nameserver 193.140.192.40

5. Backup and Data Recovery (Restoring)

HP-UX supports executing backup operations directly from command line and from within the SAM (System Administration Manager). Using command line interface and backup commands is a tedious task, however, more experienced system administrators still prefer using this approach because of the fact that they are used to work with these commands for several years, even decades.

HP-UX supports several backup commands such as: **fbackup, cpio, tar**.

Syntax of the cpio command is given as follows:

Command: Explanation:
----
cpio -o [cvxB] > *device_name*   Backup
cpio -i [cvxdumB] [*patterns*] < *device_name*   Restoring

Figure 9.12. /etc/resolv.conf file

search ef.boun.edu.tr cc.boun.edu.tr
nameserver 193.140.192.20
nameserver 193.140.192.21
nameserver 193.140.192.40

Examples:

 # find / -print | cpio -ocx > /dev/rmt/0m   Backup
 # cpio -icxvmd "/users/*" < /dev/rmt/0m*   Restoring
 # cpio -it /dev/rmt/0m   Provides the contents of tape

The cpio command uses a number of options than can be applied depending on the type of the backup, type of the device, and so forth, (c, v, x, d, m, u, B, etc.).

In addition to cpio and fbackup commands, another command that can be used is the tar command. It can be used for backup and restoring the files, however, this command is most frequently used by system administrators for installing the programs.

tar xvf /dev/rmt/0m

The tar command is often used in combination with uncompressing/compressing the filesets during the process of software installation. For instance, the following fileset named file_name.tgz is installed by using the following gzip command:

gzip -dc < /path/file_name.tgz|tar xf -

The gzip command (Gnu zip routine) is used for uncompressing the files.

6. Adding/Removing the Users

Adding and removing the user accounts on the HP-UX system is also a typical operation performed by system administrator. The sole operation is very simple, however, it has to be a part of a well-defined user policy on company level. By doing several settings related to user management, system admin can specify which user will have permissions on which files, directories, devices and programs.

Adding users can be done by using command line interface or the SAM GUI-based interface.

a.   Creating an user account by using HP-UX commands

This task is consisted of several activities:

1. Add information about new user into the /etc/passwd file

user_name:password:user_id:group_id:comment:login_directory:shell

Example:

nijaz:tso9hgPdfMasP:101:20:Nijaz Bajgoric:/users/nijaz:/bin/ksh

The /etc/passwd file is one of the most important administration files on HP-UX operating system since it contains information about users, their usernames, passwords, locations of user files, group settings, and so forth.

1. Add information on users into /etc/group file

group_name:password:group_id:group_list

Example:
users::20:nijaz, adnan, ermina

Create HOME directory for that user and set access permissions on it:

mkdir /users/nijaz
chmod 755 /users/nijaz

Create default setup files

cp /etc/d.profile   /users/nijaz/.profile (in case of using Bourne or Korn shell)

Change the ownerships on that HOME directory and default files:

chown nijaz /users/nijaz
chgrp users /users/nijaz /users/nijaz/.profile

7. Communication with End Users

HP-UX supports u number of ways of communicating with HP-UX users. A method of communication depends on how the message is important and urgent for end users. Most frequently used commands are as follows:

- **news** command
- **wall** command
- **motd** files

- e-mail
- instant messaging system

For messages that are identified as less important ("nice to know" messages) the sys admin can create a file and place it into /usr/news directory. For more important messages ("need to know" messages) the sys admin can create a file and place it into /usr/news directory. When user logs on, the system provides the following message:

news: *news_filename*

For more important and urgent messages, the system admin can use the wall command and send a message to all users logged onto the system. For Instance, if the server has to be rebooted or halted for any reason, the sys admin will notify all users who are currently logged on the system that the server will be shutdown in a number of minutes or seconds. This message will allow end users to save necessary data, close open files, finish some processing activities, and so forth, before the system halts down.

```
# wall [Return]
Message text
[Ctrl-D]
```

Example:

```
# wall
The system will be shut down in 5 minutes. Please log off;
```

After executing tis command by sys admin on his screen, all users will immediately get the following message on their screens:

Broadcast message from root time
The system will be shut down in 5 minutes. Please log off.

Such a message is very useful as it allows the users not to lose data. This message allows the applications to close in a regular way and reduce the risk of loosing data and corrupting application software.

The file **/etc/motd** fajl *(motd - message of the day)* is also used for informing users on some activities that are planned for a specific time period.

8. Process Management

Each user on HP-UX has some possibilities to manage processes, but only those executed within his/her user domain. System administrator can administer all processes, not only user-started processes, but also those that are initiated by the system. In that way, sys admin can manage efficiency and stability of the system. Most frequently used commands and utilities are listed as follows:

a.   Process listing
     Command ps list all active processes at a time, giving the user information about the status of those processes. Several options can be added in command line with the ps command.
     # ps -ef | more
a.   Killing processes is a task performed by an user (on its own processes) or superuser (on all kind of processes) which stops (halts) executing that process. This operation can be useful in situations when some processes (users) cause some sort of instability on the system. The syntax of the kill command is:
     # kill process_id
b.   Process priority change. Administrator can change the priority of the processes or users in a way that some specific process or user is given higher or lower priority. The commands used to change process priority are: nice and renice.
     # renice -n 13 *user_name*

9. Protecting Vital Information on HP-UX

An example is /etc/passwd file—a file which contains all information about the users (their names, user accounts, passwords, etc.). This file, like all other /etc files can be used only by super user.

The format of this file with regard to user permissions (owner, group, other) is as follows:

Figure 9.13. ps command

```
   UID   PID  PPID  C    STIME TTY       TIME COMMAND
   root    0     0  0   Feb 20  ?        0:05 swapper
   root    1     0  0   Feb 20  ?        0:00 init
   root    2     0  0   Feb 20  ?        0:02 vhand
   root    3     0  0   Feb 20  ?       10:20 statdaemon
   root    4     0  0   Feb 20  ?        0:31 unhashdaemon
   root    7     0  0   Feb 20  ?        0:00 ttisr
   root   13     0  0   Feb 20  ?        0:00 lvmkd
```

- r- - r- - r- -

Which means that not only owner of this file, bit other users as well can read the contents of the file. For instance:

nijaz:**abr6sjLdfKfrG**:101:20:Nijaz Bajgoric:/users/nijaz:/bin/ksh

An ordinary user can not understand (decrypt) this format, however, it is possible to do that by using some programs than can be found on the Net even as freeware programs.

However, if /etc/passwd file is hacked, then a hacker can do all kind of super user – assigned tasks and cause significant problems. Some solutions are available, though, that is, creating an /etc/shadow file by using pwconv utility on UNIX systems. This utility hides password info even in encrypted format from seeing it. Newly created /etc/shadow file has the following file protection scheme:

Figure 9.14. The content of /etc/shadow file

```
erdem:it5OTUIPTJS8U:10735:::::::-1
ergun:1VABwRYMHSifM:10735:::::::-1
nijaz:JpPB26j/YWMhQ:10735:::::::-1
automod:XiW8xRKdr.4Xo:10735:::::::-1
```

Figure 9.15. The contents of /etc/passwd file, after applying pwconv command

```
erdem:x:303:20:/Ugur Murat Erdem,Bogazici University,,,,,BUPHM:/usr/people/assis
t/erdem:/bin/tcsh
ergun:x:307:44:/ergun:/usr/people/stud/ergun:/bin/csh
nijaz:x:335:0:Nijaz Bajgoric,,,,,,,:/usr/people/spec/nijaz:/bin/csh
automod:x:340:20:Automod Users:/usr/people/stud/automod:/bin/csh/
```

Figure 9.16. pwconv routine on HP-UX

```
# pwconv
Creating secure password database...
Directories created.
Making default files.
System default file created...
Terminal default file created...
Device assignment file created...
Moving passwords...
secure password database installed.
Converting at and crontab jobs...
At and crontab files converted.
```

-r- - - - - - - -

which means that the content of this file can be read only by super user.

After applying pwconv utility and creating an /etc/shadow file, standard /etc/passwd file has the format shown in Figure 9.15.

This operation is performed by using the pwconv utility on HP-UX operating system shown in Figure 9.16.

The newest release of HP-UX11i version 3 provides the newest set of security technologies that can provide greater access control. These technologies include:

- **Compartments**—some applications can be isolated into what is called "compartment" in order to prevent catastrophic damages to the server as a whole. When put into isolation (compartment) an application has restricted access to computer resources outside its compartment.
- **Fine-Grained privileges**—new approach in setting root-based privileges which grants processes only those privileges needed for a specific task.
- **Role-based Access Control**—enables non-root users some root privileges for specific tasks.
- **Bastille** is a security tool that is used to enhance the security of the HP-UX operating environment. Bastille was originally developed by the open source community for Linux systems. HP has implemented this product on its HP-UX operating platform and is provided as a bundled software. The initial implementation is based on using bastille command and bastille configuration file. (/etc/opt/sec_mgmt/bastille/config). This security tool makes necessary configurations on system settings, daemons, services and servers (Web servers, Domain Name Service—DNS, system of shadowed passwords, trusted systems, IP filtering, and so forth.

10. System Shutdown

System shutdown is an operation which halts the system down. End users working on desktop computers with desktop Windows operating system are familiar with this operation. However, as Microsoft's desktop operating system matured during the last 15 years, the number of necessary reboots (resets) and shutdown operations has been reduced. Halting a desktop computer has as a result disconnecting only one user from that computer, however, shutting down a server which is running mission critical application is completely different story. Therefore, the shutdown operation should be avoided as much as possible on server systems, because of the downtime and negative results of it. However, this operation is still necessary, although server vendors seek for the solutions that can reduce the number of situations in which the shutdown is needed.

Only ten years ago, even in UNIX world, shutdown was absolutely needed in the following situations:

- Adding a new hardware (processor, memory, disk, network card)
- Backup operations, in which the server had to be brought to so-called *single-user* mode, which meant that end users do not have access to data during the backup operation.
- File system checking, mounting and unmounting the file systems.
- Kernel reconfiguration.

In addition to a standard (normal) shutdown operation, there exists also an abnormal system shutdown. Abnormal system shutdown or system crash may also happen due to several reasons.

The newest versions of HP-UX, other UNIX versions and proprietary server operating systems allow performing most of system administration activities even without shutting down the system, which is very important from continuous computing and business continuity perspectives.

Figure 9.17. System administration manager (SAM) on HP-UX 10.10

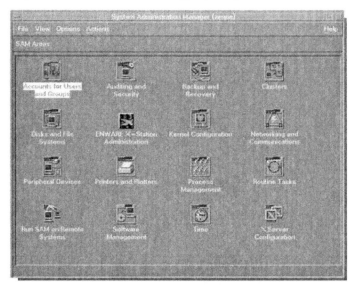

GUI-BASED SYSTEM ADMINISTRATION ON HP-UX

As said before, system administration tasks on HP-UX and on any other UNIX operating system can be performed by using a) command line (for more experienced UNIX system administrators) and b) graphical user interface.

For example, performing a backup operation can be done by using the following command:

find / -print | cpio -ocvxB > /dev/rmt/0m

Instead of memorizing such commands and their numerous options, a GUI-based system administration program (System Administration Manager – SAM) can be used, not only for backup, but for other most common system administration activities and tasks.

SAM windows contains several areas that represent most commonly used system administration tasks such as: Accounts for Users and Groups, Auditing and Security, Backup and Recovery, Disks and File Systems, Clusters, Kernel Configuration, Networking and Communications, Peripheral Devices, Printers and Plotters, Process Management, Routine Tasks, Software Management, and so forth.

Another product that can be used for backup is called HP OpenView OmniBack, particularly for faster backups, centralized backup management, performing backup of large numbers of systems, creating a database of backup information, backup customization, and so forth.

Another section of HP's System administration manager that is intended for managing networking and data communication platform is shown on Figure 9.19.

Figure 9.18. Settings for backup operations

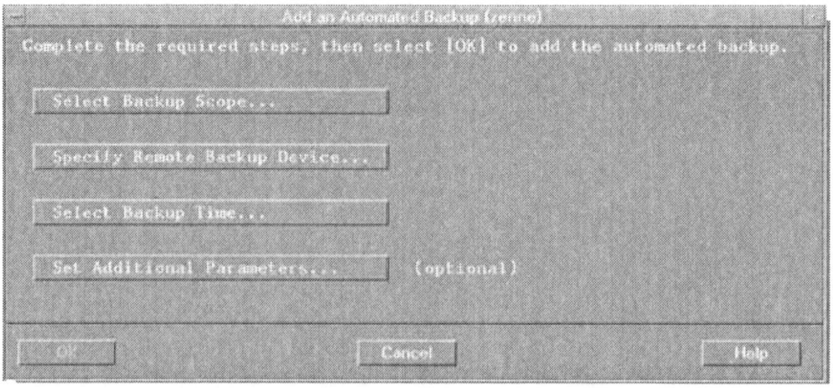

Figure 9.19. SAM Windows for network settings

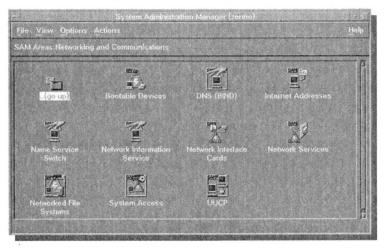

Instead of using HP-UX command line interface, this window can be used for administering the following networking devices, protocols and appliances:

- Network Interface Card
- DNS and BIND services
- Bootable devices
- Internet addressing
- NFS and NIS services
- Network services
- UUCP, and so forth.

System administration manager (SAM) is replaced by HP System Management Homepage (HP SMH) in HP-UX 11i v3. HP SMH as an enhanced version of SAM, provides Graphical User Interface (GUI), Text User Interface (TUI), and Command Line Interface (CLI) for managing HP-UX.

HP SMH provides the following system management features and capabilities:

- A common cross-platform solution is available for HP-UX 11i, Windows, and Linux.
- It is bundled with HP-UX 11i Foundation Operating Environment.
- It uses operating system-based Secure Sockets Layer (SSL) and host-based authentication to protect web-based system management tools.

- User accounts and groups are managed on a local and network information service (NIS) system.
- Can be used to configure and administer disks, file systems, and logical volumes.
- Query error details using the Error Management Technology that includes the Common Error Repository.
- View and administer various Web-based enterprise management (WBEM) events that are generated on an HP-UX 11i v3 system.
- Perform tuning operations on the HP-UX kernel.
- Configure network interfaces on HP-UX installed systems.
- Configure and manage partitions on HP server systems.
- View all devices on a host system, add and replace cards, and configure the slots and cards for that system.
- Configure security attributes of local and network information service (NIS) users, both system-wide and per-user values.
- Monitor, administer, and configure cluster systems by using Serviceguard cluster.

ADVANCED SYSTEM ADMINISTRATION TOOLS AND ROUTINES ON HP-UX FOR HIGH AVAILABILITY

Advanced business continuity technologies that can be used on HP-UX operating platform are explained.

In addition to most commonly used system administration utilities, HP-UX supports additional, more advanced technologies, tools, routines and utilities that can be used in order to ensure higher levels of availability. Most of them are supported by HP's advanced system administration modules for high availability, including integrated and dedicated high availability suites such as: **Ignite-UX, Bastille, HP Serviceguard, and so forth.**

Some of them are listed as follows:

- Creating the system recovery image by using the command **make_recovery**.
- Checking whether the system recovery image has to be recreated: **check_recovery**.
- **Hardware mirroring**. Hardware mirroring is a method of providing high availability by duplicating data on redundant hard drives.
- **Software mirroring.** Unlike hardware mirroring, the software mirroring is used to make identical copies of data on several locations, by using logical volume manager (LVM), Veritas Volume Manager (VxVM), MirrorDis/UX.

- **Hot spared disk**—it is a disk that is reserved for swapping with a broken disk that has no mirrored data.
- **Data encoding** performed by a hard disk array controller when a disk drive fails.
- **Hot Spared Disks.**
- **High Availability Storage System**s. These systems as typical hardware redundancy technology are based on using two SCSI buses, each of them with their own SCSI connectors, power supply units and fans. This set includes also hot-pluggable disks that enable inserting and removing disks without removing the array terminator.
- **High availability monitors**. HA monitors work on detecting the problems on disks, network devices, other system resources, and so forth, and alerting the system administrator to correct the problem.
- **Clustering technologies** are supported by HP's integrated clustering solution that includes support for several clustering configurations such as: Metro Cluster and Continental Cluster. The Enterprise Cluster Master Toolkit as a component of this integrated solution contains a set of templates and scripts for configuring Service Guard solutions.

OTHER IT-PROFESSIONALS FOR BUSINESS CONTINUITY

Having a system administrator is not enough for achieving high availability ratios and particularly for a comprehensive, efficient and effective business continuity management. A business willing to implement BCM solutions needs several BCM specialists on both managerial and specialist level.

As continuous computing and business continuity become more and more important in modern business, a number of new IT-professions have been introduced. It has become evident that employing only traditional system and network administrators is not enough for ensuring a comprehensive business continuity solution enterprise-wide. Therefore, businesses that implemented business continuity solutions seek BS specialists on different organizational levels. Some of them are listed as follows:

a. Managerial Level:
- Business Continuity Manager
- Enterprise Business Continuity Manager
- Associate Director for BC Programs
- Manager—Business Continuity Planning
- Manager—Corporate Security and Business Continuity
- Director of Business Continuity Program

a.   Business Architect/Analyst/Specialist level:
*   Business Resilience Architect
*   Business Continuity Analyst
*   Business Analyst for Business Continuity Program
*   Business Continuity Specialist
*   Business Continuity Administrator
*   Disaster Recovery Specialist
*   Emergency Preparedness Specialist

These specialists are expected to have the following skills:

*   Professional certification from reputable institutions such as: Disaster Recovery Institute, Business Continuity Institute.
*   Understanding of BCP methodologies
*   Skills of BCP tools such as Paragon or LRDPS.
*   Understanding of IT architectures (mainframe, c/s) and computer systems
*   Understanding of multiple operating systems
*   Understanding of LAN and WAN network environments, and so forth.

CHAPTER SUMMARY

System administrator or "super-user" is a person who administers the whole server system and has all kinds of privileges in regard to files, applications, users, and so forth. He/she uses the "root" or sys-admin account, which represents one of the most exploited vulnerabilities on IT platforms because of the unlimited power of system administrator's "super-user" commands. Should the root account fall into the wrong hands, the security of the whole server configuration becomes compromised, hence the reason of explaining this profile in separate chapter in this book. System administration tasks and role in business continuity is explained in more details on the example of HP-UX operating system platform.

REAL WORLD CASES

PlusNet admits customer emails lost forever
By John Oates
Thursday 3rd August 2006
*Adapted from: http://www.theregister.co.uk/2006/08/03/plusnet_loses_deleted_*
emails/print.html

PlusNet has today admitted that it will not be able to restore 700GB of lost customer emails. Never. Ever.

A PlusNet engineer accidentally deleted the emails on Sunday 9 July and the company has been struggling to restore them ever since.

That struggle is now over.

The PlusNet site explains why it has taken so long to (not) sort things out. The screw-up involved a Sun NAS device which runs on StorageTek's proprietary operating system which meant data recovery experts had to alter the tools they usually use.

Other than the weird operating system it said the biggest problem was caused by the unfortunate engineer's first attempt to fix the original mistake.

The engineer tried to recover the data by creating a volume of the same size, and in the same place, as the first volume - "an old sysadmin trick," PlusNet tells us. But the system uses the first volume to create a master inode - essentially a map of where all the other data is kept. Because this was deleted, finding the rest of the data in the second and third volumes is very difficult.

They did get some information back from these other volumes but without the master inode it is all but impossible to tell which emails belong to who.

Within three hours the Sun NAS was on its way to data recovery specialists.

A statement on the PlusNet website claims that half of the email was spam and that 48 per cent of it had already been read - leaving just one or two per cent of actual deleted unread email.

PlusNet is now getting its Sun kit back so it get on with setting up a new email storage system.

Adapted from: http://www.microsoft.com/casestudies/casestudy.
aspx?casestudyid=201009

HSBC Group is one of the largest banking and financial service organizations in the world, with 9,500 offices in 76 countries and territories, and an IT infrastructure that includes 300,000 desktops and 15,000 Windows®-based server computers. In the past, decisions on which technology to use were made at the local level, with each of the hundreds of companies in the HSBC Group potentially having its own data center, Windows domain, desktop standard, software deployment tools and processes, and monitoring and alerting solutions.

In 2004, HSBC launched its Common Windows Desktop initiative, with a goal of reducing the U.S.$500 million annual cost of maintaining and supporting 300,000 desktop computers by 20% through rigorous standardization. From a technical perspective, the initiative called for a single worldwide desktop image based on the Windows XP Professional operating system and a single worldwide directory forest based on the Active Directory® directory service in the Windows Server® 2003 operating system.

Along with the new desktop infrastructure itself, HSBC also needed the tools to best manage and support that new environment, including a solution for the centralized deployment of new software and software updates. In the past, the various HSBC companies used a number of tools and processes, none of which offered the levels of reliability, scalability, and integration needed to support a unified global environment.

Business Situation

HSBC needed desktop management ans erver monitoring solutions that were scalable enogh tu support a globally distributed environmnent with 300,000 desktops and 15,000 server computers.

Solution

HSBC met its needs with Microdoft System Center solutions, including Systems Management Server 2003 for desktop management and Operations Manager 2005 for monitoring critical Windows based servers.

Benefits

- Strong reliability and security
- Imprved service for internal customers
- Expected 20% reduction in desktop cost of ownership
- Strong integration of desktop and server

Software and Services

- Microsoft Active Directory
- Microsoft Operations Manager 2005
- Microsoft Systems Management Server 2003
- Microsoft Windows Server 2003 Enterprise Edition
- Microsoft Windows XP Professional

Siemens
Siemens Manages 417,000 Users with Windows Server System
Adapted from: http://www.microsoft.com/casestudies/casestudy.
aspx?casestudyid=52540

Today, Siemens has 417,000 people, 340,000 desktops, and 8,900 servers in 130 business units in 190 countries. A few years ago, Siemens supported its business with 1,000 domains in a highly decentralized structure. It wanted a single, centralized Active Directory to streamline user management, e-mail, and collaboration. Siemens was also developing an Entitlement

Architecture based on a Siemens DirX solution for its corporatewide Identity Management infrastructure. Siemens achieved its goals, thanks to Microsoft Windows Server System integrated server software that incorporates innovations to help companies do more with less.

Siemens has deployed a single-forest architecture and directory that simplifies and facilitates management, saves tens of millions of dollars annually, and helps Siemens to add new business value that it could not otherwise consider. Siemens expects to reduce file/print server count by 75%. The end result was a business solution where Windows Server System and Siemens DirX complement each other.

Situation

The information technology challenge facing Siemens is vast—as vast as the company itself. Today, Siemens employs 417,000 people in 190 countries, with some 340,000 desktops and 8,900 servers in a global network that supports 130 Siemens units in six business segments: Information and Communications, Automation and Control, Power, Transportation, Medical, and Lighting. With support from regional units, each unit is responsible for its own operations and has the flexibility to make its own decisions and build strong relationships with its customers.

A few years ago, Siemens's decentralized and constantly changing structure—the company had 1,000 domains in 1998—made it challenging to foster the cooperation among business units and regions that is critical to enabling the company to provide comprehensive customer-focused products, solutions, and services at competitive prices. It also made it challenging to provide a comprehensive, coordinated, and highly manageable IT infrastructure to support the enterprise and its growth.

Solution

Siemens is adopting a single-forest, single Active Directory infrastructure based on Microsoft Windows Server System, including Windows Server 2003 with Active Directory and Exchange Server 2003.

Benefits

- 417,000 user accounts in single Active Directory
- Millions of dollars in annual savings
- 75% file/print server consolidation
- Ability to add business value

Hardware

- Fujitsu-Siemens Primergy Servers
- HP Proliant Servers
- Dell PowerEdge Servers

Software and Services

- Microsoft Active Directory
- Microsoft Exchange Server 2003
- Microsoft Office Live Communication Server 2003
- Microsoft Office Professional Edition 2003
- Microsoft Windows Server 2003 Enterprise Edition

DISCUSSION QUESTIONS

1. Why might a system administrator affect the IT infrastructure?
2. Explain the main duties of a system administrator.
3. What is a difference between UNIX sys admin and Windows Server sys admin guys.
4. List major systema dministration activities on HP-UX.
5. What are the main file systems implemented on HP-UX?

6. Explain the difference between reboot and shutdown operation.
7. Explain briefly the importance of the /etc/passwd file.
8. What are advanced system administration utilities on HP-UX from business continuity perspective?
9. How can a manager ensure that a negative impact of disgruntled system adminintrator be minimized?
10. What new IT job profiles help a business continuity project in a company?

ENDNOTE

[1] The section on HP-UX-based system administration is based on the author's experience on administering HP-UX and other UNIX systems while working at the Department of Industrial Engineering, Bogazici University, Istanbul, Turkey. All screenshoots are taken by author on the IE Dept.'s HP K220 server running HP-UX 10.10 and 10.20.

Chapter X
Backup and Recovery Technologies for Business Continuity

CHAPTER OVERVIEW

Chapters V-IX dealt with server operating environment and its role in ensuring business continuity mostly in cases of ongoing data processing operations. Having a server down and making it up as soon as possible in order to minimize the costs of downtime was the topic in these chapters. Chapter X deals with technologies for ensuring higher levels of data availability in cases of data loss by having data recovered ASAP. Several backup and recovery technologies are explored with focus being on the traditional backup.

INTRODUCTION

An introduction to data protection technologies from business continuity perspective is given.

In addition to server configurations, server operating systems and ServerWare solutions, the second set of business continuity drivers as defined in Chapter III is presented here as a set of data protection technologies. It represents the second layer of an information infrastructure that can be implemented to enhance continuous computing and business continuity. The whole model based on three layers of business continuity technologies is shown on Figure 10.1. Layer 2 in this model contains the technologies that are used for data backup and recovery.

Several information technologies are used in order to store data in data centres in an efficient and effective way and protect it such that business does not suffer if, for any reason, data is lost. Primarily, this set comprises three main groups: data storage, data backup and data recovery technologies.

Just like using several what-if scenarios in financial management (e.g., in Excel or any personal productivity tool), in the area of data (information) management there is a need of building several „what-if" scenarios such as:

1. What if we our application server goes down; can we do our business without business critical applications running properly? Can we still keep our business „in business" if main application server is down, or if data is lost?
2. What if our messaging server goes down and stay inactive for couple of hours? What is going to happen if an important e-mail went to spam messages that are automatically removed from the messaging server?
3. What if our Web server goes down and is unreachable for several hours?
4. What if our CRM server gets into a „blue screen of death"; how long our existing customers and our prospectives will not be able to connect to our server and get necessary data about the products they want to buy?

Figure 10.1. The layers of the continuous computing infrastructure

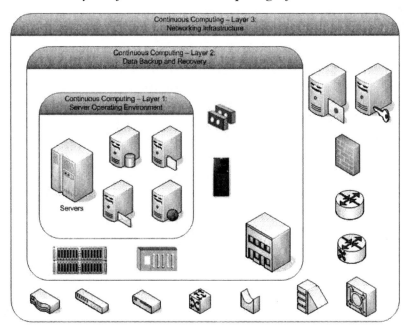

5. What if our primary data storage (har disk) crashed? Do we have backup, on which media, how long will it take to recover from that situation?

6. What if we get a hardware glitch on our RAID system? What is going to happen with our data stored on it?

7. What if our main data backup medium is broken and there is no way to restore data onto hard disk?

8. What if we have a problem on our LAN/WAN infrastructure? Network switch, router, modem, and so forth, is broken and we can not reach our data?

9. What if we have lost our backup tape (or the whole tape library), on-site due to some sort of disaster or off-site during the transport to a remote location?

10. What if a major hardware glitch occured on our main server and it caused all data is gone. We have backup taken last night, is it enough from data freshness - validity perspective? How long it will take to recover from that situation, recover data and continue with data processing?

11. What is going to happen if one of our managers lost his or her notebook with business-critical data on it?

12. What if we have lost all power in our building? What if we have lost main Internet connection and all Web servers are down?

13. And so forth.

Traditionally, during the period of more than thirty years, data management was treated in terms of primary data storage in the form of disk-based data management for data processing and secondary data storage in the form of tape-based data management system (tape backup). Storing files on hard disks, taking regular tape backups, having data restored (recovered) in case of data-file corruption or data-file loss, was a standard approach used for more than three decades.

However, in today's e-economy era, modern business is characterized by a saying "YOUR DATA IS YOUR BUSINESS – PROTECT IT!" As Michael Croy (Ybarra, 2006) pointed out: "After Katrina, companies need a different paradigm. The heart of American business is now IT. Business continuity needs to be part of daily operations. It's not an IT issue, it's a business issue, it's a corporate governance issue."

Barraza (2002) pointed out that " … with worldwide buyers and sellers operating on a 24/7/365 basis, the need for building information systems that approach 100% uptime and data availability is more acute that ever. Simply put, the global economy runs on information. More importantly, it runs on available information".

In addition, almost every business operates today under some sort of regulatory requirements related to data protection and application availability. Businesses are asked to implement several technologies, policies and techniques in order to protect data. In addition to having data backed up, modern business computing must ensure that data is protected from hackers' activities as well.

Technologies used for storing data (data storage), data backup and data recovery play crucial role in information management. Several trends in data/storage management have been identified as follows:

- Data has become a multidimensional item with different new formats that are rich in content and rich in media type.
- More and more data is converted from standard paper-based formats into electronic form in order to be stored, searched and retrieved more efficiently.
- Continuing demand for storage capacity, performance, and faster data access.
- Continuing demand for storing (keeping) data for longer period of time.
- E-mail has become an inevitable form of data that has to be stored and managed as well.
- Compliance requirements and regulations with regard to data management are issued on national and international levels asking the businesses to comply the regulations.
- Prices and power consumption of data storage devices are decreasing, while capacity, data access time and reliability of these devices are increasing.

Today's data management technologies comprise not only traditional structure that is based on a hard disk as a primary data storage and tape-based backup and recovery but also more advanced technologies such as: RAID, mirroring, online backup, replication, snapshots, data vaulting, and so forth. As a primary storage medium, hard disks are combined into arrays (groups) that can improve performances of data writing and data reading and ensure data redundancy in the events of disk failures. Larger businesses combine these disk arrays with networking technologies by forming LAN and WAN based storage infrastructures called storage area networks and networked area storage.

Traditional hard disk technology is still used as a primary storage medium. Depending on the capacity and rotational speed measured in rotations per minute (rpm) several models are available today: hard disks with speed of 5,400 rpm and 7,200 rpm are mostly used on desktop machines, while those disks with 10,000 and 15,000 rpm are installed and used on servers and integrated storage systems. The performances of hard disks are influenced also by the type of the controller interface that is used: from traditional parallel ATA and SCSI interfaces to Serial ATA (SATA) and SAS interfaces that are commonly used today. These serial connections provide faster data rates than parallel technologies.

In addition to ATA, SCSI, SATA and SAS interfaces, Fibre Channel is also used as data transfer architecture in storage systems. Fibre Channel transfers data at the speeds of 2/4 Gbps. Several disks, dozens to hundreds of disks can be grouped and organized into storage systems (storage arrays) that can store hundreds of gigabytes, terabytes, even petabytes of data. Another interface which is used in storage systems is iSCSI (Internet SCSI or SCSI over IP) which is cheaper than Fibre Channel but slower.

BACKUP AND RECOVERY: CONCEPTS AND TECHNOLOGIES

Backup concepts and technologies are explained in this section. The traditional backup technologies based on using magnetic tapes are presented from business continuity perspective. Most widely used backup scenarios are briefly explained.

In modern business, it is crucial for an organization to define and adopt a strategy of data management or, in broader sense, information management strategy on organizational level. In that sense, several policies or strategies should be carefully developed and implemented in order to define properly a set of the following data management activities:

a. Data Storage
b. Data Backup
c. Data Recovery

Efficient and effective organizational data management represents one of the main prerequisites for assuring continuous computing and business continuity. Information technology provides a number of data storage and backup solutions for achieving continuous computing as a basis for business continuity. Several technologies are used:

a. Traditional disk-based storage solutions
b. Optical storage
c. RAID technologies
d. Traditional tape - based backup technologies,
e. Online backup
f. Clustering
g. Snapshot/mirroring technologies
h. Data vaulting technologies, and so forth.

From business continuity perspective, an organization has an option to select one or more of the following data management solutions:

1. Standard hard disk-based data storage for continuous data storing in the form of primary copy of data.
2. Solutions based on disk redundancy (RAID – Redundant Array of Inexpensive/ Independent Disks) for situations if single primary copy disk crashes.
3. External devices and media such as optical devices and tape devices, that are used to back up data in the form of secondary copy of data. These devices and belonging media types are used assuming that some sort of failure or fault that may happen to a computer will cause a data loss from its primary copy of data (hard disk).
4. Advanced solutions such as fault-tolerant systems that are installed and implemented with the assume that a fault on computer system or its component will not produce data loss.
5. Advanced solutions in the form of disaster-tolerant systems that are implemented in order to provide data survival even if some sort of natural disaster occurs.
6. Off-site data protection as a way of sending business-critical data to an off-site location. In most cases data is transported off-site in the forms of traditional backups taken to magnetic tapes. However, another approach which is based on transferring data electronically to off-site facilities can be used as well. Off-site data protection is also known as data vaulting as data sets are stored in vaults.

Most of these technologies bring some sort of business risk as well. Just to give two examples:

1. **CitiFinancial**, the consumer finance subsidiary of Citigroup, notified 3.9 million customers that unencrypted tapes containing their personal financial data have been lost while in transit to a credit bureau (see New York Times, June, 2005, http://www.nytimes.com/2005/06/07/business/07data.html).
2. In Dec. 2004. **Bank of America** "lost" computer tapes containing charge card account information for 1.2 million government card holders during transfer to a backup data centre (see at: http://findarticles.com/p/articles/mi_qa3937/ is_200505/ai_n13638955)
3. **HSBC** bank admitted losing a computer disc containing the details of nearly 400,000 customers. The disc went missing after being sent via a couries from a HSBC office in Southampton to the reinsurer Swiss Re at the beginning of February 2008 (see at: http://www.itpro.co.uk/security/news/185112/hsbc-loses-disc-with-370000-details.html).

These three examples provide an additional insight on how complex is information management today. However, businesses are continuously seeking the new ways of IT risk mitigation.

Data backup or simply backup is an operation of making a copy of data from its original location on a hard disk to one or more external storage media located in an appropriate storage device in order to have it recovered (restored) in case of data corruption/destruction/theft resulted from any kind of failure/disaster that might happened on hardware, software, computer room, building, region, and so forth.

These copies of data are in most cases called "backups" in a narrow sense.

The term "backup" has been in use today as:

a.   an operation of copying data from its original – primary location (usually hard disk) onto another storage media
b.   data stored on external storage media that can be restored to a hard disk in case of data corruption/failure/disaster on original data.

Having in mind the importance of data for modern business, every organization has to develop its own backup strategy, policy, or at least, a regular backup scheme. Such a strategy (scheme) should be:

•   Regular, in terms of doing it on regular basis (hourly, daily, etc.).
•   Efficient, in terms of both backup and recovery operations. Data should be taken to the backup unit as soon as possible and without disturbing applications and end users. The same applies and even is more important when data recovery operation is considered.
•   Safe and secure, and
•   Cost – effective.

Backup differs from standard data storage or data archives in a sense that a data archive is the primary copy of data while backup is the secondary copy of data.

Backup operation can be used or performed on several levels, depending on the type of computer system on which data reside:

•   Home PC
•   Desktop PC in the office
•   Portable/mobile computers
•   Set of computers in a LAN environment (office or department)
•   Server (application, e-mail, Web, etc.)
•   Company level.

Figure 10.2. Backup—local (desktop or server)

Figure 10.3. Local backups on LAN (each desktop or server has its own tape)

Figure 10.4. Backup on LAN via backup server (only one tape)

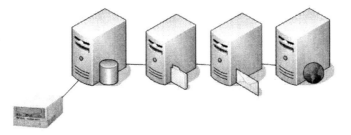

Figure 10.5. Integrated LAN-based backup solution including several servers and all kinds of end users' computer devices

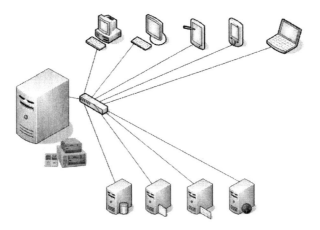

While personal/home backup becomes more important in Internet era, it is not as crucial as backup performed within the organizations, particularly when "business-critical applications" or "mission-critical applications" are considered.

Which data/application is mission-critical depends on the type of business and significance of several types of data to a specific business. Aberdeen Group (2007) presented some results from their recent report related to the importance of critical data for high availability.

According to this survey, 80% of end users named e-mail applications as the top candidate for high availability, while 62% named transactional databases. Gartner concludes that business drivers behind most companies' high availability strategies are focused on reducing unplanned downtime (80%), reducing financial risk of data loss (75%) and the need for applications to be up and running 24/7 (65%). Among the 100 respondents surveyed, not one indicated a lack of plans to adopt a high availability strategy.

Swartz (2008) cited the results of the report of BridgeHead Software which surveyed the executives in the United Kingdom and North America. According to this survey, 59% said the volume of data backup is disrupting business operations. More than two-thirds (84%) said they would benefit from reducing the data they routinely back up.

Business computing organized in any kind of business information system architecture (mainframe based legacy system, client-server) should do everything in order not to allow hardware-software glitches or any kind of failure/disaster to produce data loss. Some of potential failures/disasters include:

- file system corruption
- intentional or unintentional removing the files
- hardware glitches and failures (hard disk, RAM, processor, network card, communication device)
- operating system failures and crashes
- software failures (application, database, network, system management software)
- data loss (lost or stolen data)
- end users' errors
- system administrator's errors
- natural disasters (floods, fires, hurricanes, tornados, earthquakes)

There are several types of backup, depending on:

- Backup media/device
- Backup type (full, incremental)
- Backup operation (off-line, on-line).

In regard to backup media, there exist several approaches depending on the technology used:

- Magnetic tape-based backup
- Disk-based backup
- Optical storage-based backup
- Online backup

Magnetic tape devices and media are most widely used backup technology. The capacity of magnetic tapes are expressed in gigabytes and terabytes.

Disk-based backup uses standard magnetic disk technology, the tehnology that is used for primary data storage.

Optical storage technology (compacd disks, DVD) can also be used, depending on the computer configuration and memory space requirements.

Online backup is sometimes used instead of the traditional one, if a business decides on using application service providers' services. The data is transmitted over data communication lines to remote storage locations, backe up and stored off-site.

New approach that emerged recently called "**Virtual Tape Library – VTL**" is a technology which uses a physical disk storage that emulates a tape library. The disk is used by backup software and applications/data to be backed up as a virtual tape or virtual tape library. However, both backup and recovery operations on data are performed significantly faster.

Backup strategy should be defined on the enterprise level and should contain the following sections:

- Backup technology that will be used
- Backup type (full or partial: differential or incremental backup)
- Backup timing (hourly, daily, weekly), including the start time
- Persons responsible for backup operations
- Location of storing backup media
- Data recovery.

While preparing a backup strategy, several factors should be taken into consideration:

- How important are data on the server; which data are critical; how to store them?
- Are the data frequently modified?
- How fast and how frequent the backup should be?
- Do we have necessary equipment for backup?
- Who is in charge of backup and recovery?
- Is it needed to protect backup media on off-site basis?

The technologies that are used today for backup operations include:

- Magnetic Tape
- Hard Disk (Disk-based backup)
- Floppy Disk
- RAID Technologies
- Optical Technologies (Compact Disc, DVD)
- Memory Stick - Flash Memory technology
- Storage Area Networks (SAN)
- Network-Attached Storage (NAS)
- Direct Access Storage
- Server-based storage
- Off-site storage
- Continuous Data Protection

The selection of the appropriate backup technology which includes backup device and backup media depends on several factors such as:

- Capacity of the backup media
- Price of devices and media
- Reliability of devices and media
- Possibility of automating backup operations
- Possibility of upgrading backup devices
- Easiness of operating with media and devices
- Hardware and software performances
- Compatibility.

TAPE-BASED BACKUP

The most widely used backup – the tape backup is explained in more details, including current tape drive technologies such as: DDS/DAT, DLT, LTO, AIT),

QIC, IBM 3590 and 3570, Travan, AIT, VXA, LTO Ultrium, SAIT, Tape libraries, and so forth.

Tape-based backup is a backup in which data is periodically copied from hard disk to a tape which is inserted into a tape device (see Figure 10.7). If a hard disk crashes, the data on hard disk will be damaged or lost, however, the data can be easily recovered, copied back from the tape to a new (purchased and replaced) disk.

Tape-based data storage technology uses the tape cartridges for storing data on the sequential mode. Tape cartridges are used within a tape drive. The tapes have to be inserted into a tape drive before starting backup operation and removed after backup operation, in order to be stored onsite or offsite. The device that performs data writing and data reading is a tape drive which can be installed within a computer case or aside and connected to it by using communication cable. In addition to a stand-alone tape drives that are used in small data processing environments, big data centres use tape libraries or auto-changers in order to automate multiple tape exchanging.

The three main advantages of the tapes include:

• Tape can be removed and stored or transported to an offsite location which is important from continuous computing perspective.
• Tape can store a huge amount of data.
• Tape is considered to be a cost effective storage solution.

The primary difference between tape storage technology and disk storage technology is that tape-based approach uses sequential method of storing and retrieving the data while hard disk uses random access method of storing and retrieving the data. This difference is very important both from user perspective and data management perspective. Data access rates are much slower with tape technology than in hard disk storage.

Figure 10.6. Backup tape drive connected to a server or desktop computer

Magnetic tape has been used as a data storage media for the last 30 years. Different types of tapes, different tape technologies have been used in that period, even in the 1960s. Unlike the first years of commercial computer history (early fifties and sixties of the 20th century) when magnetic tapes were used for recording and storing data in the form of primary external memory, today, magnetic tapes are primarily used for backup operations. This technology was first used in 1951. on the UNIVAC I computer.

Today, there exist several tape drive technologies such as:

- Digital Data Storage (DDS/DAT)
- Digital Linear Tape (DLT)
- Linear Tape-Open (LTO)
- Advanced Intelligent Tape (AIT)
- Quarter Inch Cartridge (QIC).

The following table presents major types of some magnetic tape systems that are based on DDS/DAT standard. This standard was introduced in 1989.

In addition, there are also some other standards (technologies) such as:

IBM 3590 and 3570, Travan, AIT, VXA, LTO Ultrium, SAIT, T10000, and so forth.

Digital Data Storage (DDS) is based on the helical head technology and the 4mm digital audio tape cartridges. Several models (generations) of DDS format are available, such as 2 GB, 8 GB, 24 GB, 36 GB, 72 GB, … .

Digital linear tape (DLT) is based on the linear head technology which uses the system of recording data along a series of 128 or 1280 data tracks. DLT cartridges can store up to 160 GB of data, with SuperDLT cartridges that can store up to 800 GB of data.

Linear Tape-Open (LTO) is an open-format (open tape, open standard) linear tape technology created by HP, IBM and Quantum Corporation. There are several

Figure 10.7. DDS/DAT tape formats (Source: http://en.wikipedia.org/wiki/Digital_Data_Storage)

Format	Tape Length (m)	Capacity (GB)	Speed (MB/s)
DDS-1	60/90	1.3/2.0	0.6
DDS-2	120	4.0	0.6
DDS-3	125	12.0	1.1
DDS-4	150	20.0	3.2
DAT-72	170	36.0	3.2
DAT-160	150	80	6.9

generations of this technology. LTO consortium (www.lto.org) provides major features of these generations according to capacity and transfer rates:

- Generation 1. First licensed in 1998, with product appearing in 2000, Ultrium format Generation 1 provides cartridge capacities of up to 200 GB (2:1 compression) and up to 100 GB native with data transfer rates of up to 40 MB/ second (2:1 compression).
- Generation 2. With a cartridge capacity of up to 400 GB (2:1 compression) and up to 200 GB native, Ultrium format Generation 2 provides data transfer rates of up to 80 MB/second (2:1 compression). Generation 3. Featuring capacities of 800 GB (2:1 compression) and up to 400 GB native per cartridge, Ultrium format Generation 3 provides data transfer rates of up to 160 MB/second (2:1 compression) for the third generation of the 8-channel version.
- Generation 4. Delivering 1.6TB (2:1 compression) and up to 800 GB native per cartridge, Ultrium format Generation 4 provides data transfer rates of up to 240 MB/second (2:1 compression), the LTO Ultrium format generation specification was made available to licensees in late December 2006.
- Generation 5. Capacity: 3.2 TB (assuming a 2:1 compression) with data transfer speed up to 360 MB/s.
- Generation 6. Capacity: 6.4 TB (assuming a 2:1 compression) with data transfer speed up to 540 MB/s.

Advanced Intelligent Tape (AIT) technology uses helical head technology for recording data on 8mm tape cartridges. This technology can store up to 400 GB with data transfer rates up to 48 Mbps. Sony has released its fifth generation of the AIT technology called AIT-5. This tape cartridge offers 400GB native/1.04TB compressed storage capacity (see for example Sony AIT technology at www.sony. com).

Travan. The Travan technology uses helical tape format which was standardized by the Quarter Inch Cartridge (QIC) Consortium (www.qic.org). QIC was an international trade association established in 1987 with the primary objective to standardize and promote use of the quarter-inch tape technology. The latest models are based on 40 GB (compressed) storage capacity.

The highest capacity tape technologies such as: DLT-S4, LTO-4, SAIT-2, can store up to 800 GB of data.

Traditional backup operation is performed in two ways:

a. **Offline backup,** a backup operation which represents the most traditional backup operation. It is usually performed during the night in so-called "single-user" mode when all end-users are logged of from the system. The main advantages of this approach are: backup is taken faster, there is no open files during the backup operation and consequently no corrupted files. The main disadvantage of the approach includes the fact that the applications can not be used by end users during the backup operation.

b. **Online backup**, a backup that is taken during the effective utilization of application software. This approach is used whenever an application needs to be "always-on" or available on "24x7x365" basis. The main weakness of this approach lies in the fact that such an operation can significantly slowdown the system. In addition, when this kind of backup is used, some open files that are backed up can be corrupted or just skipped and not stored.

In today's business, backup operation can be executed in several ways. Most commonly used practices are listed as follows:

a. First approach – local backup medium. Each server can have its own backup drive and storage medium (Figure 10.8). This solution can be implemented not only for in server environment with several servers (file, data, application, Web server, messaging server, etc.) but in a standard peer-to-peer PC environment. Backup is also recommended in home computing. Optical devices can be used as well.

Data is sent (backed up) directly from the server to its backup tape, LAN is not used for data transfer. This results in high speeds of taking backup. However, this model lacks an efficient centralized system for managing backup operations.

a. Second option is based on a LAN infrastructure with a dedicated backup server that is configured to serve as a main backup server. Data is transferred over

Figure 10.8. Servers with their tape drives for backup

Figure 10.9. Server-based backup

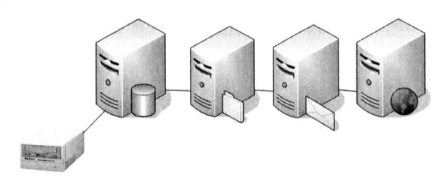

local area network toward the backup server and then stored to backup tape or any other backup device that is connected to the backup server (Figure 10.9).

A tape drive as a hardware device that can be part of a computer configuration or external device. It can only hold one tape at a time. A single tape can be used for backing up data in small business. However, in case of midsize businesses and big companies, a single tape is unlikely to hold the complete backup of such an entire organization. In these cases, when a single tape is not sufficient for storing all data stored on the hard disk, two approaches can be applied:

- A single tape drive with manually inserting, replacing and removing the tapes by an IT technician or administrator, each time when a tape is full or backup operation finished.
- Implementing an integrated tape library solution which contains multiple tape drives such that a human intervention is not needed. This solution can be extended with autoloader which is a robotic mechanism that selects a tape, inserts into a tape drive within the tape library, removes a tape from its drive and place it to a specific location.

With the auto-loader tape system the tapes are automatically changed during the process of backup and recovery. Another technology that can be used is called a Tape Jukebox (for instance, the MDL Tape Jukebox and Tape library, see at: www.mdlcorp.com).

For example, the HP StorageWorks Enterprise Systems Library (ESL) E-Series Tape Libraries (www.hp.com) has the capacity of up to 1400 TB native and 5670 TB compressed. In a single cabinet, the ESL E-Series contains from 322 to 712 LTO cartridges or 286 to 630 SDLT cartridges and has the ability to scale to twenty-four drives. The ESL E-Series supports a mixture of LTO-4 Ultrium 1840 Fibre Channel, LTO-3 Ultrium 960 Fibre Channel and SDLT 600 tape technology. HP StorageWorks E-Series Tape Libraries are fully integrated into HP StorageWorks Extended Tape Library Architecture (ETLA).

Another example is the IBM System Storage TS3310 Tape Library (www.ibm. com). It is a modular, scalable tape library. It is designed to scale vertically with expansion for LTO tape cartridges, drives and redundant power supplies. The base library module, model L5B, contains all of the necessary robotics and intelligence to manage the 5U high library system, which contains up to 36 cartridges and two LTO generation 4 and/or generation 3 tape drives.

The table on Figure 10.10 contains HP solutions in the range of business class libraries.

Figure 10.10. HP business class libraries, adapted from http://h18006.www1. hp.com/products/storageworks/msl6000/index.html

	HP StorageWorks MSL6000 Tape Libraries	HP StorageWorks MSL8096 Tape Library	HP StorageWorks MSL4048 Tape Library	HP StorageWorks MSL2024 Tape Library
Tape Drives Supported	LTO-4 Ultrium 1840 Ultrium 960 SDLT 600	LTO-4 Ultrium 1840 LTO-3 Ultrium 960 LTO-3 Ultrium 920	LTO-4 Ultrium 1840 LTO-3 Ultrium 960 LTO-3 Ultrium 920 LTO-2 Ultrium 448	LTO-4 Ultrium 1840 LTO-3 Ultrium 960 LTO-3 Ultrium 920 LTO-2 Ultrium 448
Number of Tape Drives	1-16 LTO-4 Ultrium 1840 (multi-unit) 1-16 Ultrium 960 (multi-unit) 1-16 SDLT 600 (multi-unit)	2-4 LTO-4 Ultrium 1840 2-4 LTO-3 Ultrium 960 2-4 LTO-3 Ultrium 920	1-2 LTO-4 Ultrium 1840 1-2 LTO-3 Ultrium 960 1-4 LTO-3 Ultrium 920 1-4 LTO-2 Ultrium 448	1 LTO-4 Ultrium 1840 1 LTO-3 Ultrium 960 1-2 LTO-3 Ultrium 920 1-2 LTO-2 Ultrium 448
Number of Cartridge Slots	30 to 240 (Ultrium-based library, multi-unit) 26 to 208 (SDLT-based library, multi-unit)	96	48	24
Maximum Capacity	384TB	153.6TB	76.8TB	38.4TB
Maximum Sustained Transfer Rate (compressed)	13.8 TB/hr (16 drive, multi-unit configuration)	3.4TB/hr (4 LTO-4 Ultrium 1840 drive config)	1.7TB/hr (2 LTO-4 Ultrium 1840 drive config)	864GB/hr (1 LTO-4 Ultrium 1840 drive config)
Form Factor	5U or 10U	8U	4U	2U

continued on following page

Figure 10.10. continued

	HP StorageWorks MSL6000 Tape Libraries	HP StorageWorks MSL8096 Tape Library	HP StorageWorks MSL4048 Tape Library	HP StorageWorks MSL2024 Tape Library
Interface	4Gb Fibre Channel (LTO-4 Ultrium 1840 / Ultrium 960 2Gb Fibre Channel (SDLT600) Ultra320 LVD/SE SCSI (Ultrium 1840/960) Ultra160 LVD/SE SCSI (SDLT 600)	4Gb Native Fibre Channel Interface (LTO-4 Ultrium 1840 & LTO-3 Ultrium 960) Ultra320 LVD/SE SCSI (LTO-4 Ultrium 1840 & LTO-3 Ultrium 960) 3Gb/second SAS (LTO-3 Ultrium 920)	4Gb Native Fibre Channel Interface (LTO-4 Ultrium 1840 & LTO-3 Ultrium 960) Ultra320 LVD/SE SCSI (LTO-4 Ultrium 1840, LTO-3 Ultrium 960 & LTO-3 Ultrium 920) Ultra160 LVD/SE SCSI (LTO-2 Ultrium 448) 3Gb/second SAS (LTO-3 Ultrium 920	4Gb Native Fibre Channel (LTO-4 Ultrium 1840 & LTO-3 Ultrium 960) Ultra320 LVD/SE SCSI (LTO-4 Ultrium 1840, LTO-3 Ultrium 960 & LTO-3 Ultrium 920) Ultra160 LVD/SE SCSI (LTO-2 Ultrium 448) 3Gb/sec SAS (LTO-3 Ultrium 920)

INTEGRATED BACKUP SOLUTIONS FOR BUSINESS CONTINUITY

As traditional backup has some disadvantages, more advanced and integrated backup technologies are introduced such as: off-site data storage, disk-based backup, online backup, optical technology, solid state technology, and so forth. This section provides some basic info on these technologies within the business continuity framework.

Off-site Data Storage. Taking data backup onto magnetic tapes is just a first step in a comprehensive backup strategy. The process of managing backup tapes has to be addressed as well. If backup tape is stored only on-site, in case of any local disaster such as fire or flood, data stored on both hard disk and tape can be destroyed. Therefore, there needs to be a solution which includes storing tapes on remote location as well. The following figure (Figure 10.11) shows such a solution:

Traditional backup is only first step (first stage) toward an integrated storage solution that helps in enhancing the levels of business continuity. Continuous computing requires better solutions than a standard – traditional backup. Having mission critical data on a tape in the form of traditional backup is much better than loosing data completely, however, recovering from hardware/software glitch or any kind of failure that caused interrupting data processing in the form of restoring data from a tape usually take a significant time, depending on the amount of data. Therefore, businesses seeking higher levels of application availability and continuous computing need more sophisticated and, with regard to data backup and data recovery

Figure 10.11. Tape—offsite and/or out-of-reach

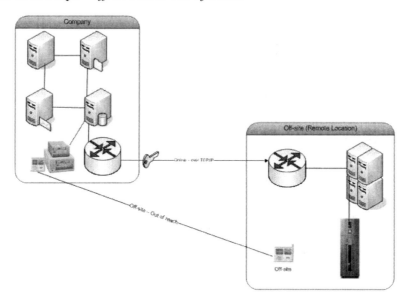

speed, much faster solutions. Software vendors such as HP, IBM, Quantum, and so forth, offer such integrated solutions as well.

For instance, HP offers a range of data protection and recovery solutions called "HP StorageWorks solutions for Business Continuity and Availability" that include the following technologies:

- traditional backup solutions,
- two-stage backup-recovery solutions
- local replication
- remote replication
- near-continuous and continuous data protection
- clustering.

Disk-based Backup. To date, for a period of more than forty years, the magnetic tape technology has been the default solution for backup operations. However, the need to recover mission critical data faster has influenced the emergence of new technologies that can be used instead or in a combination with tapes. Moreover, as more and more data centres experienced the problems with "damaged" or "unreadable" magnetic tapes, together with the problems of lost or stolen tapes for any reason, IT specialists from customer side and hardware vendors from the other side, initiated several projects of replacing the tape as a major data backup medium.

One of the main disadvantages of tape-based backup is its sequential technology with regard to data writing/reading operation to and from the tape. To get to a specific file or folder that is at the end of the tape, users have to forward through the entire tape until that peace of data is reached.

While the tape-backup has been the most widely used backup technology and method of archiving data, the fact that it is based in sequential data access forces businesses to seek for some other solutions that provide faster backups and data recoveries. In order for data to be restored from the tape, tape has to be inserted into its device, a recovery operation has to be started, the drive has to start the process of forwarding through the entire tape until the data (file, folder, the whole tape content) to be restored is copied to the disk. This operation, depending on the capacity, speed, can take several hours, some times even days, to complete.

Disk-based backup reduces the backup and restoring operations compared to tape-based backups because of its direct (random) data access technology. In addition, since the disks have higher reliability than magnetic tapes, much more incremental backup operations can be performed with regard to full-backup operation which takes much more time.

Disk Backup is backup which is performed to a disk-based storage medium, instead of using tapes. However, disk-based backup or disk-to-disk (D2D) backup, allows much faster data restoring. Therefore, from the RTO (Recovery Time Objective) perspective, disk-based backups become more appropriate and more cost-effective solution compared to the tape-based backup solutions. In addition, hard disk technology is considered as more durable and more reliable that magnetic tape, they are not affected by the environmental factors. Tape drive gets dirty and has to be cleaned by using a special tape - cleaning tape. In addition, magnetic tape can brake while inserting/removing operations and is generally considered as vulnerable device and media to several environmental factors such as: humidity, dust, heat, and so forth.

Disk-based backup comprises several technologies (Figure 10.12).

Figure 10.12. Disk-based backup technologies

Technology	Explanation
Disk-to-Disk (D2D)	Second tier of disk storage
Virtual Tape Library	Hard disk or set of hard disks that act as a tape (set of tapes).
Mirroring	Copying the contents of hard disk to two or more disks systems simultaneously. can be synchronous and asynchronous.
Snapshot	Making a copy that allows recovery to a specific RPO.

Mirroring, Virtual Tape Library and Snapshot technologies are also considered separately as advanced data backup and recovery technologies, even though, in the end, these three approaches use disk technology to backup data.

Some businesses employ an approach which includes performing disk-based backup and storing data to tape as well. This backup strategy is called Disk2Disk2Tape.

A hybrid solution is also possible: using tape-backup technology and implementing hard-disk backup as a second solution since hard disks have been getting les and less expensive.

For example, The HP StorageWorks D2D Backup System provides reliable, consolidated data protection for up to four servers in a single, self-managing device. It works with backup software application to fully automate daily backup jobs, requiring less manual handling – a real benefit for organizations with limited IT resources. The HP D2D Backup System also increases the reliability of the backups by reducing the risk of human error and problems with tape drive hardware and media, the two major causes of failed backups.

The HP D2D disk-to-disk backup solution can easily restore lost or corrupted files from online backups, reducing downtime costs. The HP StorageWorks D2D Backup System uses disk to emulate up to four tape autoloaders and works with backup software to provide automated backup for multiple servers.

According to HP (www.hp.com), the main features of the HP StorageWorks D2D Backup System are listed as follows:

"Hands-free" daily backup: Automating the backup process simplifies the data protection processes.

More reliable backups: Automation makes data protection processes more dependable by reducing the risks of human error and problems associated with tape hardware and media.

Restore lost data faster: Disk-based backups provide faster access to backup data, allowing lost or corrupted files to be restored in minutes rather than hours or days. Such an operation reduces downtime significantly.

Possibility of integrating and using the two approaches in the same time. Implementing disk-to-disk backup and keeping tape backups as well is an option that reduces the risks of losing data.

Optical Technology. In addition to magnetic tapes, optical technologies such as recordable CD and recordable DVD can be used as a backup device (see for example the DVD Library and CDROM/RW Library from MDL Corp. www.mdlcorp.com).

Solid state technology. Another type of data storage – so called "solid state storage" with main representatives in the form of USB Flash Memory, USB Flash Drives, Digital Cards, and so forth, can also be used as a backup device. These devices are costly with regard to their low capacity, however, they are extensively used in personal computing for their portability user-friendly architecture and interface.

Online Backup. With the advances of Internet technologies and high speed communication lines, online backup appeared as an approach in finding more efficient and effective ways of backing up and restoring data. Instead of copying files and storing them on magnetic or optical media, data can be sent over the Internet to another computer which in turn can act as a remote backup. In case of loosing data for any reason, the system gets connected to that remote computer in order to restore data. Remote backup is always accessible over the Net, data can always be downloaded, which is an advantage especially for mobile users.

This approach has some disadvantages though, that is, when user has a lot of files to backup or restore (measured in gigabytes or terabytes) that could take a long time or when network/Internet connection breaks down for any reason. Even in these cases, online backup providers can provide backups on standard off-line devices and media. Web-based backup is a version of online backup and allows users to do backup/restore operations from web browsers.

Main advantages for a company include the following:

- No need to buy backup hardware, store it, maintain, and so forth.
- All backup files are always online, from anywhere
- Can be cost-effective
- Simple to manage

Figure 10.13. Online backup

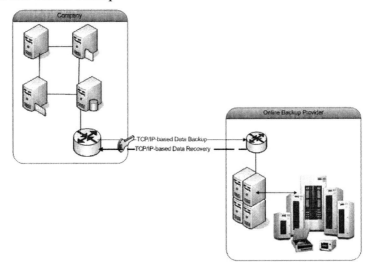

Another approach used in online backup is based on using disk-to-disk backup or disk-based online backup. Instead of using magnetic tapes, the online backup provider uses disk-based backup technology. Such a solution delivers faster backup, faster or even immediate data recovery, immediate transmission to an offsite location, and archive creation.

APPLICATION SOFTWARE FOR BACKUP AND RECOVERY OPERATIONS

Application software plays a significant role in any backup strategy. Backup software is a critical management tool that interfaces backup hardware with corporate data, allowing administrators to decide when and where to backup selected files, folders, drives, servers or even entire data centers. Backup software also supports backup automation so backups can be performed and verified on a preset schedule (e.g., nights or weekends) without direct human intervention. Some backup software will support encryption, protecting data at the backup server before sending the encrypted data off to the tape drive or library. Most contemporary enterprise backup tools can easily send pager and e-mail alarms to a technician or administrator in the event of a backup problem.

Backup software depends on operating system that runs the server. For instance, on HP-UX machines, two approaches can be used in order to perform a backup operation:

a.   Command-line interface

UNIX commands that can be used for backup and recovery are:

- **fbackup**
- **cpio**
- **tar**

As an example, we give a syntax of the cpio command for a) backup and b) restoring:

a.   backup: cpio -o [cvxB] > *device_name*
b.   restoring: cpio -i [cvxdumB] [*patterns*] < *device_name*

Examples:

*# find / -print	cpio -ocx > /dev/rmt/0m*	Backup
# cpio -icxvmd "/users/*" < /dev/rmt/0m*	Restoring
# cpio -it /dev/rmt/0m	Gives the tape contents

b.   GUI-based backup

The following UNIX command is used to start a backup operation on UNIX servers:

find / -print | cpio -ocvxB > /dev/rmt/0m

HP-UX operating system supports several commands for backup operations. In previous example, cpio command is used. The "find" and "print" parts of the backup command are used in order to search all the files starting from the root directory (/) and list them on the screen. the section which follows the cpio command (-ocvxB) consists of several characters that determine the type of backup operation. The "greater than sign" or "right bracket sign" is used to identify the type of operation (backup) while the "less than sign" or "left bracket sign" would be used in case of the recovery operation. the section of the command which follows ">" sign (/dev/rmt/0m) is used to determine the type of the device (tape) and logical name assigned to that device (0m).

Instead of using such a command, a GUI based system administration tool (program) can be used. The program is "user-oriented", includes some wizard-like tools and allows the system administrator to set and perform backup and/or recovery operation more easily.

Within the scope of a traditional backup operation, there exists several (at least four) levels of data protection, with each higher level meaning better data protection (see Figure 10.14).

- Data is stored on magnetic tape within a traditional backup operation. The tape is stored on the same location where the server is located. This is the lowest level and approach that should be avoided.
- Backup data is stored on magnetic tape, however, the tape is transported and stored on a remote site.
- There exist two copies of data: one is on the same location with the server, the other is dislocated and stored on another location. This approach requires additional resources, including human resources, in order to transfer (transport)

Figure 10.14. HP-UX system administration manager (SAM) on v. 10.10

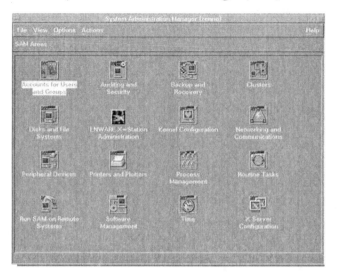

Figure 10.15. Defining a backup on HP-UX 10.10 (selecting the type of backup, backup scope, backup device, backup time, etc.)

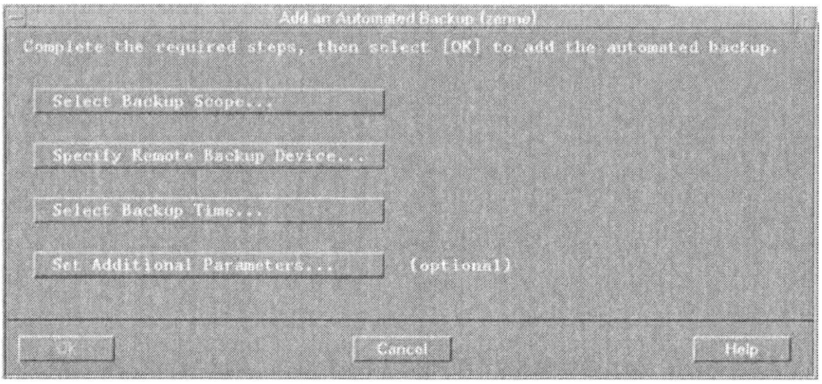

the tapes to a remote location. The operation of moving data tapes to remote location always bring some sort of risk such as theft or tape lost.

• Two backup copies are created, one is stored on the same location with the server, the other copy is transferred to a remote location by using local area network, wide area network and Internet infrastructure.

CHAPTER SUMMARY

Several information technologies are used in order to store data in data centres in order to protect it such that business does not suffer if, for any reason, data is lost. These technologies can be divided into three main groups: data storage technologies, backup technologies and data recovery technologies. Traditional backup technologies and their role in enhancing business continuity are explained in this chapter.

REFERENCES

Aberdeen report (2007). The importance of high availability. Aberdeen Group, Retrieved on April 4, 2008 from http://extranet.neverfailgroup.com/download/Aberdeen%20%20The%20Importance%20of%20High%20Availability.pdf.

Barraza, O. (2002). Achieving 99,9998% + storage uptime and availability. DotHill Systems, Retrieved on August 7, 2006 from http://www.dothill.com/products/white-papers/5-9s_wp.pdf.

Swartz, N. (2008), Backup data dogging businesses. *Information Management Journal, Jan/Feb 2008, 42*(1), ABI/INFORM Global, pp. 19.

Ybarra, M. (2006). The long road back. *CIO Decisions magazine, January 2006*, Retrieved on July 31, 2006 from http://searchcio.techtarget.com/magItem/0,291266,sid19_gci1154418_idx3,00.html.

REAL WORLD CASES

Motorola, Inc.
Compiled and adapted from: http://www.emc.com/cp/pdf/motorola_cp_ldv.pdf

Business Challenge

To implement a new storage solution that would eliminate bottlenecks and scale effortlessly to accommodate rapid growth.

EMC Solution

The high-performance, high-capacity EMC Symmetrix DMX system with EMC PowerPath path management software, has more than doubled the rate of I/Os per second and reduced component build uploads by 12 hours. Simplified storage management is facilitated through EMC ControlCenter software and EMC Solutions Enabler APIs. EMC TimeFinder is used to clone data. EMC SRDF software will be used for data migration.

Business Benefits

- **High availability**—The EMC Symmetrix DMX system supports 24x7 availability.
- **World-class service**—EMC's dial-home capability—a remote diagnostic service—identifies problems and potential risks and escalates resolution before they can impact operations.
- **Centralized storage management**—EMC ControlCenter simplifies storage management and monitors the performance of the EMC Symmetrix DMX and host servers.

Toyota Motorsport
Compiled and adapted from: http://www.emc.com/cp/pdf/H1968_Toyota_CF_ldv.pdf

Business Challenge

To implement a business continuity strategy that cost-effectively protects racecar performance, engineering, and operational data.

EMC Solution

EMC Services' experts helped Toyota Motorsport design and implement comprehensive replication, backup, recovery, and archiving strategies. Core applications are kept on high-end Symmetrix DMX systems in a SAN and NAS environment that is integrated with EMC Celerra CNS. SRDF mirrors its critical applications and TimeFinder/Mirror helps create business continuance volumes. A CLARiiON CX system at the race track gathers statistics. Centera provides long-term archival storage.

Business Benefits

- **Reduced backup time**—Aged data is moved from Symmetrix to Centera reducing production data backup time by more than 25%.

- **Decreased storage costs**—Toyota is saving 52% in storage acquisition costs by freeing capacity on the Symmetrix system.
- **Fast recovery**—Recovery of core applications has gone from nearly three days to a maximum of two hours for a complete failover.

DISCUSSION QUESTIONS

1. Have you ever lost your data on the system? What went wrong?
2. Have you been involved in the process of data recovery?
3. What is the difference between backup device and backup media?
4. Explain briefly tape-based backup technology.
5. Why do we use tape libraries?
6. It is sometime argued that disk based backup is more reliable than tape-based backup. Do you agree?
7. What is the difference between online and ofline backup?
8. Describe the process of taking backup on UNIX macjines.
9. What commands are used to take backup on HP-UX?
10. Explain the process of data recovery.

Chapter XI
Advanced Storage Technologies for Business Continuity

CHAPTER OVERVIEW

In addition to standard storage and traditional tape-based backup technologies explained in Chapter X, businesses employ advanced storage technologies in order to achieve higher levels of applications and data availability. Most widely used advanced storage technologies such as direct access storage (DAS), storage area network (SAN), network attached storage (NAS), RAID technology, mirroring and data replication, data vaulting, continuous data protection, and clustering are explained in Chapter XI.

DAS, SAN, AND NAS

Direct access storage, storage area network, and network access storage technologies are briefly explained in this section.

Contemporary business is forced to cope with demands for more efficient and effective storage solutions as part of its efforts to recover faster and more efficiently from any type of failure and/or disaster. Apart from standard backup technologies, business computing employs additional technologies in finding the ways of managing data in an efficient and effective way. With advances in data communications, networking technologies and high speed coomunication lines, in addition to traditional primary storage technologies, several new approaches called "advanced storage systems" have been developed.

Most widely used advanced storage technologies are: a) direct access storage, b) storage area network (SAN), and c) network attached storage (NAS).

SAN and NAS technologies are mainly based on a) Fibre Channel as a mature storage backbone technology and/or b) newly developed Internet SCSI (iSCSI) and Serial ATA technologies. SANs that use iSCSI protocol are gaining acceptance as a supplement or even complete replacement for Fibre Channel-based SANs. Today, these storage solutions and services are being integrated into server operating platforms. For instance, HP decided to integrate Smart Array serial controllers, storage enclosures, Hot-Plug Serial Attached SCSI and Serial ATA hard drivers with HP ProLiant servers (Singer, 2005). Such an operating environment does not require separate connection devices/protocols for interconnecting servers, storage, networking devices. Support for storage scalability includes support for RAID systems and scalability clustering options.

Direct access storage (DAS) is a solution that is based on a direct connection between a server and its storage system. Hard disk installed on a standard computer is also considered as a direct access storage system. This approach does not use a lot of networking devices, it is implemented onsite. Hence, it is characterized as a high performance solution with regard to data transfer rates. Several technologies are used within this model of storing data:

- SCSI (Small Computer System Interface)
- RAID systems (Redundant Array of Independent/Inexpensive Disks)
- Serial or Serial Attached SCSI—SAS
- Fibre Channel technology.

Figure 11.1. Direct attached storage (DAS)

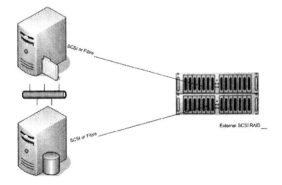

Storage area network approach is based on sharing a storage system among several servers and storage devices by using SCSI, iSCSI, and Fibre Channel communication technology. Remote storage devices (disks, disk arrays, tape devices, tape libraries) can be attached to servers. SAN model uses file-based protocols such as NFS, SMB-SAMBA (Small/Server Message Block) and CIFS that allow attaching and sharing file systems over the network.

Storage area network is a network that is usually isolated from the local area networks and wide area networks. It employs high-speed networking technologies (Gigabits/sec).

NFS is an acronym for network file system developed by Sun and is used as a main networking platform on UNIX servers and workstations. Another product called NIS (network information services) was also developed by Sun and is distributed today together with NFS, in the form of NFS/NIS protocol. A version for connecting PCs called PCNFS was developed as well and is used in order to connect PCs to UNIX/Linux servers and share file systems.

SAMBA is a distributed as an open source code under the GNU General Public License system (www.samba.org). It is available for most UNIX versions including: HP-UX, AIX, IRIX, Solaris, SunOS, Ultrix, NetBSD, FreeBSD, OpenBSD, SCO-UNIX, proprietary systems such as OpenVMS and IBM MVS (OS/390—z/OS). It is supported by Linux community, as well. SAMBA is used as a powerful tool for interoperability between UNIX/Linux servers, proprietary servers and Windows-based servers and clients. However, this protocol can be used as a platform for SAN platforms.

CIFS is an acronym for common internet file system as another protocol created by Microsoft in order to improve interoperability of Windows operating systems and other OS-platforms.

From business continuity perspective, SAN technology provides several advantages:

- Enhances application and data availability
- Increases storage capacity
- Allows booting and rebooting servers from the SAN environment
- Enables duplication features such as "Business Continuity Volumes," "data-volume cloning," and other real-time duplication technologies.
- Reduces hardware costs
- Reduces data management costs.

Network attached storage (NAS) is an advanced storage technology comprised of several storage media called NAS filers that are connected to servers via a set of data communication—networking devices (switches, routers, etc.). The concept is shown in Figure 11.2 and 11.3.

One of the most important characteristics of the NAS infrastructure from business continuity perspective is that data stored within NAS filers remains available even if server is down. Figure 11.4 depicts these three concepts and technologies.

RAID TECHNOLOGY

The section contains a short explanation of the RAID concept and technology.

The RAID concept and technology is known as: a) Redundant Array of Independent Disks and b) Redundant Array of Inexpensive Disks. There are three main concepts in RAID:

1. Data Striping—the splitting of data and storing it across more than one hard disk

Figure 11.2. Network attached storage—An infrastructure that connects one server to a NAS filer system

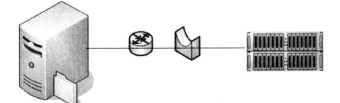

Figure 11.3. Network attached storage—An infrastructure that connects multiple servers to a NAS filer system

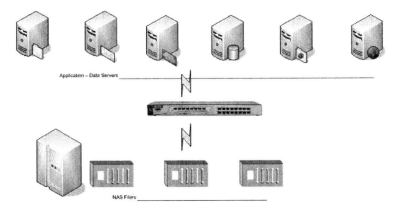

Figure 11.4. Storage technologies: A comparison of DAS, SAN, and NAS

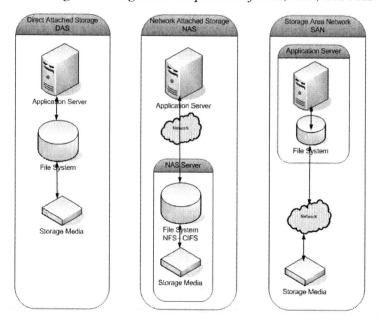

2. Mirroring—the copying of data and storing it to more the one hard disk
3. Error correction—the technology which is based on storing redundant data in order to detect and resolve the problem.

RAID was first introduced by Digital. It can be implemented as a hardware RAID and software RAID. Hardware RAID is installed by using the specific hardware controller, while software RAID can be implemented only if there is a special software for it or if operating system has appropriate support for it.

There exist several RAID technologies (layers, levels):

RAID 0 (Figure 11.5) is based on a striped disk array, data is broken into several blocks, each block is copied to a separate hard disk. This layer is called "Striped Disk Array without Fault Tolerance." Therefore, it is not considered to be a true RAID.

RAID 1 (Figure 11.6) writes data on two disks in the same time. If for any reason, one disk drive crashes, the data can be found on another disk. This process is called mirroring and duplexing. It is recommended for mission critical applications and all other applications – data that require higher levels of availability.

There exists a system of ten RAID layers (RAID 0, RAID 1, RAID 2, RAID 3, RAID 4, RAID 5, RAID 6, RAID 10, RAID 50, RAID 0+1). They are implemented depending on data processing, data availability and protection requirements.

Figure 11.5. RAID 0

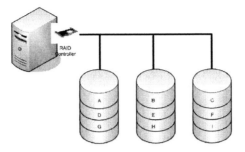

Figure 11.6. RAID 1

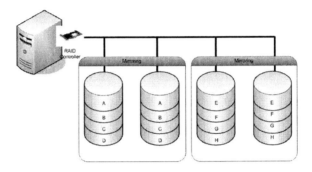

Figure 11.7. RAID 10—RAID For High Availability and High Performance

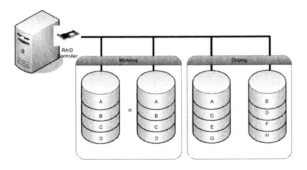

For instance RAID 10 (Figure 11.7) is a combination of data striping and data mirroring and is recommended for database servers, servers that require high availability, high performances, and fault- tolerance.

RAID at layer 10 requires a minimum of four drives to be implemented.

RAID "0+1" is also a combination of striping and mirroring, in a way that it creates a mirrored array whose segments are RAID 0 striped arrays.

MIRRORING AND DATA REPLICATION

Mirroring and data replication are new technologies that emerged 5–6 years ago. They are most frequently used as additional, second-level backup technologies, in addition to standard tape-based backups.

Mirroring is basically a process of making an exact copy of data and placing it on another – remote location. The basic difference between mirroring and standard backup is in that a mirrored data is an exact copy of the original data and, being a copy, it is immediately available for re-using, without a program for data recovery. In this way, the whole database can be copied into its mirrored version, and this version is held on a separate disk. The server (data base management server) updates automatically the contents of the database on both hard disks. Incase of a failure of database on hard disk A, the server automatically uses another (mirrored) database (B).

Data Replication is another approach and is based on duplicating the whole servers, not only databases on different hard disks. The data replication is shown on Figure 11.8.

If some sort of server failure happens on primary server, its clients are redirected onto secondary server (see Figure 11.9).

Figure 11.8. Data replication—two servers before the failure

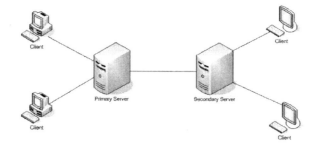

Figure 11.9. Data replication: the situation after the primary server failure

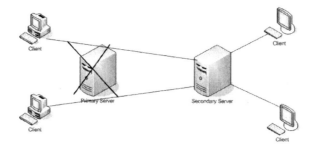

Figure 11.10. Mirroring

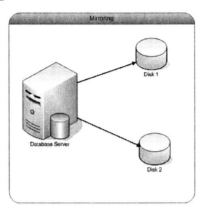

Figure 11.11. Data replication—One Server

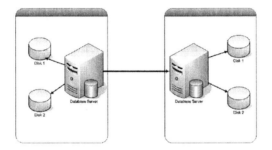

Figure 11.12. Data replication—Multiple servers

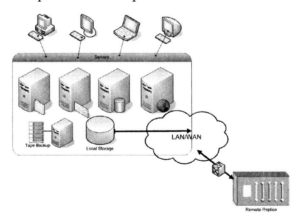

Mirroring and data replication are similar concepts. However, there exist some differences shown on Figure 11.12.

Data mirroring refers to a process of making a mirror of a database or the whole disk to another one. In data replication model, the whole database server is replicated on another (remote) machine.

DATA VAULTING

Data vaulting is an advanced data archiving technology that permits an automated backup of data to a remote location, archiving, and recovery.

In data vaulting, data transfer is made via high speed communication lines that connect business' data centers with "data vaults" as purpose built vaults. This approach (technology) is also called "Off-site Data Protection." Data is usually transferred to remote sites electronically, however, it can be transported to off-site locations by using removable storage media such as tapes. Transferring data electronically to off-site locations is also known as Electronic Vaulting. Businesses can choose to have their own off-site backup locations and manage their way of doing off-site data protection, however, they can use third party services, companies specialized in off-site data protection. An example is a company Iron Mountain (www.ironmountain.com).

Companies providing data vaulting services fit into three categories:

- Underground vaults (disused military facilities, or disused mines)
- Insulated chambers sharing facilities
- Dedicated vaults.

Figure 11.13. Electronic data vaulting

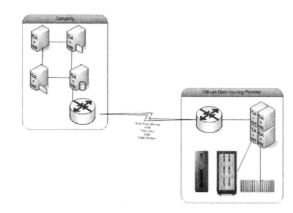

CONTINUOUS DATA PROTECTION

Continuous data protection is a similar approach to data vaulting and another alternative to doing standard backups. This technology used an approach of a continuous storing of data changes on a remote location.

Instead of backing up data on regular basis - scheduling periodic backups, in a continuous data protection approach, the system logs every change on the host system immediately. Continuous data protection (see Figure 11.14) is a technology that is based on a continuous storing of data changes. It allows the following features:

- Data recovery to any point
- Data recovery adjusting
- Continuous access to changed data
- Combining with offline backup.

CLUSTERING

Clustering as an established IT technology is used in data storage and data management as well.

Cluster is a configuration of two or more computers that are interconnected in order to provide higher levels of availability, reliability and scalability. Dozens, hundreds and thousands of computers can be connected into a cluster configuration. Google, for example, has more than 450,000 computers connected into several cluster configurations.

Figure 11.14. Continuous data protection

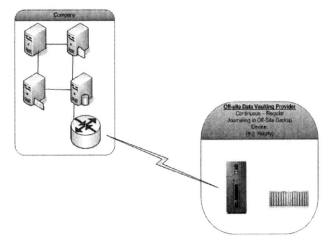

If in the system a partial failure happens, the failover process begins automatically, the processing can be shifted or redirected to another machine so that the process continues on the cluster level, the whole workload can be redistributed. If there is a problem observed on one server of the cluster, resources are redirected and the load is redistributed to other servers in the cluster.

Cluster configurations have the abilitiy of adding computers and other devices and resources in order to increase the overall performances of the system. This is especially important from scalablitiy perspective: the system can be scaled up by adding more hardware resources (processors, RAM), or by adding new computers.

Clustering refers to using multiple computer configurations (servers, workstations, PCs) in order to create a single highly available system. Cluster components can be on the same location, but in most cases, cluster is composed of dispersed configurations. The distance can be as long as 500 miles. The configuration includes not only computers but multiple storage devices, redundant components, redundant interconnections.

Cluster-based computing model is mainly used for the following purposes:

a. High availability
b. High reliability
c. High scalability
d. Workload management and Load balancing
e. Storage

A most common use of clustering today is to load balance traffic on Web sites organized and managed by Internet service providers. When a standard Web page request is sent by user to what is called a "manager" server, which is a server that receives requests, that server has to determine which of several Web servers in the cluster to forward the request to for handling.

Network load balancing is another technique used within cluster configurations in order to manage the network traffic on Web servers, FTP servers (see Figure 11.15).

Clustering technology was introduced first by Digital in the beginning of 1980s with its VAX machines that worked under VMS operating system. Later, Digital replaced VAX computers by Alpha processor based systems, while VMS became OpenVMS. Digital pioneered OpenVMS Clusters as a key enabling technology for high scalability and availability in 1983.

OpenVMS systems are today under HP's umbrella, however, they are still considered as the most reliable operating platform for cluster systems. According to a Harvard Research Group there existed more than 25.000 OpenVMS-based cluster

Figure 11.15. Cluster configuration within an ISP provider with the Load Manager for load balancing

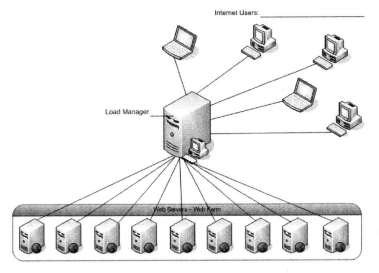

configurations deployed al over the world and approximately 450,000 OpenVMS systems. In addition, more than 75% of Fortune100 companies use OpenVMS clusters. Computers forming OpenVMS cluster can be up to 500 miles away, interconnected by T3 communication lines. OpenVMS clusters support up to 96 nodes that can span up to 500 miles (800 kilometres), providing such a kind of availability that, even if a local disaster occurs, servers can be up and functioning.

Today, HP offers a portfolio of solutions based on its HP foundation clustering software, HP Serviceguard. The cluster configurations use HP Integrity servers based on Itanium 2 processors and HP 9000 servers bases on PA-RISC processors. The portfolio includes the following cluster configurations: HP Extended Cluster, HP Metro cluster, and HP Continental clusters.

- Extended Distance Cluster is a host-based data replication configuration that can span up to 100 km.
- Metrocluster offers real-time infrastructure with automatic failover and failback of mission-critical applications between data centers.
- Continentalclusters feature bi-directional, push-button failover, giving IT staff complete control over when to initiate failover.

Microsoft Windows Server platform supports clustering capabilities as well. After hiring David Cutler and his team in 1988, Microsoft started the project of developing the "New Technology" operating system. With the first NT version released in 1993, Windows NT Server 4.0 in 1996, Windows 2000 Server in 2000, Microsoft developed a powerful server platform that is used today Windows 2003 Server or Windows Server. Microsoft introduced clustering technologies as well as the key technology to improve availability, reliability and scalability. With Windows Server 2003, Microsoft uses a three-part clustering strategy that includes:

Server cluster provides failover support for applications and services that require high availability, scalability and reliability. With clustering, organizations can make applications and data available on multiple servers linked together in a cluster configuration. Back-end applications and services, such as those provided by database servers, are ideal candidates for Server cluster.

Network load balancing (NLB) provides failover support for IP-based applications and services that require high scalability and availability. With Network Load Balancing, organizations can build groups of clustered computers to support load balancing of Transmission Control Protocol (TCP), User Datagram Protocol (UDP) and Generic Routing Encapsulation (GRE) traffic requests. Web-tier and front-end services are ideal candidates for NLB.

Component load balancing (CLB) provides dynamic load balancing of middle-tier application components that use COM+. With Component Load Balancing, COM+ components can be load balanced over multiple nodes to dramatically enhance the availability and scalability of software applications.

Figure 11.16 shows Cluster Administrator screen on Windows Server 2003.

Windows Compute Cluster Server 2003 is a cluster of servers that includes a single head node and one or more compute nodes. The head node controls and

Figure 11.16. Clustering on Windows Server 2003

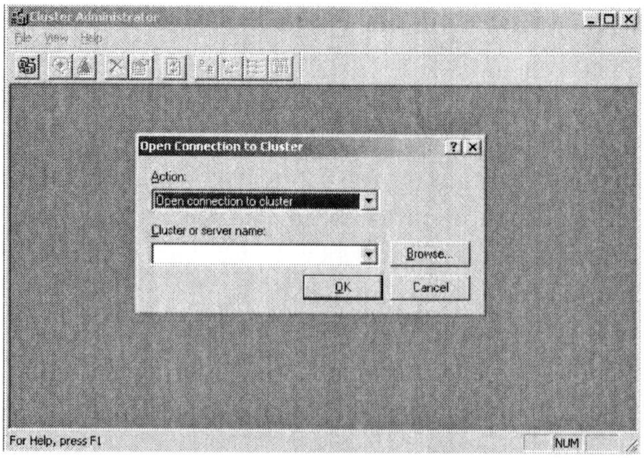

mediates all access to the cluster resources and is the single point of management, deployment, and job scheduling for the compute cluster.

The cluster service runs on the Windows Server 2003 or Windows 2000 operating system using network drivers, device drivers, and resource instrumentation processes designed specifically for server clusters and its component processes. These closely related, cooperating components of the cluster service are:

- **Checkpoint Manager**—saves application registry keys in a cluster directory stored on the quorum resource.
- **Database Manager**—maintains cluster configuration information.
- **Event Log Replication Manager**—replicates event log entries from one node to all other nodes in the cluster.
- **Failover Manager**—performs resource management and initiates appropriate actions, such as startup, restart, and failover.
- **Global Update Manager**—provides a global update service used by cluster components.
- **Log Manager**—writes changes to recovery logs stored on the quorum resource.
- **Membership Manager**—manages cluster membership and monitors the health of other nodes in the cluster.
- **Node Manager**—assigns resource group ownership to nodes based on group preference lists and node availability.
- **Resource Monitors**—monitors the health of each cluster resource using callbacks to resource DLLs. Resource Monitors run in a separate process, and communicate with the cluster server through remote procedure calls (RPCs) to protect cluster server from individual failures in cluster resources.
- **Backup/Restore Manager**—backs up, or restores, quorum log file and all checkpoint files, with help from the Failover Manager and the Database Manager.

All off-site and long-distance backup technologies transfer large amounts of data, therefore, they have to provide the following requirements:

a. High throughput
b. Low latency time
c. Zero or minimal data loss

Figure 11.17. Off-site (remote) backup technology requirements (Source: Ciena White Paper, www.ciena.com, 2005)

Application	Typical Throughput	Latency Requirement	Loss Tolerance
Synchronous Disk Mirroring	10 to 40 MB/s	Low, fixed latency	Zero loss
Asynchronous Disk Mirroring	10 to 40 MB/s	Low latency	Zero loss
Remote Backup	10 to 40 MB/s	Low latency	Low loss
Clustering	5 to 20 MB/s	Low, fixed latency	Zero loss
SAN Extension	10 to 40 MB/s	Low latency	Zero loss

The requirements are shown in Figure 11.17.

DATA RECOVERY

Data Recovery as an operation of copying data back to hard disk from backup media and the two most important attributes of data recovery (RPO, RTO) are briefly explained.

Data backup is used primarily in order to have data recovered (restored) in case of data corruption. Data Recovery is an operation of copying data back to hard disk from backup media in order to use it again by applications and end users.

Two most important dimensions of data recovery are:

a. Recovery Point
b. Recovery Time

and within this framework, two major objectives:

*   RPO (Recovery Point Objective)
*   RTO (Recovery Time Objective).

Recovery Point Objective (RPO) describes a point in time to which data must be restored, while RTO (Recovery Time Objective) is the time limit within which data must be restored.

Figure 11.18 shows main dimensions of data recovery operations as well as major technologies. In between tape backup and advanced backup Technologies, several technologies are used, more or less costly, with more or less time for data to be restored, and with higher or lower value of data.

Figure 11.18. Data recovery: RPO and RTO

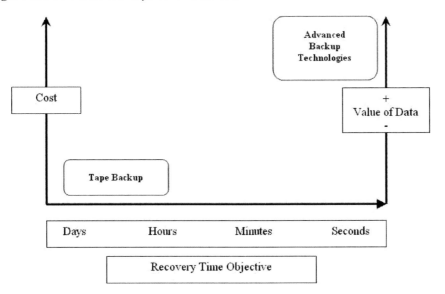

Assempra Technologies (www.asempra.com) developed an evaluation metrics in order to evaluate a solution with regard to recovery time characteristics. They argue that focusing only on RTO and RPO is not enough. Instead, they propose a metric which contains ten attributes classified into three groups, as follows:

Recovery Time Characteristics

1.   Recovery Time Objective (RTO)
2.   Recovery Time Granularity (RTG)

Recovered Data Characteristics

1.   Recovery Point Objective (RPO)
2.   Recovery Object Granularity (ROG)1
3.   Recovery Event Granularity (REG)
4.   Recovery Consistency Characteristics (RCC)

Recovery Scalability Characteristics

1.   Recovery Service Scalability (RSS)
2.   Recovery Service Resiliency (RSR)
3.   Recovery Location Scope (RLS)

4.   Business Continuity Cost (BCC)

Here are the explanations of these attributes according to this model:

RTO defines how quickly the solution is capable of recovering the data and application it is designed to protect.

RTG determines the time spacing for selecting a recovery point.

Recovery Point Objective defines the minimum time gap between the last physical failure and the point-in-time where data can be recovered. The smaller the time gap, the less data are lost.

Recovery Object Granularity measures the level of object granularity a business continuity solution is capable of recovering.

Recovery Event Granularity measures the capability of a business continuity solution to track events and to recover a failed application or missing data to a specific event.

Recovery Consistency Characteristics define the usability of recovered data by the associated application. The RCC of a business continuity solution depend not only on how data is captured and stored, but also on the data type being protected.

Recovery Service Scalability is important in evaluating a business continuity solution. A business continuity solution must be able to scale with the applications and the data it protects.

Recovery Service Resiliency defines how well a business continuity solution tolerates failures. A business continuity service must not cause an application to fail. It must be more reliable than the application it protects.

Recovery Location Scope defines where the protected data must be presented when recovery takes place.

Business Continuity Cost defines the cost efficiency of a business continuity solution. Data services such as backup, snapshot, replication, hierarchical data management, information lifecycle management, and archive are traditionally separate tools with very different architectures.

Figure 11.19. Storage—Backup solutions summarized and compared

	Data Saved	Application Running on Always-on Basis	Downtime	Data Recovery: Time and Complexity	Total Costs of Ownership
Tape Backup	Yes	None	Days	Hours, Days High	Low
Online Tape Backup	Yes	None	Hours	Hours Medium	Medium

continued on following page

Figure 11.19. continued

	Data Saved	Application Running on Always-on Basis	Downtime	Data Recovery: Time and Complexity	Total Costs of Ownership
Disk-based Backup	Yes	None	Minutes	Minutes Low	Medium
SCSI	Yes	None	Minutes		Low
Off-site Data Protection	None	None	Hours	Hours, Medium	Medium
Clustering	High	High	Minutes	Minutes	High
Fault-Tolerant Solution	High	High	High	Seconds, Low Complexity	High
Fault-Tolerant and Disaster-Tolerant Solution	100%	100%	Zero	Seconds, Low Complexity	High

The table in Figure 11.19 summarizes most commonly used standard and advanced storage technologies.

CHAPTER SUMMARY

İn addition to traditional backup technologies, contemporary computing is forced to employ additional technologies in finding the ways of managing data in more efficient and effective way. With advances in data communications, networking technologies and high speed coomunication lines, several new approaches called "advanced storage systems" have been developed. These technologires that include the solutions such as NAS, SAN, DAS, RAID, online backup, data vaulting, data miroring, and so forth, are briefly explained from business continuity perspective.

REFERENCES

Singer, M. (2005). HP Vows Server, Storage Marriage Available, Retrieved on August 7, 2007 from http://itmanagement.earthweb.com/erp/article.php/3489651.

REAL WORLD CASES

HP Integrity Servers help keep planes and passengers in the air
Compiled from: http://h71028.www7.hp.com/ERC/downloads/4AA0-8037EEW.pdf

Every minute an aircraft is on the ground it is losing money and unplanned delays can destroy flight schedules. Getting the right parts to the right place at the right time is crucial and that is the expertise of Lufthansa Technik Logistik (LTL).

Part of the Lufthansa Technik Group, a world leading provider of maintenance, repair and overhaul (MRO) to the air transport industry, LTL services more than 450 airlines and aircraft operators.

From the smallest electrical switch for a Boeing 737 coffee machine to a seven tonne Boeing 747 Jumbo engine, it has over 420,000 stock items. Its total supply chain management systems include transportation, materials sourcing, storage and distribution and providing 24-hour Aircraft On Ground (AOG) services worldwide.

If those systems fail, the knock-on effects can have serious consequences for the world's airports, airlines and passengers. To prevent this, LTL needed highly available systems with the power, flexibility and capacity to support its complex software stack.

This is a mix of both standard and bespoke systems. It includes standard SAP Enterprise Resource Planning modules, Oracle databases with customised applications such as tracking and tracing, and application integration platforms like DataStage and WebLogic from BEA systems. There are also many specialised logistics applications for such activities as shipping, forwarding, warehouse management and customs.

LTL also needed the scalability to cope with its rapid growth, the best price/performance ratio and a reduction in management complexity. Situated in Hamburg, Germany, the company's IT department supports some 1,000 users at its two main locations in Frankfurt and Hamburg and its service provider Lufthansa Systems ticked all the right boxes with a combination of HP Integrity Business Critical Servers (BCS) and HP storage solutions.

Objective

Lufthansa Technik Logistik GmbH (LTL) supplies maintenance, repair and overhaul (MRO) services to 450 airlines worldwide. Its heterogeneous server environment delivered low performance and high maintenance costs and also had availability and scalability issues.

Approach

Working together with HP, Lufthansa Systems consolidated the 18 old PA-RISC machines down to two HP Integrity Business Critical Servers (BCS).

It transitioned LTL from PA-RISC to Itanium.

HP MSL tape libraries and EVA storage arrays were provided for backup and storage.

They were formed into two identical server and storage systems, connected by SAN switches to create a high availability mirrored environment.

Business Benefits

- Maintenance and support costs have been reduced by 10% providing excellent price/performance ratio.
- Crucial system availability means that LTL can keep its customer's planes flying.
- This increases its ability to compete in its aggressive market.

DISCUSSION QUESTIONS

1. What is difference between SAN and NAS?
2. What are SAMBA and CIFS technologies?
3. What does RAID stands for?
4. Explain briefly main RAID levels.
5. What is data vaulting?
6. Explain the data replication technology.
7. Make a short assessment of the Iron Mountain's data protection services.
8. Explain the main data recovery dimensions.
9. What is server clustering and why it is used for?
10. List briefly major advantage and disadvantages of major storage and backup technologies.

Chapter XII
Networking Technologies for Business Continuity

CHAPTER OVERVIEW

Continuous computing technologies explored in previous chapters, in many cases, are located on different locations. However, they depend on each other and are bound to data communication and networking technologies that are used in order to ensure data transfers. Therefore, the data communications technologies are crucial in ensuring continuous computing each time when computing devices and users are located in different locations. Chapter XII provides some explanations on them and their role in business continuity.

NETWORK INFRASTRUCTURE AND NETWORK DOWNTIME

Networking infrastructure is a prerequisite for any kind of e-business in networked economy. It consists of several data communications and computer network technologies that are implemented in order to come up with appropriate data communications—computer network platform. Computer network infrastructure is very important from business continuity perspective since any disconnection failure that occurs on it can cause data unavailability.

As shown in Figure 12.1, these technologies make the third layer of an information system that enables continuous computing.

They include technologies such as communication devices, communication media, communication protocols, network operating systems, networking protocols, data protection and security standards. Network cards, modems, cable modems, DSL modems, routers, bridges, switches, hubs, firewalls, and so forth, are used to connect computers within local area networks, wide area networks, virtual private networks, campus networks, metropolitan networks. Several communication media, guided and non-guided, such as leased lines, ISDN, ATM, frame-relay, wireless communications devices and protocols, satellite communications, and so forth, are used in order to establish several types of computer networks. These networks are in turn basis for networked enterprises, e-business, e-government and e-economy. Hunter (2008) noted that recent Internet outages in the Middle-East bring customary boom in business continuity.

In addition to data communication hardware and software glitches and failures, another threat with regard to business continuity is in network attacks. Network attacks today can come in the form of competitive espionage, disgruntled ex-employees, hackers, crackers, other forms of outsiders willing to use our servers to store music, movies, pornography, pirated software and so on.

In modern Internet era, in what is called "networked business," the network security in an organization that operates in such a kind of environment is a business continuity problem. A famous saying, "A chain is only as strong as its weakest link" applies as a rule in modern e-business.

Network downtime caused by security attacks is costing large enterprises more than $30 million a year, according to a recent study by Infonetics Research.

Figure 12.1. Continuous computing layers: The role of networking infrastructure (Layer 3)

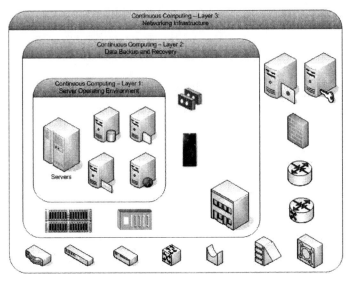

According to the study, "The Costs of Network Security Attacks: North America 2007," large organizations are losing an average of 2.2% of their annual revenue because of security attacks. That may sound relatively small, but when coupled with the extra few percentage points of revenue companies lose to non-security related downtime, the loss is much higher.

Large companies take the biggest hit from security-related downtime, but results show that small and midsized businesses (SMBs) stand to lose about half a percent of their annual revenue to security-related downtime, which can translate to hundreds of thousands of dollars annually. Cisco provides a framework of the impacts of network failures (Cisco White Paper, 2004).

Measures that have to be implemented in order to have the networking infrastructure more secure include:

- Having anti-virus protection on enterprise-wide basis and up-to-date.
- Implementation of two-fold firewalls: software firewall on the system and a hardware firewall in the networking infrastructure. Implementation includes proper installation, configuration, upgrading and updating.
- Allowing root access only from system console that is physically secure. This is a useful method that is used in reducing security breaches on servers. On UNIX servers, this is done by using /etc/securetty file with the single-entry console.
- Maintaining the server security by setting restrictive permissions on the file /etc/exports.
- Setting "allow" and "deny" options on accessing and using networking services by using /var/adm/inetd.sec security file.
- Denying access to ftp and telnet services.
- Continuous monitoring of the network activity, comparing an "usual" traffic and the one that can be caused by an attack. Several software packages called anti-sniffers can be used in order to indicate abnormal network activity. Ethereal is an example of a network protocol analyzer (www.ethereal.com).
- Continuous monitoring and assessing all data communication technologies that are used within a networking platform. This includes several methods and techniques used to verify the security levels of the communication devices, communication lines, networking protocols, networking software, and so forth.
- Implementing an intrusion detection system
- Implementing properly password policies and educating end users on the importance of user authentication.
- Secure the wireless networks.
- Having both server operating system and desktop operating system platforms updated with patches and updates.

- Using on regular basis standard and advanced system and network administration tools and techniques such as: ping, whois, netroute, netlinkrc, traceroute, netstat, nslookup, and so forth.
- Using port scanners

The utilities that are listed above are UNIX-based, implemented and used on UNIX operating platforms. However, similar solutions can be found on other server operating systems as well.

NETWORKED BUSINESS ENVIRONMENT, VIRTUAL BUSINESS

The terms of virtual business, virtual enterprise and virtual organization are introduced and most commonly models are explained.

To cope with increasing market demands, many corporations are turning to information technology in order to boost establishing some kind of e-business or virtual business (virtual enterprise—VE). Such businesses can be formed in different ways, depending mainly on the primary goal of entering virtual business. The main requirement is to connect several geographically separated entities involved in VE business (people, companies) in a way that they can communicate among each other and run the business. That is where information technology comes in, providing a set of resources for an efficient and effective virtual business.

Pearlson and Saunders (2006) define a virtual organization as a structure that makes it possible for individuals to work for an organization and live anywhere. They argue that the virtual organization is not to be confused with the virtual corporation which is a temporary network of companies linked by information technology to exploit fact-changing opportunities.

Recent interest in the topic of virtual enterprises has been enormous, and continues to grow. Almost since the Internet era began, researchers and IT-professionals have considered its application in business to be one of Internet's most valuable contributions. Not surprisingly, since the term "virtual enterprise" and its several aspects has become one of the hottest topics in the second half of the '90s.

Virtual reality in contemporary business has also changed the way managers do their job. The term "agile management" has been introduced with the concept of virtual enterprise with an emphasis on information agility or informational efficiency. In virtual enterprises, information agility represents the major prerequisite for agile management and means eliminating inefficiencies in accessing, exchanging and disseminating of all kinds of information. Information technology provides managers with a set of tools that eases access to corporate information.

Figure 12.2. A networked business infrastructure

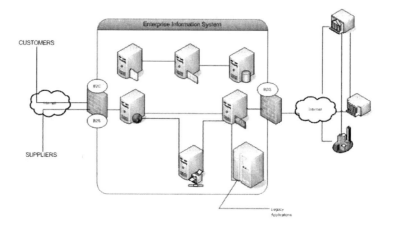

The concept of "virtual enterprise" has been introduced as a result of an explosive growth of computer communications in the '90s, particularly with the emergence of Internet and Web technologies. In fact, it was the concept of electronic data interchange (EDI), which " ...made a first step towards automating online business-to-business commerce, but fell short of providing the comprehensive communication environment needed (Dunn & Varano, 1999).

Camarinha-Matos, Afsarmanesh, Garita, and Lima (1998) described the steps towards an architecture for virtual enterprise. They provided several definitions of the term "virtual enterprise" and other similar terms that are used in this context such as: extended enterprise, supply chain management, electronic commerce, cross border enterprise, network of enterprises, virtual corporation. All these terms represent related concepts. Byrne (1993) defined a virtual corporation as a "temporary network of independent companies—suppliers, customers, even rivals—linked by information technology to share skills, costs and access to one another's market." In a similar definition, Wijk, Geurts, and Bultie (1998) noted that "within the network, all partners provide their own core competencies and the co-operation is based on semi-stable relations. The products and services, which a Virtual Organisation provides are dependent on innovation and strongly customer based." A broader definition given by Jansen, Steenbakkers, and Jägers (1998) explained a virtual organization as a "Combination of various parties (persons and/or organizations) located over a wide geographical area which are committed to achieving a collective goal by pooling their core competencies and resources." This definition introduces a possibility of applying the concept of virtuality in all organizations, not only enterprises, including such organizations consisting of several persons. In our work we will mainly rely on this definition of VE.

Goldman, Nagel, and Preiss (1995) defined the six reasons why a company would form a virtual enterprise:

- Sharing infrastructure, risks, and costs.
- The linking of complementary core competencies.
- A reduction in the concept to cash time.
- An increase in facilities.
- Gaining access to other markets.
- The transition from selling products to selling solutions.

Song and Nagi (1997) proposed a framework for an agile manufacturing information system (AMIS) and introduce the concept of virtual information system for agile manufacturing (VISAM).

Virtual enterprises can be formed in different ways. The most common approaches are:

- **Groupwork-based VE.** Group of people working together separated geographically can form a virtual enterprise (Figure 12.3). Doing such a kind of business is possible thanks to contemporary communications-networking and Internet technology (phone, fax, GSM, e-mail, Web, talk, videoconferencing).
- **Business specialization-based VE.** Group of small or large companies that specialize in some specific business activities can establish a new company on temporary or permanent basis (Figure 12.4).
- **Virtual manufacturing-based VE.** Business based on outsourcing some manufacturing operations can be done within a virtual framework (Figure 12.5). Actually, this is a new approach within agile manufacturing philosophy which is called virtual manufacturing. Virtual enterprise framework enables such a business.
- **Extranet-based VE.** Virtual enterprise can also be the case in which a company decides to form special relationships with its customers and/or suppliers through an extranet infrastructure (Figure 12.6).
- **Distributed computing-based VE.** We can also consider a case in which distributed objects are used between two or more companies usually connected through Internet, as some sort of virtual business. These are applications created using distributed computing standards such as CORBA and DCOM (Figure 12.7).

In the section that follows, these models of virtual enterprises are briefly described. In either case, the main prerequisite for virtual enterprise is an efficient and effective IT infrastructure which is based on fast and stable communication backbone. Virtual enterprise information system (VEIS) is then established to support virtual business.

Groupwork-based virtual enterprise is very simple type of VE and its information architecture is based on two or more computers connected through Internet. Users from geographically separated sites share data and applications by using communication technology.

In the second case (Figure 12.4), a new company—virtual company is established from the partnering companies A, B, and C which enter a partnering business. Virtual enterprise consists of the segments of the existing businesses. Communication-network infrastructure can be based on either WAN or Extranet.

The solution from Figure 12.5, the virtual manufacturing-based VE model can be applied when companies enter a partnering business which requires much closer relationships among companies. Virtual enterprise is set as superset of the existing businesses. Model makes use of the concept of virtual manufacturing and in short means that a manufacturing company may outsource some of its work to subcontractors. Communications are provided either by Wide Area Network, Extranet or even standard Internet connection.

Figure 12.3. Groupwork-based VE

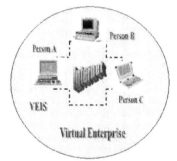

Figure 12.4 Business specialization-based VE

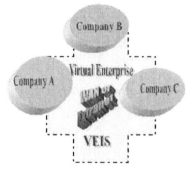

In Figure 12.6, the Extranet-based model of virtual enterprise is presented. In this model, Company A forms a virtual enterprise with its customers and suppliers, mainly through a well established Extranet. This model is sometimes called "extended enterprise" in which a dominant enterprise "extends" its boundaries to all or some of its suppliers (Camarinha-Matos et al., 1998).

Distributed computing (Figure 12.7) is a special case of virtuality in running computer applications. It is a new, object-oriented and Internet based framework in which different modules of an application may be running on separate computers on Internet. Applications can also share some objects so that they ask for some services from them. As can be seen from Figure 12.7, several distributed objects from different locations communicate among each other participating within the same application or coming from different applications.

The appropriate design of a virtual enterprise information system, referred to here as VEIS, is of central importance in applying IT in virtual enterprises. In any type of VE model, its VEIS must provide a set of IT facilities that support VE business efficiently and effectively. The organizational requirements depend on the type and complexity of VE, therefore, a contingency approach should be respected. VE-related

Figure 12.5. Virtual manufacturing-based VE

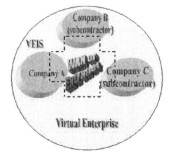
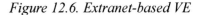

Figure 12.6. Extranet-based VE

Figure 12.7. Distributed computing-based VE

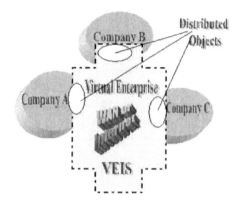

contingency factors can be extracted from the models defined above (group of people or group of companies, temporary or permanent business, virtual manufacturing, relationships with customers and suppliers, etc.). On the other side, the following requirements are expected to be fulfilled by information technology:

- Multiple hardware platform support (different hardware platforms can be used in companies involved in VE).
- Data and application integration support (support for different data formats and application platforms).
- Support for high-speed LAN and WAN technologies.
- Support for multiple hardware and software communication protocols.
- Efficient remote access for telecommuters.
- Secure data transfer.
- Efficient access to all kinds of information.

These requirements can be grouped into the following IT dimensions or IT-related contingency factors for establishing an efficient and effective VEIS architecture:

- Hardware/operating system platform
- Communications-networking platform
- Application platform
- User Interface platform

From VE perspective, the hardware/OS platform is important from the following aspects:

- Application servers, data servers, e-mail servers, and Web servers should run on reliable machines with high availability ratio.
- Servers must be scalable enough, because as time goes on, new companies with new users may wish to enter VE business.
- Servers supporting VE business must support open hardware-software communication protocols in order to be able to exchange data.
- Servers must support remote access capabilities.

NETWORK TECHNOLOGIES (DATA COMMUNICATIONS TECHNOLOGIES)

The data communications and computer network technologies that are used in designing and implementing networking infrastructure are described.

With the enormous growth in computer networking, business data communications, and particularly Internet, the demand for fast, reliable and cost-effective data communications backbone has also been growing. For purposes of a networked environment and virtual business, several high-speed communication technologies are used such as Fast Ethernet, Gigabit Ethernet, FDDI, ISDN, ATM, xDSL, cable modems, wireless technologies, and so forth. Most of these technologies are costly to implement and maintain, therefore the selection of the appropriate one is a critical point in creating an information architecture. Many factors have be involved, some of them are: type of the business, geographical distances among the offices, branches and companies involved in business, hardware platforms of partners involved, application platforms, number and characteristics of remote users, availability of specific LAN/WAN technologies provided by national Telecom company, and so forth.

From the viewpoints of virtual business and business continuity, the technologies that improve LAN and WAN performances and remote access capabilities are of most importance. In the section that follows, these high-speed networking technologies are shortly explained.

Technologies for WAN Infrastructure

Leased lines have been traditionally used as a WAN backbone for establishing inter-company network infrastructure. In a virtual business, they are also suitable for connecting companies that form virtual manufacturing-based or Extranet-based models of virtual enterprises. From technological perspective, they are telephone lines that are leased for private use forming a dedicated phone line between two points. Leased lines are capable of carrying data at several rates, ranging from 56

Kbps, up to several hundreds of Mbps, even Gbps. T1 lines are widely used as major data transfer backbone in the USA and have a capacity of 1.544 Mbps, T2 lines have 6.312 Mbps, T3 lines transmit data at 44.736 Mbps, while T4 lines work at 274.176 Mbps. For small businesses with few users who rely on standard utilization of e-mail messaging system and Internet a T1 line would be enough. Businesses that rely on heavy e-mail messaging traffic and heavy use of Web technologies should select a T3 or T4.

FDDI (Fibre Distributed Data Interface) is both LAN and WAN technology. It is mainly used as a network backbone connecting two or more LAN segments in range up to 200 kilometers. A simple backbone might connect two servers through a high-speed link consisting of network adapter cards and cable.

Fibre channel refers to a relatively new technology with the most common usage being in connecting devices within Storage Area Networks and clustered servers in distributed computing environment. FDDI and Fibre channel support data transmission speeds of 100/200 Mbps. Fibre Channel is a high-performance data communication technology that can be used for high-performance data transfer and network infrastructures. It was originally based on standard optical fibre technology. Today, Fibre Channel networking environments can be established by using optical fibres (mono-mode and multi-mode) and standard data communication media such as coaxial or twisted-pair cables. The newest Fibre Channel technology provides the 4Gbps fast and high-performance interconnection platform for supporting mission-critical applications within cluster based environments and LAN and WAN based Storage Area Networks. Depending on the media used, maximum distances between nodes range from 10m to 10km. The three main network topologies that are based on Fibre Channel are: Point-to-point connections, Arbitrated loop architecture (FC-AL), and Switched architecture (FC-SW). Fibre Channel technology is used today not only for Local Area Networks and Wide Area Networks but for LAN and WAN-based storage architecture such as Storage Area Networks, Network Attached Storage and Direct Access Storage.

X.25 and Frame Relay packet-switched network protocols. X.25 is a simple, commonly used and inexpensive WAN technology. Although it is widely available, X.25 is slow compared to newer technologies. Frame relay works at the data-link layer of the OSI model and provides data transfer rates from 56 Kbps to 1.544 Mbps. Frame relay services are typically provided by telecommunications carriers. This technology is less expensive than other WAN technologies because it provides bandwidth on demand, rather than dedicating lines whether data is being transmitted or not. A version of Frame Relay called International Frame Relay is suitable as a WAN backbone for those VE companies with partners abroad.

Cell Relay or ATM (asynchronous transfer mode). ATM is also both LAN and WAN technology which is usually implemented as a backbone technology.

ATM is very scalable networking platform, with data transfer rates ranging from 25 Mbps to 2.4 Gbps.

Synchronous optical network. Synchronous optical network (SONET) is a WAN technology that works at the physical layer of the OSI model. It provides data transfer rates from 51.8 Mbps to 2.48 Gbps.

VPN. Virtual private network (VPN) is a way or organizing a WAN infrastructure by using public switched lines with secure messaging protocols. Actually, public Internet infrastructure is used for business data communications. It should be noted here that the attribute "virtual" does not mean necessarily that it is a dedicated platform for virtual business. VPN infrastructure can be used in any type of business, not only virtual business. With the VPN, users from remote locations (branch-offices) not only access a company messaging system (e-mail and faxing), its intranet, they also can use applications running on servers. WAN-VPN platforms are usually established, maintained and managed by telecom companies or ISPs. They are then outsourced to companies willing to use this type of WAN. If a company wants to keep control over its WAN-VPN infrastructure it may chose to build its own VPN, instead of outsourcing it. This approach is cost effective for companies with a number of remote offices, not only because of making an efficient network connection but also because of the possibility of a centralized network management.

The VPN-based WAN usually includes:

- Gateway that encrypts data packets and authenticates users. VPN gateways sit behind firewalls that at most sites are incorporated into the routers.
- VPN management software that lets network managers configure and manage VPNs from a single computer. This software is usually sold in the form of integrated suite which integrates hardware, software, and services, in order to

Figure 12.8. SONET technologies and data rates

OC Name—Number of Channels	Nominal Data Rate	Effective Data Rate
OC-1	51 Mbps	48 Mbps
OC-3	155 Mbps	143 Mbps
OC-12	622 Mbps	571 Mbps
OC-48	2.488 Gbps	2.3 Gbps
OC-192	9.953 Gbps	9.1 Gbps
OC-768	39.812 Gbps	36.4 Gbps

simplify deployment of VPNs. VPN system requires Firewall and Tunneling software with LZO compression utility which improves dial-up connection.

- Client software for users to connect remotely. It allows telecommuters, mobile workers, and other remote users to take advantage of Internet connections for convenient, low-cost, secure remote access.

VPN concept has though some disadvantages. VPN-based WANs are slow because of data compression, less robust and vulnerable to hackers. Recently developed the three IP VPN technologies are used to design network environments:

- Multi protocol label switching (MPLS)—as a baseline technology
- IP security (IPSec) and
- Secure socket layer (SSL) for secure transactions over the Net through a Web browser.

Technologies for Remote Data Access

56 Kbps Dial-Up Modem Connection. Technology called x2 introduced by U.S. Robotic, together with V.90, a data transmission recommendation developed by ITU (International Telecommunications Union), provides a specification for achieving data transfer speeds of up to 56 Kbps over the standard public telephone lines. With standard V.42 compression, 56K modem technology can download at speeds up to 115 Kbps.

ISDN. ISDN is a set of protocols that integrate data, voice, and video signals into digital telephone lines. ISDN offers data transfer rates between 56 Kbps and either 1.544 Mbps or 2.048 Mbps, depending on the country telecom infrastructure. It requires special equipment at the users' site; user can talk on the phone and make file transfer at the same time. In addition to remote access, ISDN can also be used as WAN backbone.

Cable Modem. Cable modem technology makes use of cable-TV infrastructure by hooking up computer to a local cable-TV line. In many countries, cable modem and DSL technologies replaced standard dial-up and ISDN connections since data transfer speed can reach several Mbps. The cable system is a shared medium, which is a fact that should be taken into consideration when thinking of such a type of connection. The cable modem usually has two ports: Ethernet port for attaching to a standard Ethernet card in the computer, while the other port is Coaxial port which is used for plugging in-coming cable-TV wire.

xDSL Technology. In the recent years several versions of DSL technologies (digital subscriber line) have emerged. Because of several possible models, this technology is often referred to as xDSL technology. The xDSL is a digital packet technology like ISDN, but technology that usually uses a dedicated rather than a switched connection. With the appropriate devices, it can deliver signals at the speeds in the range from 1.5 to 6 Mbps over the current telephone wiring system. Therefore, Asymmetric DSL or ADSL, is often considered as an alternative to dial-up and even ISDN.

Wireless LAN and wireless Internet. With a wireless LAN technology, mobile users can connect to a local area network through a radio connection. A wireless LAN is a data communication system that uses electromagnetic waves for transmitting data over the air. It can be implemented either as an extension to the existing standard LAN, or as an alternative for it. It has gained a public interest with the emergence of remote access computing devices such as notebooks, hand-held computers, personal digital assistants (PDAs), mobile phones, smart phones, and so forth. These devices can be used for more efficient and effective communication among users, as well as for data exchange with host systems. Wireless Internet access is also supported. For example, hand-held PCs running Windows CE operating system include the Pocket Internet Explorer browser for remotely accessing Web or company's Intranet.

Two types of wireless connection are used: a) Wireless device connection and b) Wireless networking.

Wireless device connections are supported by protocols such as: IrDA, Bluetooth, IrDA-FIR/IrDA-VFIR and Wireless USB—WUSB (up to 480 Mbps). Wireless networking solutions range from 802.11 standard (2 Mbps), 802.11b (11 Mbps), 802.11a (54 Mbps), 802.11g (54 Mbps), 802.11n (540 Mbps).

WiMAX technology. New technology introduced recently—"WiMAX" (Worldwide Interoperability for Microwave Access) refers to the IEEE 802.16 standards for broadband wireless technology with the transfer rate of 1.3 Mbps.

Figure 12.9. xDSL acronyms

Type	Definition
DSL	Digital subscriber line (generic)
SDSL	Single line/Symmetric digital subscriber line
ADSL	Asymmetric digital subscriber line
HDSL	High bit (data) rate digital subscriber line
VDSL	Very high data rate digital subscriber line
VADSL	Very high speed digital subscriber line (another term for VDSL)

LAN Technology: Ethernet, Fast Ethernet, Gigabit Ethernet

Ethernet protocol is a typical LAN technology and most widely used LAN technology. The first installations of Ethernet-based local area networks used to transmit data at speed up to 10 Mbps. Ethernet cards known as Fast Ethernet (standard 100Base-T, IEEE 802.3u) represent high-speed LAN technology as they can provide data transfer rates of 100 Mbps and 1 Gbps (1000Base-T or IEEE 802.3z). Two new Ethernet standards recently developed are 10 Gigabit Ethernet (up to 10,000 Mbps) and 100 Gigabit Ethernet (with data transfer rate of 100,000 Mbps). As Ethernet cards are used for connecting computers to LANs, they are in the same time an entry point in establishing connection to a WAN and Internet, hence their importance in VE business. Ethernet cards are today used in a combination with other communication devices for remote access, for example, xDSL and cable-modem technology.

Communication Protocols and Applications for Virtual Enterprises

Communication protocols and applications are in fact what drives a virtual business. Protocols are, in short, the sets of hardware/software rules that communication endpoints must follow in order to exchange some sort of information. Transport protocols ensure a reliable data transfer over computer networks. Most widely used are:

- IBM's APPN
- TCP part of the TCP/IP protocol
- SPX part of the Novell NetWare IPX/SPX protocol
- Microsoft NetBIOS and NetBEUI
- AppleTalk

Network protocols represent a set of conventions and rules that are needed for two operating systems to communicate. Major network protocols are:

- IP section of TCP/IP protocol
- IBM SNA
- DECnet
- IPX (Novell's network protocol)
- NetBIOS (Microsoft protocol)
- AppleTalk (Apple's network protocol)

Starting from e-mail, other Internet services (telnet and FTP), Web-based technologies, videoconferencing technology, transactions-oriented applications such as EDI and electronic commerce, together with both hardware and software communication protocols, these applications enable companies to organize virtual business. Communication applications usually come in pairs with software protocols that enable them. For virtual enterprises, the following combinations are the most important: TCP/IP-Internet, e-mail/SMTP, Web/HTTP-HTML, WAP (Wireless Application Protocol). Web technology, for example, provides a platform for establishing intranet and extranet applications through which companies create virtual enterprises. The following table represent major networking protocols according to OSI layers:

The tables in Figures 12.11 and 12.12 summarize major technologies, standards, devices that are used in implementing local and wide area networks.

As a supplement to standard e-mail messaging technology, videoconferencing technology enables remote users not only to communicate among each other, exchange standard data, but organize virtual meetings, exchange video and audio data, and share data and applications as well. In order to be able to use this technology, in addition to a standard PC, additional set of hardware-software facilities is needed. It includes a camera that is usually installed on top of a PC, speakers, a microphone, and a videoconferencing software. Using videoconferencing technology in contemporary business is on the rise, as prices for equipment and communications fall. This technology is especially suitable for Groupwork-based model of virtual enterprise, but can be used in other models as well.

Making a Business-to-business electronic commerce may take many forms, depending on technology that is used. Over the last two decades, electronic data interchange—EDI has been used as a form for exchanging business documents over private networking infrastructures, using a pre-defined data-document format. With the explosion of Internet and Web technology, EDI has been replaced partially

Figure 12.10. OSI layers and network protocols

OSI Layer	Protocols
5-7. Application Layers (Session, Presentation, Application)	HTTP, HTML, XML MPEG, IMAP, POP
4. Transport	TCP (TCP/IP) SPX (Novell)
3. Network	IP (TCP/IP) IPX (Novell)
2. Data Link	Ethernet
1. Physical	Twisted Pair RS-232 Modem

Figure 12.11. LAN technologies

Media:	Devices:	Backbone technology:
☐ Twisted-pair	☐ Cards	☐ Ethernet
☐ Coaxial	☐ Hub	☐ Token-Ring
☐ Fibre optic	☐ Switch	☐ FDDI
☐ Wireless	☐ Router	☐ Fibre optic
	☐ Bridge	☐ ATM
	☐ Transceiver	☐ Wireless

Figure 12.12. WAN Technologies

Media:	Devices:	Backbone Technology:
☐ POTS lines	☐ Router	☐ POTS lines
☐ ISDN	☐ Repeater	☐ ISDN
☐ Fibre optic	☐ Bridge	☐ X-25, Frame Relay
☐ Satellite	☐ Modem	☐ T1, T2, T3, T4
☐ RFI	☐ ISDN adapters	☐ FDDI
☐ xDSL	☐ Cable Modem	☐ ATM
	☐ VPN devices	☐ VPN
	☐ xDSL devices	☐ xDSL
	☐ Wireless devices	☐ Wireless

by Internet-based electronic commerce applications, which include several forms like: online catalogs, virtual malls, online buying and selling, and so forth. The main advantage of e-commerce over EDI is that no additional equipment is needed, transactions can be made over public network infrastructure, whereas the primary concern with e-commerce is still security.

CHAPTER SUMMARY

In today's business, which is called "networked business," the network security in an organization that operates in such a kind of environment is a business continuity issue as well. Network downtime caused by communication devices' glitches, security attacks, and so forth, may affect the business as a whole. Networking technologies are briefly explained in this chapter in order to identify potential vulnerable points from business continuity perspective.

REFERENCES

Infonetics Research (2007). Reducing Downtime Costs with Network-Based IPS, http://www.mcafee.com/us/local_content/white_papers/wp_infonetics.pdf.

Cisco White Paper: Network Availability: How much do you need? How do you get it?, 2004.

Pearlson, K. E. & Saunders, C. S:, (2006). *Managing and Using Information Systems: A Strategic Approach*, Wiley

Dunn, J. R. & Varano, M. W. (1999). Leveraging Web-based information systems. *Information Systems Management*, Fall 1999.

Hunter, P. (2008). Eastern Internet outage brings customary boom in business continuity. *Computer Fraud & Security*, March 2008, pp. 16-17.

Camarinha-Matos, L. M., Afsarmanesh, H., Garita, C., & Lima, C. (1998). Towards an architecture for virtual enterprises. *Journal of Intelligent Manufacturing, 9*(2), April, 1998.

Byrne, J. A. (1993), The virtual corporation. *Business Week*, February 1993.

Jacoliene van Wijk, drs Daisy Geurts, ing René Bultje (1998). 7 steps to virtuality: Understanding the Virtual Organisation processes before designing ICT-support, http://www.cs.tcd.ie/Virtues/ocve98/proceedings/005.html.

Jansen, W., Steenbakkers, G. C. A. & Jägers, H. (1998, July). *Coordination and use if ICT in virtual organisations. PrimaVera working paper Series.* Paper presented at the EGOS Conference, Maastricht.

Goldman, S. L., Nagel, R. N. & Preiss, K. (1995). *Agile Competitors and Virtual Organizations: Strategies for Enriching the Customer.* New York, NY: Van Nostrand Reinhold.

Song, L. & Nagi, R. (1997). Design and implementation of a virtual information system for agile manufacturing. *IIE Transactions on Design and Manufacturing, special issue on Agile Manufacturing, 1997, 29*(10), pp. 839-857.

REAL WORLD CASES

Data Center 3.0: Enhancing Business Resilience and Agility
*Compiled from: http://www.cisco.com/en/US/netsol/ns708/networking_solutions_*
solution_segment_home.html

Cisco offers products, services, and programs to support a holistic view of the data center, adapting to your current and future business needs, including:

- Better manage data center resources
- Deploy more robust business continuance
- Build cost effective storage area networks
- Enhance data security
- Improve efficiency and increase business productivity

With the introduction of the Data Center 3.0 initiative, Cisco and our partners set the new standard for "Data Center Class" networking and IT solutions and help customers to create next-generation data centers.

Cisco Data Center Lays Foundation for Greater Business Agility and Resiliency
Compiled from: http://www.cisco.com/web/about/ciscoitatwork/featured_content/
fc_may_june_2007_article03.html

A greenfield opportunity...if you could create whatever you wanted in a data center, what would you build? Here's what Cisco IT envisioned: an entirely new business data center, one that bolsters Cisco's ability to move into new markets, can easily support US$8 billion in business revenue generated quarterly, and that increases recoverability of the data center in a natural or other disaster.

This new Cisco data center is now under construction in Richardson, Texas, and will support all North American operations. It will be Cisco's first fully operational data center that adopts the Cisco IT service-oriented data center model and test runs the impact such a model can have on its business.

To make the service-oriented data center model work, Cisco IT has focused considerable effort on operations, specifically governance-the policies that ensure compatibility and security of applications as well as their ability to minimize use of resources. The focus on governance arose in part from a realization that Cisco needed to align its IT operations to 21st century demands and to improve them overall, says Brett Colbert, senior director of IT at Cisco. Basic blocking and tackling in fundamental areas such as incidents, change releases, and configuration management drew early attention, as the IT group developed policies and standards to which applications must adhere.

One of the first steps the group took was to ask existing production data center users and partners what single thing they would change about operations if they could. From their responses, the IT group developed a list of 40 proposed policies and submitted them to Cisco's Enterprise Architecture Council, which has so far approved more than 30 of them.

One of these policies, for example, states that all applications must pass a security vulnerability assessment to be served by the new data center. Another requires all databases to run on a platform supported by the data center. And another policy states that an application must be able to run in a service-oriented environment to migrate to the new data center or provide a compelling business reason why it should be maintained on a standalone server.

Resiliency also factors into the policies, even down to the application level. To be served by the new data center, every application must have a disaster recovery plan stating, at a minimum, who should be called if data is corrupted, how the data will be restored, and how long the application can be down without affecting customers or other critical business processes.

So, the IT staff has worked diligently to educate clients about the advantages of a service-oriented data center environment, identifying risks and ways to mitigate them in the process. Several clients have experienced benefits through early-stage service-oriented architecture operations at Cisco's production data centers in San Jose, California, and Research Triangle Park, NC. At the same time, Cisco IT is standardizing its own activities. People in IT operations do not necessarily speak the same language across the company, notes Colbert, leading to misunderstanding and confusion. For example, he says, "People use 'incident,' 'problem,' and 'issue' to describe the same thing. Some will do a root cause analysis; others will not. Some will document fixes; others do not. We're setting uniform policies for our own operations as well."

Cisco's new data center in Richardson, Texas, will contain 29,000 square feet of raised floor space, divided into four "halls" that support the business needs of not only Cisco IT, but also of Linksys, Scientific Atlanta, and Cisco's government services group. Halls will be divided into pods, each containing all the processing, storage, and networking resources needed to support a number of applications. Resources will be virtualized and dynamically reassigned as needed.

"At a minimum, the data center will function at Tier III availability, up from Tier II. This is the terminology used by the Uptime Institute, an industry organization, to describe the redundancy and recoverability of a data center," Colbert explains. "You can go up to a Tier IV." The new data center will be served by two communications carriers and two power suppliers. Generally, Tier III data centers demonstrate 99.98 percent availability. The new data center will be served by two communications carriers and two power suppliers.

Cisco IT supports just under 10,000 servers, roughly 3,800 applications, and about 800 databases. So far, more than 1,000 of those applications have been evaluated and approved to migrate to the Richardson facility, which is expected to employ approximately 4,500 servers.

"You don't need more server and storage capacity to do more work in our service-oriented data center model. Because of virtualization, you can get a great deal more work out of what you have," emphasizes Todd Glenn, IT manager at Cisco. In addition, the Richardson data center will be as "green" as Cisco can make it. This is an especially high-priority goal given that 80 percent of data center challenges are related to power, cooling, or space, according to Gartner estimates.

The data center will make use of a number of Cisco tools for application load balancing and server and storage management. Applications and databases themselves will also be virtualized whenever possible. For example, customer relationship management (CRM) and order fulfillment software can share the same database of customer information. Based on the latest construction schedules, Cisco's Workplace Resources Group expects to turn the physical plant over to IT in August 2007. The next step, which should stretch through the end of 2007, is "Wave 0," in which all of the processing, storage, network, infrastructure services, and middleware needed are moved into the center and proved in. At the beginning of 2008, "Wave 1" will see the first movement of applications into the new data center, followed by successive waves over the next few years.

The biggest return on investment (ROI) in the Richardson data center will come from its ability to adapt to Cisco's changing business needs.

"IT systems can be a significant barrier to a company's ability to move into new markets," according to Colbert. "If an application and its supporting resources were designed to handle enterprise sales, they may not support the company's move into consumer or small business markets. We want our IT systems to enable every move the business wants to make." For example, consumers purchasing online do not want to struggle with page after page of configuration options when they are looking for a simple home router. So, the software application should be capable of hiding the configuration pages intended for enterprise purchasers.

Specifically, they want an infrastructure and services that will support applications that consist of loosely coupled modules, rather than monolithic ones. This is among the new business capabilities Cisco will derive from the Richardson data center—in effect, the ability to mix and match modules, perhaps even from different applications, to suit the customer, the product, and the market segment.

Cisco IT will try out such a loosely coupled application architecture in a new e-commerce platform at the Richardson data center, in which ordering, tracking, pricing, discounting, and related applications will be designed within modules that can be pulled up to satisfy specific customer needs. "We want to make it much easier for people to buy from us," says Colbert.

Cisco IT is examining specific ROI and performance metrics in new ways, as well. For example, can operational metrics, such as system availability, problem resolution within guaranteed service-level agreements (SLAs), and the usage percentages for servers and storage networks, be tied to business agility and resiliency goals? This is the type of business-benefits metric the IT group wants to cultivate.

"This new data center is a transformational opportunity," notes Colbert. "We will build in and demonstrate architectural and operational excellence, and we will prove how much IT affects—and can support—business goals in the 21st century."

DISCUSSION QUESTIONS

1. Given the growth in data communications technology, how might that technology affect the way how business is operated today? How secure is telecommuniting and mobile work?
2. Explain the main components: devices, media, and protocols that form the layer 3 of the contnuous computing platform.
3. Identify the most critical points of the networking infrastrucure from the business coninuity perspective.
4. Explain the main points of the Cisco's model: the list of the impacts of network failures.
5. List the main measures that should be implemented in order to get more secured network infrastructure.
6. Explain the main models of virtual business and virtual enterprises.
7. Make an assessment of most commonly used WAN technologies that are used in your business and are available in your region.
8. What are advantages and disadvantages of virtual private networks?
9. Explain the difference between xDSL and cable modem technology.
10. List the man networking protocols that are supported by your dektop PC and its operating systems.

Chapter XIII
Business Continuity Management

CHAPTER OVERVIEW

After explaining several continuous computing technologies in previous chapters, the book focuses on business continuity management in Chapter XIII. Ensuring higher levels of data and applications availability and hence improving the business continuity is not one-time job. Contrary, it represents a process that has to be managed in an efficient and effective way. It encompasses numerous activities that have to be planned and managed. This chapter introduces the main concepts, standards and approaches of business continuity management.

THE SYSTEMS PERSPECTIVE OF BUSINESS CONTINUITY: EXTENDED CHURCHMAN'S DEFINITION

In order to give more comprehensive definition of business continuity from the perspective of systems approach, additional dimensions of the second Churchman's system definition cited in the beginning of the book will be used in this section.

According to Churchman **"...**there exists **a client** whose interests (values) are served by S in such a manner that the higher the measure of performance, the better the interests are served, and more generally, the client is the standard of the measure of performance." In our case, the entire business system represents the client of its information system. The higher the measure of performance (e.g., availability ratio) provided by information system, the better the interests of an organization are served.

Churchman continues with the following dimension: "...there exists **a decision maker** who - via his resources—can produce changes in the measures of performance of S's components and hence changes in the measure of performance of S." Decision maker in our case will be one or more IT specialists including system administrator, network administrator, IT manager, business continuity manager, including CIO as well. All of them, via their resources that they use, administer or manage (information technologies), can make decisions and produce changes in the measure of performance of S's components and S as a whole (information system). System administrator, by using system administration tools, techniques, utilities, and so-called "tips-and-tricks" on the system operating platform can "produce changes in the measures of performance of the system" (enhance the system availability ratio).

Churchman's **designer**, who conceptualizes the nature of S in such a manner that the designer's concepts potentially produce actions in the decision maker, and hence changes in the measures of performance of S's components, and hence changes in the measure of performance of S, in our case, will be an IS designer, IS system developer, CIO or even CEO, who may propose or create such solutions or define such business objectives that can be later implemented by IT specialists. The designer's intention is to change S (IS) so as to maximize IS' value to the client (business system, organization). Designing and implementing a business continuity plan is a typical example of such activity.

INTRODUCTION TO BUSINESS CONTINUITY MANAGEMENT (BCM)

Business continuity management (BCM) involves several measures (activities) that have to be planned in order to achieve higher levels of the system/application availability ratios. The section introduces the main BC concept and standards.

Over the past decade, information has become an organizational resource that has to be managed in an efficient and effective way just like any other resource. In practice, however, many organizations still keep information management activities within computer centres even though information has become a corporate asset. Organizational management cannot be effective if it does not integrate organization-wide information management as well. This is in particular important for contemporary businesses, which require continuous computing platform as a main prerequisite for business continuance. Therefore, modern business needs an efficient integration of business continuity management into organizational management, the process which is done by integrating of continuous computing technologies into enterprise information system.

In today's information age, information management comprises numerous activities with data processing/data management being the core component. In addition to data management, information management includes the following components as well: system management, network management, security management, and so forth. Recently, with advances in Internet technologies and e-business, the need for achieving "a near 100%" level of business computing availability was brought up yet again. Consequently, the term of "business continuity management" was coined up and became a significant part of organizational information management.

Business Continuity Management as a separate discipline emerged 10 years ago. Since then (mid of '90s), this discipline emphasizes the role of BC Management and BC planning in modern business, with the main goal being "Keeping Business in Business".

Business continuity has been treated as both IT and managerial issue in the last ten years particularly after the e-business boom and the "9/11" event.

According to a survey done by the Security Services practice of Deloitte & Touche/TPM (2006), the number of companies that have developed formal business continuity management programs within the last six years has nearly tripled. According to this report, whereas just 30% of organizations had corporate business continuity plans in place six years ago, more than 83% of 273 survey respondents representing a cross section of industries say they now have formal business continuity plans. Within the last year alone, 70% of respondents reported having business continuity management (BCM) programs for most, if not all, of their critical business functions, up from 41% a year ago.

According to the "2007 AT&T Business Continuity Study" (2007), which contains results based on a telephone survey of 1,000 information technology executives in 10 U.S. metropolitan/regional areas:

a. Business continuity planning is seen as a "priority" by more than two-thirds (69%) of IT executives across the United States. Four out of ten (40%) indicate it has always been a priority for their business, and more than one-fourth (29%) indicate it has become a priority in recent years due to natural disasters, security, and terrorist threats.
b. Seven out of ten (72%) executives indicate their companies have a business continuity plan. One-fourth (26%) indicate their company does not have a plan.
c. Eight out of ten (82%) executives indicate that cyber security is part of their company's overall business continuity plan.

d. Of the 10 market areas, New York and Houston rank the highest in terms of business continuity preparedness while Cleveland ranks the lowest.

Business Continuity Institute (http://www.thebci.org) defined Business Continuity Management as a holistic management process that identifies potential impacts that threaten an organization and provides a framework for building resilience with the capability for an effective response that safeguards the interests of its key stakeholders, reputation and value creating activities. Its primary objective is to allow the Executive to continue to manage their business under adverse conditions, by the introduction of appropriate resilience strategies, recovery objectives, business continuity and crisis management plans in collaboration with, or as a key component of, an integrated risk management initiative.

BCI defined a list of 10 BC standards:

1. **Initiation and Management.** Establish the need for a business continuity management (BCM) Process or Function, including resilience strategies, recovery objectives, business continuity and crisis management plans and including obtaining management support and organizing and managing the formulation of the function or process either in collaboration with, or as a key component of, an integrated risk management initiative.
2. **Business Impact Analysis.** Identify the impacts resulting from disruptions and disaster scenarios that can affect the organization and techniques that can be used to quantify and qualify such impacts. Identify time-critical functions, their recovery priorities, and inter-dependencies so that recovery time objectives can be set.
3. **Risk Evaluation and Control.** Determine the events and external surroundings that can adversely affect the organization and its resources (facilities, technologies, etc.) with disruption as well as disaster, the damage such events can cause, and the controls needed to prevent or minimize the effects of potential loss. Provide cost-benefit analysis to justify investment in controls to mitigate risks.
4. **Developing Business Continuity Management Strategies.** Determine and guide the selection of possible business operating strategies for continuation of business within the recovery point objective and recovery time objective, while maintaining the organization's critical functions.
5. **Emergency Response and Operations.** Develop and implement procedures for response and stabilizing the situation following an incident or event, including establishing and managing an Emergency Operations Centre to be used as a command centre.

6. **Developing and Implementing Business Continuity and Crisis Management Plans.** Design, develop, and implement BC and Crisis Management Plans that provide continuity within the recovery time and recovery point objectives.

7. **Awareness and Training Programs.** Prepare a program to create and maintain corporate awareness and enhance the skills required to develop and implement the business continuity management program or process and its supporting activities.

8. **Maintaining and Exercising Business Continuity and Crisis Management Plans.** Pre-plan and coordinate plan exercises, and evaluate and document plan exercise results. Develop processes to maintain the currency of continuity capabilities and the plan document in accordance with the organization's strategic direction. Verify that the Plan will prove effective by comparison with a suitable standard, and report results in a clear and concise manner.

9. **Crisis Communications.** Develop, coordinate, evaluate, and exercise plans to communicate with internal stakeholders (employees, corporate management, etc.), external stakeholders (customers, shareholders, vendors, suppliers, etc.) and the media (print, radio, television, internet, etc.).

10. **Coordination with External Agencies.** Establish applicable procedures and policies for coordinating continuity and restoration activities with external agencies (local, state, national, emergency responders, defense, etc.) while ensuring compliance with applicable statutes or regulations.

Research papers on BCM focus either on frameworks or separate technologies that are used in order to improve the availability levels.

Botha and Von Solms (2004) proposed a cyclic approach to business continuity planning. Gibb and Buchanan (2006) defined a framework for the design, implementation and monitoring of a business continuity management program within the context of an information strategy.

Pitt and Goyal (2004) see BCM as a tool for facilities management. Walker (2006) considers outsourcing options for business continuity. King (2003) introduced a term of "Business Continuity Culture" and underscored the fact that "If you fail to plan, you will be planning to fail".

Williamson (2007) found that in business continuity planning, financial organizations are ahead of other types of businesses. Bertrand (2005) researches the relationships between business continuity and mission-critical applications. He emphasizes the role of Replication Point Objective (RPO) and Replication Time Objective (RTO) in recovering from disasters. He stresses the role of replication technologies in providing better RPO and RTO values.

Yeh and Tsai (2005) tried to identify the factors affecting continuity of cooperative electronic supply chain relationships with empirical case of the Taiwanese motor industry. Gerber and Solms (2005) emphasize the need for a holistic approach that should include a carefully planned security policy, the use of technology and well-trained staff. Finch (2004) revealed that large companies' exposure to risk increased by inter-organisational networking and that having SMEs as partners in the SCM further increased the risk exposure.

Wann, Chwan, Ya, and Hui (2004) identify continuity as a behavioural factor No1 on business process integration in SCM. Bartel and Rutkowski (2006) proposed a fuzzy decision support system for IT service continuity management. They argue that IT service continuity management (ITSC) is typically part of a larger BCM program, which expands beyond IT to include all business services within an organization. ITSC management allows an organization to identify, assess and take responsibility for managing its risks or threats to IT.

In their article, Herbane, Elliott, and Swartz (2004) examined the organizational antecedents of BCM and developed a conceptual approach to posit that BCM, in actively ensuring operational continuity, has a role in preserving competitive advantage.

Cerullo and Cerullo (2004) states that, "...there is no single recommended plan for business continuity; instead, every organization needs to develop a comprehensive BCP based on its unique situation. The BCP process should address three independent objectives: identify major risks of business interruption, develop a plan to mitigate or reduce the impact of the identified risk, and train employees and test the plan to ensure that it is effective". Lewis, Watson, and Pickren (2003) pointed out that disaster recovery is receiving increasing attention as firms grow more dependent on uninterrupted information system functioning. Technologies called "hot-sites" and "cold-sites" used in disaster recovery management are variants and combinations of the technologies already explained in Chapters X and XI.

Hepenstal and Campbell (2007) provide some insights on transforming Intel's worldwide Materials organization from crisis management and response to a more mature BC approach. According to these authors, the BC-oriented approach improved Intel's ability to quickly recover from a supply chain outage and restoring supply to manufacturing and other operations.

Craighead, Blackhurst, Rungtusanatham, and Handfield (2007), considered business continuity issues within the supply chain mitigation capabilities and supply chain disruption severity. They proposed a multiple-source empirical research method and presented six propositions that relate the severity of supply chain disruptions. Stanton (2007) states "Fail to Plan, Plan to Fail".

All these works deal with BCM either from managerial or organizational perspective. However, they lack some guidelines for implementing numerous information technologies that can provide a platform for business continuity. It is an integrated operating environment which consists of several continuous computing technologies that plays crucial role in achieving high availability ratios and represents a main building block of an "always-on" enterprise information system.

Business continuity management consists of strategies, policies, activities and measures that business undertakes in order to survive when some sort of catastrophic event occurs. Even though it represents a managerial activity, at the end, business continuity in information age relies on high-ratios of application/data availability, reliability and scalability that should be provided by server operating environment. Therefore, business continuity management, being a part of the fifth dimension of Churchman's definition of the system, as defined in introduction, should be based on continuous efforts of integrating business continuity drivers into contemporary enterprise information systems.

In that sense, an enterprise information system should be managed from business continuity perspective in a way that it includes managerial and system administration activities related to managing the integration of business continuity drivers.

BUSINESS CONTINUITY PLAN AND DISASTER RECOVERY PLAN

Disaster recovery planning can be part of BCM, however, it can be defined separately. Several software packages, both stand-alone and client/server-based applications can be used while preparing a business continuity plan. Most of them are template-based, end-user oriented, and can be used by managers with no or less technical experience. An example of such a tool is the BCP generator (www.bcpgenerator. com). Continuity Central (www.continuitycentral.com) and Disaster Recovery Journal (www.drj.com) provide the lists of tools and packages that can be used for business continuity planning. Each of these tools puts an emphasize on some specific aspects of business continuity management. However, in general, there are some sections that each business continuity plan should have, such as:

- an explanation of BC philosophy and its importance for an organization, its vision and mission;
- short explanation of all risks and threats for a specific business, including IT-related risks and threats;
- identified critical IT resources, allowable downtime and outage times;
- failure/disaster assessment, notification and plan activation procedures;
- communication and escalation scheme, diagrams and "if-then" flowcharts, showing all necessary information on how to behave and what to do in case of a specific failure or disaster;
- human resources assigned for business continuity and their responsibilities;

- "how-to" explanations for some specific situations;
- information about IT-vendors, notification methods, response times;
- information about backup media locations, off-site backup locations;
- sys admin contacts, system administrator's and network administrator's passwords;
- recovery strategies, data recovery priorities, including activation time for specific hardware and software resources;
- emergency operating sites and their activation;
- and so forth.

Brett, Landry, and Koger (2006) defined a list of 10 common disaster recovery myths:

- Myth 1: The Only Disasters to Plan for are Natural Disasters
- Myth 2: A Mock Test Really Tests Disaster Recovery
- Myth 3: Attacks and Hacks Are Only External Threats
- Myth 4: Untested Disaster Recovery Hot Sites
- Myth 5: Conference Rooms Are Adequate Disaster Recovery Sites
- Myth 6: Disaster Recovery Can Be Implemented Later
- Myth 7: Equipment Will Be Available During and After the Disaster
- Myth 8: Back-Ups Work
- Myth 9: Disaster Recovery Can be Planned Individually
- Myth 10: Everyone Knows What to Do

They argue that by dispelling these 10 common myths, organizations can better plan, develop, and test true DR plans. DR planning is an ongoing task, not a one-time goal, so capital budgets must include items for maintaining DR sites and equipment.

CERT (COMPUTER EMERGENCY RESPONSE TEAM)

The growth of Internet accompanied by development and proliferation of Internet technologies, increasing levels of business' reliance on Internet, sophisticated Internet-based intrusion techniques, created a need for additional technologies and facilities that are to be installed and implemented on national levels. Addressing the problems with availability, reliability and security of computing facilities and infrastructures attracted an attention by scientists, businesses, developers, IT vendors and state organizations. This led to establishing of the organizations on national levels in order to help businesses in coping with IT-related risks and threats coming from Internet and business environment (attacks, accidents, failures, etc.).

CERT is such a project. It stands for computer emergency response team and refers to an organization or US-federally founded research project operated by Carnegie Mellon University (www.cmu.edu) and its Software Engineering Institute (SEI, www.sei.cmu.edu). This project aims at using appropriate system management technologies and best practices in order to resist attacks on networked systems, reduce potential damages and ensure continuance of critical computing operations and services. Another term—CERT/CC is a component of the CERT program and is devoted to CERT Coordination Centre.

The United States Computer Emergency Readiness Team (US-CERT, www.us-cert.gov) is a partnership between the Department of Homeland Security and the private and private sectors established in 2003 to protect the nation's Internet infrastructure. Similar centres exist in other countries as well, for instance Aus-CERT is the national Computer Emergency response Team for Australia (www.auscert.org.au).

STANDARDS AND LEGISLATION RELATED TO RISK MANAGEMENT AND BUSINESS CONTINUITY MANAGEMENT

Businesses apply several approaches in order to avoid (reduce, mitigate, manage) the IT-related risks and other business risks. This section attempts to offer a solution to the issue of avoiding IT risks and/or reduce consequences of events that present IT risks. There exist several standards and/or recommendations that specify the best methods for managing information resources. In addition to standards prescribed by international standardization agencies, various national standards and recommendations and best practices of various private companies are used. Some of the standards that include the function of managing information resources are explained in this section.

All kinds of risks that are related to information technologies and their potential threats to business should be a part of an integrated risk management on organizational level. Risk management is an ongoing process designed to assess the likelihood of an adverse event occurring, implement measures to reduce the risk that such an event will occur and ensure the organization can respond in such a ways to minimize the consequences of the event. IT security is a key area for risk management in modern organizations (Slay & Koronios, 2006).

There are several ways of controlling and managing risks, however, it has to be identified as an ongoing process which comprises the following steps.

- Identifying the risk in order to act proactively (in advance), rather than react to an event that already occurred.
- Risk assessment—assessing the importance of the risk to a specific business. If the risk is assessed to be a serious one, then some future actions should be planned.
- Risk mitigation in two forms: risk reduction and impact reduction. Risk reduction measures should reduce the probability of the risk occurring while impact reduction efforts try to reduce the costs of some bad event.

The first point to stress is that IT risks must be viewed as a part of the whole process of risk management. Therefore, IT risk management must be a part of ERM program. On the other hand, since IT risks are distinctive, there exists a set of dedicated tools for managing IT risks. The level of protection provided by the security management system is significantly higher than in cases of ad-hoc approach or implementation of only technical and system-related mechanisms.

STANDARDS FOR INFORMATION SYSTEMS SECURITY MANAGEMENT

Today's business is constantly under a pressure not only from customers, suppliers and competitors but from regulatory requirements as well. Table shown in Figure 13.1 summarizes some of these regulations.

Today, there exist several standards and sets of recommendations that specify the best methods for managing IT functions of a company. In addition to standards prescribed by international standardization agencies, various national standards and recommendations and best practices of various private companies are used. Some of the standards that include the function of managing information security are:

- ITIL (Information Technology Infrastructure Library) is a collection of best-practice solutions achieved in practice of managing IT services issued by the British Office of Government Commerce
- COBIT (Control Objectives for Information and related Technology) issued by ISACA (Information Systems Audit and Control Association) created as a framework for establishing control of the relationship of IT processes and business requirements.
- **NFPA 1600** The North American business continuity standard (www.nfpa.org). NFPA 1600 is the Standard on Disaster/Emergency Management and Business Continuity Programs, was prepared by the Technical Committee on Emergency Management and Business Continuity. It was issued by the Standards Council on December 1, 2006, with an effective date of December 20, 2006, and supersedes all previous editions.

Figure 13.1. Regulatory requirements for electronic data (Source: Transform Magazine 08/2004)

Regulatory Requirements for Electronic Data	
Regulation/ Data Type	**Data Covered**
Uniform Electronic Transactions Act/ All	Electronic signatures, e-mail, and records; same validity as manual signatures and paper transactions
Sarbanes-Oxley Act/Financial	All records, including e-mails and all audit-related documentation (accounting firms) retained for five years
SEC 17 CFT Part 210/ Financial	All work papers and other audit-related documents for financial statements retained for seven years
SEC Rule 17a-3, 17a-4/ Financial	Certain business records retained for three years, memos, e-mails, and other correspondence; all information related to the opening or maintenance of a customer account retained for six years
NASD 280(b)(17)/ Financial	Log of all options-related background and financial info maintained at both branch office and supervisory office of branch retained for three years
Fair Labor Standards Act; Nat'l Labor Relations Act/ HR	Certain HR records retained three years
Employee Retirement Income Security Act/HR	Any correspondence relating to eligibility and wage and hour records for determining retirement benefits retained indefinitely
ADA/HR	Personnel records of those who are involuntarily terminated for one year
OSHA/HR	Records of medical exams and records of hazardous materials exposure monitoring retained for duration of employment plus 30 years.
HIPAA--Healthcare	E-mail and correspondence related to patient request to modify records retained for 6 years. All patient records for two years after death in data center with guaranteed uptime and security

- ISO/IEC 17799:2005 (The Code of Practice for Information Security Management)—is an international standard for managing information security.
- ISO/IEC TR 1335 (Guidelines for the Management of IT Security) is a technical document that includes information and instructions on IT security, both from management aspect and from implementation aspect.
- ISO/IEC 15408 (Security Techniques—Evaluation Criteria for IT Security) is used as reference for review and certification of IT products and services.
- Risk Management Standard (IRM) as a result of the efforts made by the major risk management associations in the UK including the IRM, AIRMIC and ALARM.
- TickIt was issued by the British standards institute and is use for review and certification of software quality management systems.

- Internal Control—Integrated Framework was issued by COSO and includes a framework whose application will improve the process of financial reporting through improved internal control processes.

Implementation of risk management methods, techniques and procedure depends on the type of business. Several industries developed specific frameworks for risk management. These frameworks include regulations, methodologies, technologies, and so forth. In the section that follows, an example related to banking sector will be described.

One of the greatest risks that IT can introduce to banking is inadequate use of capabilities offered by the constant improvement process taking place in this area, and consequently reduce the bank's competitive power. Therefore, from the risk management point of view, it is necessary to view IT operations as a whole, and information security management as a part of that whole. Bielski (2008) states that some think of business continuity as doing what is necessary to set up a "shadow" organization that will take you from incident response through various phases of recovery.

For the majority of above-mentioned security principles there are technologies that can contain the solution or a part of the solution for certain security issues in an organization. For certain smaller organizations implementation of adequate technological solutions can present the solution for most IT risks; for banks, however, that is not the case, but technology must be used within an ordered system that can rely on standards examined in the previous section.

Who is responsible for creating the plan, implementing information security standards and applying technological measures for improvement of information security system?

It has to be emphasized that every employee of the company and the company itself has a duty to develop the culture of business risk awareness resulting from faulty management of information security. From this point of view, information security is not only responsibility of the IT department, but it also includes many non-technological aspects: business continuity management, physical security and fraud risks. This proves that information security is a part of the integrated risk management process as a whole on company level whose structure has been explained in the risk management section.

The peculiarity of the information security management is the staff sufficiently knowledgeable for maintaining specific aspects of planning and administration. The organization of this function depends on the size and the type of the company. In case of banks, for instance, this function should be performed on at least two levels. The first is the manager level (or department level—depending on the size of the bank), whose responsibility is planning, managing and monitoring the operations related to information security and, in cooperation with managers of other business units and branch offices, applying into practice policies and guidelines approved by the management and supervisory board. The second level is the security professionals working on the implementation and administration of technological solutions.

However, although there exist formal responsibilities, effective security organization depends on cooperation between the management, auditing, legal department, heads of business units, physical security staff, IT managers, administrators, and all employees.

THE BASEL II REGULATIONS[1]

Today's businesses must comply with legal regulations. Companies operating on multinational markets have to comply with several legal regulations created by public laws on national or international level. For instance, the Sarbanes-Oxley Act (SOX) in the USA and Basel II in Europe.

New Capital Accord, also known as Basel II, is a set of recommendations issued by "The Basel Committee on Banking Supervision" (hereinafter: the Committee) regulating the adequacy of banks' capital in relation to risk exposure. Basel II provisions apply to internationally active banks in G10 countries. The European Union adopted a Directive (CAD3) rendering the provisions of the Accord compulsory for all banks in EU member countries by 2007.

Basel Capital Accord of 1988 is the first internationally recognized agreement that defines the measures for establishing minimum capital requirements for banks. The Basel Committee designed the Capital Accord of 1988 in the manner that it could have been applied in several banks and several legal systems. The essence of the Accord was to advise banks to divide their clients according to type (governments, corporations, population, etc.). Each risk exposure resulting from business relationships (loans, guarantees, letters of credit, etc.) with the same types of clients, disregarding possible differences for each individual loan, carries the same risk weight factor when determining the capital requirements. The framework established by the New Accord puts more emphasis on risk management in banks and "rewards" the banks with better risk management with lower capital requirements. This will be achieved by bracing the capital requirements and potential credit loss and introduction of new capital requirements aiming to cover any potential loss resulting from operational errors. In order to reconcile the requirements for improved risk management and wide acceptance of the Accord, the New Capital Accord includes several approaches, from those easily applicable, to more advanced ones taking into account improvements in risk management and adjusting the minimum capital requirements accordingly.

Basel II is based on three pillars, each defining a different area and each logically following the previous one. The first pillar regulates capital adequacy, the second pillar defines the control of procedures and processes defined in the first pillar, and the third pillar deals with disclosure of the results.

The following section provides a short summary of the three pillars.

The first pillar deals with calculation of the minimum capital requirements for credit, operational and market risk (minimum regulatory capital—MRC). The MRC is defined as a ratio of the bank's total capital and the sum of risk-weighted assets—RW, including the components related to the credit, market and operational risk. The MRC must not be lower than 8%. The secondary capital must not exceed 100% of the core capital (Basel II, 2004).

MRC = (Total capital / (Credit risk + Operational risk + Market risk))*100% => 8%

During the transition period, scheduled to last until the end of 2009, banks will be required to calculate the MRC in accordance with the provisions of the 1988 Accord and this value will be used as the floor limiting the lowest level of the MRC calculated in accordance with Basel II.

Credit risk is the risk that an agreeing party will fail to fully settle its liabilities by maturity. The bank can perform the measurement of the exposure to credit risk by selecting one of the following approaches:

1. **Standard approach**. Standard approach (SA) has been designed to be applicable to any bank. This approach breaks down a bank's credit portfolio into a small number of risk categories. Each of the categories has a risk weight factor defined by external rating institutions. Depending on the classification of the loan in respect to individual categories, the loan is assigned a risk weight factor which is subsequently multiplied by the debt amount, resulting in an amount included in the credit risk.
2. **Internal ratings based (IRB) approach.** The main difference between the SA and IRB is that the parameters used in the process of measuring the credit risk are defined by the bank itself. These parameters are:

- Probability of default—PD is calculated on the basis of a statistical analysis of previous credit losses and represents the possibility that the loan will not be repaid during the observed time period.
- Exposure at default—EAD is calculated as the amount of the outstanding debt at default.
- The fraction of the liability that cannot be recovered following loss (loss given default—LGD).

Operational risk is a risk of loss caused by inadequate internal processes, procedural errors, human errors, system errors or external events. Basel II identifies three methodologies for determining operational risk:

1. **Basic indicator approach—BIA** implies that the amount of capital charge is calculated as 15% of the bank's average income over a period of three years.
2. **Standardized approach,** unlike the BIA, implies that the average income is divided into income generated from various business lines. For each of the lines a percentage is defined and used as a basis for determining the capital charge for the respective lines. The sum of capital charges across each of the business lines is the bank's total operational risk.
3. **Advanced measurement approach—AMA** is not based on any fixed rules, but includes a high level of flexibility and self-discipline. In the Committee's words, "Banks will be permitted to choose their own methodology for assessing operational risk, as long as it is sufficiently comprehensive and systematic". The bank's compliance with the requirements for application of AMA is the subject of supervision.

The second pillar of Basel II, the supervisory process, not only ensures the adequacy of the bank's capital for engaging in business risks (as established in the first pillar), but also supports the bank in the processes of risk management and supervision. The Basel Committee has specified four key principles of supervisory review as a complement to comprehensive regulations issued in the document "Core Principles for Effective Banking Supervision and the Core Principles Methodology".

The third pillar of Basel II aims to achieve greater market discipline by means of improved disclosure of information regarding the bank's business. The idea behind this method of achieving market discipline is that, on the basis of acquired information, the market will be able to recognize and reward adequate procedures of risk management. In this manner, an increased pressure is placed on banks to improve their risk management strategies and, when deciding on the strategies, to select those implying reduced risk.

Work on the text of the Accord began in 1998 and was completed in June 2004. According to the schedule, internationally active bank in G10 countries should commence with parallel application of the Accord during 2006.

In July 2004 (only one month following the adoption of the final text of the Accord) the European Commission adopted "The new Capital Adequacy Directive, CAD 3", a directive transforming the Basel II into European Union legislation. In its scope, CAD 3 is considerably more comprehensive than Basel II, since it will be applied to all credit institutions and investment companies, unlike only to internationally active banks as is defined in Basel II. CAD 3 is a law that will be applied in the European Union, unlike Basel II, which is a voluntary agreement between supervisors from G10 countries. This resulted in a conclusion that all banks and financial institutions in EU will be required to apply the provisions of the Accord which should be adopted (and possibly adjusted) in the meantime by legislative and regulatory bodies in all countries.

Basel II was established as an agreement applicable to G10 countries that took part in its drawing-up. This fact demonstrates that it was designed to be applied in rich industrial and post-industrial countries, and not in developing countries which are not required to apply it. However, it is expected that the leading international financial institutions, the IMF and the World Bank will encourage developing countries to implement Basel II. In addition, all developing Eastern European and Western Balkans countries, on account of their aspirations to join the European Union, are required to adjust their regulations with regulations existing in the European Union, that is, to implement Basel II.

One of the major problems the developing countries will face is the fact that most companies in such countries do not have a credit rating, and a 100% risk weight factor will be used for those companies when applying the standard approach (except in cases of delays when a 150% is used). In this case, the banks applying the standard approach for calculating capital requirements have a less favorable position when competing with banks applying more advanced methods (usually foreign banks).

The advantage of foreign banks doing business in such countries is that they will use the IRB approach (foundation or advanced) in most cases, unlike domestic competitors who will use the standard approach, thus being able to make a more accurate assessment of the risk of a placement and simultaneously creating unequal conditions in other issues, such as: greater capital requirements for loans to population, problems with supervision conducted by local supervisors and supervisors from the country of origin, by different rules (Fischer, 2004).

Requirements placed on banks by the Accord do not merely ensure a balance of capital and risk exposure, they also result in an improvement of the risk management process. The information previously known only by employees responsible for risk management will, when a bank starts implementing the Accord, be fully available to a wide range of interested parties, including regulatory bodies, the market, shareholders, clients, and so forth, which will compel the bank to manage risk in the best possible manner. In order to achieve this, it is necessary to improve the quality of data and integration of the sources of data, in other words, modifications of the bank's entire information system are necessary.

The banks are required to calculate capital requirements for covering credit risk using a complex set of methods. Applications for supporting the procedure include: application for credit rating analysis, application for database maintenance including previous loss, credit rating history; collateral, guarantors and other security instruments data; applications for future potential loss assessment (computational simulation models); application for calculating capital requirements.

In order to calculate capital requirements for covering operational risk, the bank must, at least, develop an application for separating the income by business segments defined in the Accord and, using the output received and appropriate coefficients, determine capital requirements for covering operational risk.

In case that the bank decides to apply more advanced approaches which include modeling (IRB for credit and AMA for operational risk), it must ensure full transparency of the modeling process and enable flexibility of used models in terms that it is possible to improve the model by adding new data and using new patterns discovered using the application. The bank must also test all applications based on historical data, as well as conduct stress-test.

Information system requirements which must be met in order to ensure successful implementation of the supervisory procedure as the second pillar of the Accord are mostly reflected in system flexibility requirements, so as to enable easy implementation of corrections required by regulatory bodies during the supervisory process. In order to provide the supervisory process, banks have to incorporate a monitoring option into the system so that it is possible to trace the received results at any given time. The system must enable customization of output via modification of input parameters. During supervisory process, the bank has to provide evidence for validity of all parts of the system, including the internal rating system, the application for future loss assessment and the system for recording events related to operational risk.

In order to meet the requirements posed under the third pillar (market discipline) which refer to increased volume and quality of disclosure, the bank must ensure adequate reporting system integrated with the capital requirements calculation system.

When building risk management systems, one of the main issues is the method of implementation of the system. The method of implementation depends on the size of the bank, level of development of the risk management system, and the approach selected. If the bank has decided to apply foundation approaches for credit and operational risk (SA and BIA, respectively), it is not necessary to significantly adjust the risk management system, and further consideration is given to cases when advanced approaches have been selected.

Banks that have already set up satisfactory risk management system may select the incremental approach for harmonization of the system with the Accord requirements. This approach implies an analysis of the existing system and detection of inconsistencies with the provisions of the Accord and development of the system for the purpose of overcoming them. Such corrections might include writing new interfaces for communication between the parts of the system or writing new procedures for data processing, designing capital requirements calculators, and applying adjustments and drawing up reports as required by the regulatory bodies. Applying the incremental approach assumes calculation of regulatory capital in each of the bank's units and subsequently consolidation of received results on bank level followed by reporting for the bank as a whole.

The advantages of such system implementation are the costs of implementation, since only corrections to existing system are applied, as well as the speed of implementation achieved through implementation being simultaneously conducted in several organizational units.

Potential flaws of this approach are: risk of failure to meet the requirements from the second pillar related to the bank's obligation to provide evidence for capacity for risk management, and only to ensure capital requirements; possible failure to meet the requirements of the Accord as a result of lack of consistency and integral approach; lack of an integral perspective of client data (single client's data can be placed in several organizational units); impeded exchange of information between the organizational units, particularly in terms of using common databases including operational risks data; each modification to the Accord must be implemented in all organizational units; higher maintenance expenses arising from the necessity to maintain a separate system in each organizational unit; existence of a large number of potential "single points of failure" (IBM, 2003).

This approach is possible in smaller banks with less organizational units, however its application in larger banks with numerous organizational units presents a risk.

Unlike the tactical approach, the integral approach implies a development of a new risk management information system at bank level meeting the standards set by the Accord. Such approach provides for consistency and greater control over subsystems when compared to the tactical approach. The main feature that separates these two approaches is that the integral approach implies storage of data in which data is located in a joint format and is used as entry into the capital requirement calculation system. The information system supporting such approach must be expandable, both in terms of amount of data and in terms of supporting new types of data. The system also has to be modular in order for single modules to be upgradeable in cases of modifications of regulatory requirements without interrupting other parts of the system.

Information system for an efficient implementation of the integral approach could be made from following subsystems:

- Data sources—Various internal and external sources of data necessary for assessing risk exposure.
- Integration and data collection system.

- Data storage
- Capital requirements calculation system—Performs tasks of calculating parameters necessary for assessing risk exposure. It is based on complex mathematical models and can be purchased in the market in the form of finished sets.
- Processed data storage (data marts)—contains information on certain problems simultaneously supporting end-user requirements in single organizational unit and summary data.
- Reporting system—provides reports for regulatory bodies, public, and bank management. It should use OLAP (on-line analytical processing) tools for multi-dimensional analysis and Data mining methods for detection of causes and trends in order to achieve most benefits from the collected data. In addition to hard copies, it generates reports in XML and XBRL formats which ensures system flexibility.

When examining this model, it is necessary to take into account the feedback that, based on results of potential risks, suggests corrective actions to be taken on the original system for the purpose of decreasing risk.

When planning and designing a credit risk management system, Committee recommendations need to be taken into account regarding the fact that the entire process needs to be integrated, that is the information used for assessing the risk exposure of a loan must be the basis for approving new loans. Therefore, it is necessary to integrate automated procedures into the system that follow the course from approving the loan to managing the credit portfolio.

In order to meet the requirements for credit risk management prescribed by Basel II, most banks in the region will have to invest heavily into information systems, particularly if they wish to apply the IRB approach. Financial Insight (SAP, 2003) noted that all the banks will have to make improvements in the following four areas:

- Standardisation of credit definitions—The Committee recommends that the credit rating be standardised and applied consistently across all the subsidiaries of the bank (this especially applies to large banks).
- Historical ratings data—The Committee's recommendation is to track ratings over time and compare them to defaults to determine the predictive value of the ratings.
- Credit reference data—All data related to the internal ratings (including: who determined the rating, when it was determined, where, and using which method) must be stored for future use and testing of the accuracy of ratings.

- Integration with the front-office—The ratings data used in the process of credit risk assesment should be used with the fron-office during the loan approval process.

In addition to these areas which are the focal points for all banks, information systems of banks wishing to apply the IRB approach should, in Financial Insight's opinion (SAP, 2003), include the following components:

Credit users information database including information related to their relationships to other entities that can expose the bank to credit risk,

- credit analysts should determine the risk exposure for each individual credit,
- single database of all transactions related to the entire portfolio,
- probability default estimation taking into account all available credit information,
- credit loss database,
- calculator to calculate reqired capital for capital charges on the basis of credit rating and exposure data.

The above-mentioned information clearly demonstrates that the implementation of the system for calculating the regulatory capital for securing against operational risk is more complex in cases when SA, and particularly AMA approaches are used then when implementing the BIA approach.

As is evident from the part discussing operational risks, in order to calculate the capital requirements in accordance with the BIA approach, it is only necessary to be acquainted with the total income of the bank, and in the somewhat more complex SA approach, it is necessary to know the origin of that income as divided into eight categories.

It is much more complex to calculate capital requirements in accordance with the AMA approach. This approach is based on collection and analysis of loss data and key risk indicators and this analysis are used as the basis for determining capital requirements.

As it has been clarified in the first section of the paper, the risk management system is primarily a process, and not a program set purchased on the market that will deal with all the issues of risk management. Obviously, information technologies should provide the key support during the implementation of the process. IS for determining capital requirements must include all of the following components:

- loss collection system and loss database,
- key risk indicators collection system and key risk indicators database,
- risk analysis system,

- capital requirements calculator,
- reporting system.

Using advanced information technologies in the bank information system can be observed as the key tool that ensures the operation of the bank and risk management. However, in the same time, it presents an additional risk factor. The fact that the information system presents additional operational risk for the bank has been included in the Accord as well. The methods of usage of information technologies in banking are continuously amended by new aspects, instead of detailed requirements related to the bank's information system, only general principles that need to be met have been included. The Committee only emphasizes the importance of a reliable information system, particularly in terms of information safety and system availability.

In order to define the operational risks posed by the IS in the bank, it is necessary to define the functions that the IS must include. In a nutshell, the functions can be divided into three groups (Chorafas, 2004):

- providing services to clients,
- meeting regulatory requirements,
- bank's management support (reporting, knowledge bases, etc.).

Each failure or difficulty of any of these functions presents an event that poses an operational risk to the bank's business. Such events can occur for several reasons, such as: hardware malfunctions, communication breakdown, system and application software errors, human errors, incompetent handling, internal frauds via software usage, external break-ins into the IS, natural disasters.

The main objective of the information security program is to enable the bank to achieve its business goals by implementing the IS managing all the risks related to application of information technologies. This objective can be divided into several categories. Related works usually include confidentiality, integrity and availability, also known as the CIA triangle. The central message of the CIA triangle is that IS security presents a point within the triangle, it is impossible to reach the maximum values of all three parameters of security simultaneously, but it is necessary to find a balance best suited to the needs of the company. In addition to these three principles of information security, there are several more important principles that need to be taken into account: privacy of information, monitoring, verification, and documentation.

The confidentiality principle states that private and confidential information must not be available to unauthorized persons. Confidentiality refers to stored data, data being processed and data being transmitted. Confidentiality is not concerned with whether the fact is confidential or not, but prior to applying this principle, it is useful to classify data according to secrecy levels. When applying this principle, the responsible person must decide what data should be available to whom and from what location. For example, a user can have access right for data on the internal network, but to be denied the right if remotely accessing the network. Confidentiality level has an immediate impact to availability level and can be controlled and implemented by using various mechanisms for access control. Another danger to confidentiality is the so-called social engineering, that is, attackers' attempt to get hold of authorized users' usernames and passwords using various non-technical methods.

Information system availability in banking operations is extremely important. Even the minor hang-up caused by communication problems, hardware malfunctions or software issues can cause operational losses. Internet banking and ATM networks require 24x7x365 availability of the bank's information system. Availability is the capability of authorized users to access data and having this access whenever necessary. Data availability can be limited for several reasons. In addition to limitations defined by the CIA triangle, there are many frequently unplanned reasons that reduce system availability.

Data integrity principle demands for data to be:

- protected from changes made by unauthorized users and processes,
- protected from unauthorized modification by authorized users and processes,
- externally and internally consistent (Krutz & Vines, 2001).

Apart from data, the integrity principle can be applied to the entire IS and, in that case, it denotes a system protected from unauthorized manipulation (e.g., configuration changes). In addition to various external and internal attacks aiming to alter the data in the system, integrity can also be violated by unintentional actions performed by authorized users. Privacy principle, although not being a part of the CIA triangle, has an effect on all of its parts. It determines which information can be made available to others (confidentiality), how that information is protected from manipulations (integrity) and how it can be accessed (availability).

There are different laws in different countries that govern privacy of user data. Banks are placed in a particularly sensitive position since they possess financial data that is protected, especially for private persons, in most countries. In case that certain client's financial data is available outside the bank, the bank can face legal measure, and injured reputation is a certainty. Another aspect of privacy that can be examined is employee privacy and issues arise such as: monitoring of e-mails or Internet traffic. Prior to taking such actions, they need to be defined in security policies and organizational procedures and the employees must be made aware of the existence of such controls. Apart from these two issues, another concern is the data access of IT staff, who usually have unlimited access to data and thus present a great risk to data privacy.

Outsourcing is a process when a certain organization ("outsourcer") assigns responsibility for securing certain services to another entity ("insourcer"). Outsourcing has been present in the banking sector for a period of time, but mostly in small banks that were able to expand their scope of services with acceptable operational expenses (processing of credit card transactions, e-banking services, etc.). Since recently, outsourcing is being used in all banks regardless of their size. Often, in addition to services such as e-mail, web hosting, telecommunication services, application software development, and so forth, banks tend to move entire departments to other legal entities. As a rule, outsourcing is applied for processed and services that do not present "core" services of a company, that is, the bank.

The main reasons for using outsourcing are:

- insufficient resources for implementing appropriate technologies,
- lack of competent IT staff,
- shorter implementation time,
- lower expenses of implementation of technology solutions.

The bank that uses outsourcing IT services is exposed to same types of operational risks as the bank that provides these services internally. In case of correct approach to outsourcing, a bank can significantly reduce operational risk by improving availability and quality of the system and services. Apart from the advantages that can be reached in the scope of operational risks, there exist the following dangers:

- attitude of the bank's management that outsourcing eliminates operational risks,
- failure to gain necessary knowledge and skills within the bank,
- management's belief that outsourcing solves all issues related to IT.

Prior to deciding whether to outsource certain IT services or the entire IT department, the bank's management must engage in all activities necessary for protection from operational risks. The outsourced services must be fully controlled, as if they are being performed within the bank. That is, prior to making a decision to outsource, the bank must fully comprehend the functioning of services being outsourced. The management must ensure that the major operations of risk management are being applied to outsourced services (Federal Reserve Systems, 2005):

- risk assessments,
- selection of service provider,
- contracts,
- controls,
- access to information,
- planning for backup solutions.

When selecting the service provider, it is necessary to assess the capabilities, financial power, reputation and the method of risk management of the potential partner prior to concluding the agreement. The agreement must clearly define the responsibilities of the agreeing parties, method of verification of performed responsibilities, accountability for possible damages arising from failure to meet agreement conditions.

In addition, it is necessary to examine the influence of outsourcing to the bank's operations, legal requirements, expenses, liquidity, capital, and influence on the internal reporting system. Outsourcing must not increase operational risks, nor reduce the bank's efficiency in performing everyday operations.

Over the previous several years there has been an increase in the number of users of e-banking and transactions conducted via e-banking. Simultaneously, there has been a significant increase in fraud attempts using these channels, such as the phenomenon of "phishing". For this reason, it is necessary to pay special attention to securing such services. Although the Accord does not cover this area, the Committee has issued a document under the title "Risk Management Principles for Electronic Banking" that deals with this subject. The document defines e-banking as "providing banking products and services to retail and corporate clients through various electronic channels, as well as large payments conducted electronically and other banking services that the clients can access electronically" (Basel Committee, 2003).

There are numerous other ways for application of information technologies in the bank to affect an increase of operational risk. Some of them are listed here:

- **Integration of existing applications and new modules.** When developing and implementing new applications, problems related to compatibility and integrity of data can arise, affecting not only the new application, but endangering operation of "core" systems. Also, new applications can degrade performance of the existing system.
- **Integration of information systems during mergers.** Nowadays, banks are constantly merging and growing. A specific issue related to this process is that there arise problems during integration of information systems. Since the

systems are different, often developed in different countries, it is necessary to either integrate the existing systems on reporting level or fully replace application software in one of the banks. Any of the approaches demands adequate risk management.

- **Hardware, software and communication equipment modifications or upgrades**. Each modification or upgrade of the information/communication system in the bank presents grave operational risk and must be appropriately followed by risk management measures.

An efficient and effective implementation of the information system to support Basel II is primarily dependent on the approach selected by the bank. In that sense, if the SA approach for credit risk and BIA approach for operational risk is selected, implementation of the supporting information system is simple and comes down to calculations in accordance with formulas defined in the Accord applied to data in the system without the need to implement complex BI systems and perform data transformation. In addition, in this case it is necessary to develop an appropriate reporting system for compliance with the first and the second pillars of the Accord.

In case of implementation of a more complex approach (IRB, AMA), development and implementation of the supporting information system is considerably more complicated and demands resources of various kinds (human, time, monetary) that can be sustained only by large banks.

As already pointed out, information technologies are the main tool in contemporary banking. This underscores the fact that each unexpected downtime in system functioning based on information technologies presents a risk for the bank, since it can cause a failure or difficult functioning of the operations. Such events can occur for several reasons, such as: hardware malfunctions, communication breakdown, system and application software errors, human errors, incompetent handling, internal frauds via software usage, external break-ins into the IS, natural disasters.

The Accord deals with requirements for the bank's information system as a part of the operational risk as a whole only through management principles considering that it is not possible to set strict rules on account of rapid technological changes and differences between banks. The Committee emphasizes the importance of reliability of the information system, particularly in terms of information security and system availability. This means that the stipulations of the Accord have provided banks with great freedom in deciding on the measures for reducing risk posed by implementation of information technologies as long as they are able to prove that these measures are adequate during the supervisory process.

However, in addition to reducing risks arising from implementation of information technologies, the bank must follow their development since the greatest risk that IT can pose to the bank's operations is inadequate usage and wrong implementation.

In the world of fast technological changes and new banking products based on these changes, it is of key importance that the bank is able to create a new product in a timely fashion with the least amount of risk, and this requires an IT department able to support is.

The main principles of information security between which the bank must find a balance are confidentiality, integrity and availability. It is not possible for a bank to simultaneously maximize the effects of each of the principles since they include contrary premises. In order to have a successful reduction of operational risk posed by implementation of IT in the bank's operations, it is necessary to do the following:

- implement information system management and information security standards,
- apply technological controls,
- establish adequate organization that ensures implementation of standards and controls.

The Basel II compliance regulations require using specific applications for effective risk management. These applications emerged couple of years ago, not only due to Basel II and other regulations, but as a result of several efforts of banking sector and financial institutions in coping with business pressures. They include several techniques for data collection, data structuring, data modelling, data analysis, risk management, reporting, scenario management, and so forth, to be used by financial service providers.

THE GARTNER'S BASEL II APPLICATION SOFTWARE MAGIC QUADRANT

Gartner's description of "The 2006 Basel II Capital Accord risk management application software Magic Quadrant" is presented.

The Gartner's Magic Quadrant (Gartner Report, 2006) focuses on those technology vendors that offer Basel II software applications that, at minimum, include risk engine calculation functions for credit, market or operational risk, and/or Basel II-specific data management capabilities.

Here is a list of the vendors and products included in the 2006 Magic Quadrant:

- Algorithmics: Algo Suite 4.5, Algo OpVantage
- Ci3: Sword v.6.0

- Experian: Transact SM, Probe SM (and Portfolio Monitoring Solution)
- Fermat: CAD-Basel II v.5.3
- Fernbach: FlexFinance Basel II
- FinArch (Financial Architects): Financial Studio Basel II v.3.0
- FRS: Financial Analytics Suite (version 2.12)
- IRIS: riskpro product (version 2.6)
- RCS (Risk Management Concepts Systems): OpRisk Suite v.4.0, INTECRA
- Reveleus (i-flex): Reveleus Basel II Solution v.3.0, Reveleus Operational Risk v.4.0
- SAP: SAP Basel II (April 2006)
- SAS: SAS Credit Risk Management v4.2, SAS OpRisk Monitor v3.2 SAS Risk Dimensions v4.2.1
- SunGard: BancWare Capital Manager v1.7
- Teradata: Financial Services Logical Data Model (FS-LDM) v7.0 and Value Analyzer

Gartner proposed the following set of the evaluation criteria:

Product/Service: Core goods and services offered by the vendor that compete in/serve the defined market. This includes current product/service capabilities, quality, feature sets, skills, and so forth, whether offered natively or through OEM agreements/partnerships as defined in the market definition and detailed in the subcriteria.

Overall Viability (Business Unit, Financial, Strategy, Organization): Viability includes an assessment of the overall organization's financial health, the financial and practical success of the business unit, and the likelihood of the individual business unit to continue investing in the product, to continue offering the product and to advance the state of the art within the organization's portfolio of products.

Sales Execution/Pricing: The vendor's capabilities in all pre-sales activities and the structure that supports them. This includes deal management, pricing and negotiation, pre-sales support and the overall effectiveness of the sales channel.

Market Responsiveness and Track Record: Ability to respond, change direction, be flexible and achieve competitive success as opportunities develop, competitors act, customer needs evolve and market dynamics change. This criterion also considers the vendor's history of responsiveness.

Marketing Execution: The clarity, quality, creativity and efficacy of programs designed to deliver the organization's message in order to influence the market, promote the brand and business, increase awareness of the products, and establish a positive identification with the product/brand and organization in the minds of buyers. This "mind share" can be driven by a combination of publicity, promotional, thought leadership, word-of-mouth and sales activities.

Customer Experience: Relationships, products and services/programs that enable clients to be successful with the products evaluated. Specifically, this includes the ways customers receive technical support or account support. This can also include ancillary tools, customer support programs (and the quality thereof), availability of user groups, service-level agreements, and so forth.

Operations: The ability of the organization to meet its goals and commitments. Factors include the quality of the organizational structure including skills, experiences, programs, systems and other vehicles that enable the organization to operate effectively and efficiently on an ongoing basis.

Market Understanding: Ability of the vendor to understand buyers' wants and needs and to translate those into products and services. Vendors that show the highest degree of vision listen and understand buyers' wants and needs, and can shape or enhance those with their added vision.

Marketing Strategy: A clear, differentiated set of messages consistently communicated throughout the organization and externalized through the Web site, advertising, customer programs and positioning statements.

Sales Strategy: The strategy for selling product that uses the appropriate network of direct and indirect sales, marketing, service and communication affiliates that extend the scope and depth of market reach, skills, expertise, technologies, services and the customer base.

Offering (Product) Strategy: The vendor's approach to product development and delivery that emphasizes differentiation, functionality, methodology and feature set as they map to current and future requirements.

Business Model: The soundness and logic of the vendor's underlying business proposition.

Vertical/Industry Strategy: The vendor's strategy to direct resources, skills and offerings to meet the specific needs of individual market segments, including verticals.

Innovation: Direct, related, complementary and synergistic layouts of resources, expertise or capital for investment, consolidation, defensive or pre-emptive purposes.

Geographic Strategy: The vendor's strategy to direct resources, skills and offerings to meet the specific needs of geographies outside the "home" or native geography, either directly or through partners, channels and subsidiaries as appropriate for that geography and market.

CHAPTER SUMMARY

Business continuity management as a separate discipline emerged more than a decade ago. Since then (mid of '90s), this discipline has been focusing on identifying the BC Management and BC planning in modern business, with the main goal being "Applying IT for a continuous process of keeping business in business". Chapter XIII identified shortly this field and described most important standards.

REFERENCES

Bartel, V. W. & Rutkowski, A. F. (2006). A fuzzy decision support system for IT service continuity threat assessment. *Decision Support Systems (article in press)*, Retrieved on July 18, 2006.

Basel Committee (2003). Basel committee on banking supervision, risk management principles for electronic banking. *Bank for International Settlements*, pp. 4.

Basel II (2004). Basel committee on banking supervision: International convergence of capital measurement and capital standards: A revised framework. *Bank for International Settlements,* June 2004, pp. 177.

Bertrand, C. (2005). Business continuity and mission critical applications. *Network Security, 20*(8), August 2005, pp. 9-11.

Bielski, R. (2008). Extreme risks, American bankers association. *ABA Banking Journal, 100*(3), ABI/INFORM Global, pp. 29-44.

Botha, J. & Von Solms, R. (2004). A cyclic approach to business continuity planning. *Information Management & Computer Security, 12*(4), pp. 328-337.

Brett, J. L., Landry, B. J. L. & Koger, M. S. (2006). Dispelling 10 common disaster recovery myths: Lessons learned from Hurricane Katrina and other disasters. *ACM Journal on Educational Resources in Computing, 6*(4), pp. 1-14.

Cerullo, V. & Cerullo, R. (2004). Business continuity planning: A comprehensive approach. *Information Systems Management, Summer 2004*, pp. 70-78.

Chorafas Dimitris N. (2004). Operational risk control with Basel II: Benefits and implementation procedures. *Elsevier Butterworth-Heinemann*, p. 91.

Craighead, C. W., Blackhurst, J., Rungtusanatham, M. J. & Handfield, R. B. (2007). The severity of supply chain disruptions: Design characteristics and mitigation capabilities. *Decision Sciences, 38*(1), pp. 131-155.

Deloitte & Touche/TPM Report (2006). Emphasis on business continuity management programs increases dramatically, Retrieved on July 31, 2006 from http://www.deloitte.com/dtt/press_release/0,1014,sid%253D2283%2526cid%253D109458,00.html.

Federal Reserve System (2005). Outsourcing of information and transaction processing. *Board of Governors of the Federal Reserve System*, Retrieved on May 3, 2005 from http://www.federalreserve.gov/boarddocs/srletters/2000/SR0004.htm.

Finch, P. (2004). Supply chain risk management. *Supply Chain management: An International Journal, 9*(2), pp. 183-196.

Fischer, S. (2004). Basel II: Risk management and implications for banking in emerging market countries. *Citigroup*, pp. 10-11.

Gartner Report (2006) McKibben, D. & Furlonger, D., Magic quadrant for Basel II software applications. *Industry Research*, Note, Number: G00143398.

Gerber, M. & Solms, R. (2005). Management of risk in the information age. *Computers & Security, 24*, pp. 16-30, Retrieved on July 18, 2006.

Gibb, F. & Buchanan, S. (2006). A framework for business continuity management. *International Journal of Information Management, 26*, pp. 128–141.

Hepenstal, A. & Campbell, B. (2007). Maturation of business continuity practice in the Intel supply chain. *Intel Technology Journal, 11*(2), pp. 165-171.

Herbane, B., Elliott, D. & Swartz, E. M. (2004). Business continuity management: Time for a strategic role? *Long Range Planning, 37*, pp. 435–457.

IBM (2003). IBM business consulting services, addressing the systems architecture implications of Basel II. IBM, p. 18.

King, D. L. (2003). Moving towards a business continuity culture. *Network Security, Elsevier*, pp. 12-17.

Krutz, R. L. & Vines, R. D. (2001). *The CISSP Prep Guide—Mastering the Ten Domains of Computer Security*, Wiley Computer Publishing, p. 8.

Lewis, W., Watson, R. & Pickren, A. (2003). An empirical assessment of IT disaster risk. *Communication of ACM, September 2003*, pp. 201-206.

Pitt, M. & Goyal, S. (2004). Business continuity planning as a facilities management tool. *Facilities, 22*(3-4), pp. 87-99.

SAP (2003). Technical requirements for Basel II compliance, www.sap.com/banking.

Slay, J. & Koronios, A. (2006) *Information Technology Securitiy & Risk Management*, Wiley.

Stanton, R. (2007). Fail to plan, plan to fail. *InfoSecurity, November/December 2007*, pp. 24-25.

Williamson, B. (2007). Trends in business continuity planning. *Bank Accounting & Finance, August-September 2007*, pp. 50-53.

Wu, W. Y., Chiag, C. Y., Wu, Y. J., & Tu, H. J. (2004). The influencing factors of commitment and business integration on supply chain management. *Industrial Management & Data Systems, 104*(4), pp. 322-333.

Yeh, Q. J. & Tsai, C. L. (2001). Two conflict potentials during IS development. *Information & Management, 39*, pp. 135-149.

REAL WORLD CASES

London's Community in Action
Adapted from: http://www.business.att.com/nx_resource.jsp?repoid=Topic&rtype=Article&rvalue=nv_londons_community_in_action&repoitem=business_continuity&segment=ent_biz

The London transport bombings on July 7, 2005, killed 52 people, injured a further 700 and impacted thousands of firms, large and small. But contingency preparations ensured that further catastrophe was avoided. Now recovery plans have been revised by the different sectors affected, and enhanced in light of direct experience.

Few organizations have had their disaster planning put to the test like Transport for London—the body that runs the capital's transport system. Without warning, three bombs went off in underground trains during morning rush hour near the center of London followed by another in a bus a short while later. However, regular multi-agency testing of plans, training for all staff and effective communications networks meant that Transport for London was not caught unaware by the terrorist action. "Processes stood up very well," says Nick Agnew, Head of Safety and Contingency Planning at Transport for London. Over 200,000 people were evacuated from the underground within an hour, and 85% of the services were running the following day.

Transport for London followed command and control processes laid out by the London Emergency Services Liaison Panel (LESLP)—a group set up to ensure collaboration between different agencies in planning for, and responding to, a major incident. Fortunately, a large international week-long exercise had been carried out in the capital the previous April, which was "distressingly close" to the July incident, Agnew says. A key result was that "emergency counterparts knew each other" and did not waste time figuring out who they should be liaising with on July 7th. Various types of network communications played an important role, Agnew says, including Transport for London's own internal phone network, which eased communications with the affected sites, use of the bus radio network to coordinate the transport of wounded passengers to hospitals, messages sent via pagers and, crucially, the underground train radio network itself. The bombings have "reinforced the need for effective and comprehensive underground communications," Agnew says. Moves being taken to enhance these include improvements in the coverage available to partner services working below ground and the enabling of mobile phone use in the platform areas, although some concerns were initially expressed about the possible use of the latter by terrorists. Of less doubt is the drive to improve the coverage and quality of CCTV images. All important adjustments, but one lesson in particular stands out: people often react well in a crisis, but the workforce needs prior instruction.

Preparations also paid off for the British Medical Association (BMA), the professional association for doctors in the country, with around 140,000 members. The fourth bomb exploded on a bus outside its headquarters. Recovery plans were compounded as the building was sealed off for 12 days, and no access was allowed to the IT infrastructure. "We were caught in the middle," says CIO Poli Avramidis. The business continuity plan (BCP)—non-existent when Avramidis joined the BMA four years earlier—was put into action and, following evacuation of the building, an emergency team comprising the chief executive, three directors and the CIO coordinated all efforts. Although there were delays in getting the backup site running—not to mention the difficulty of moving staff there—the BMA's network infrastructure allowed the organization to carry on. Staff were sent to satellite offices around the country or to work from home, the website was used to update staff, and BlackBerrys and other devices were pressed into service for mobile communication (although most were unusable in the first two hours after the explosion).

Avramidis calculates that the BMA lost only a fraction of a potential £2 million that would have been lost had the plan failed or not been formulated. However, he admits it would have been a different story had the BMA lost its communications infrastructure. The association has made some adjustments to its BCP. For example, radio-wave Motorola devices have been supplied to key staff to use instead of mobile phones, in light of the cellular network failures. "Battle-boxes" have also been installed, which contain, among other things, passwords that can be taken out of the office when evacuated. Deployment of its IP VPN has been accelerated, with greater use of security tools to remotely access data on PCs. The BMA is also now looking at outsourcing its communications rooms to increase resilience and improve disaster recovery.

Also caught in the crossfire was the UK retailer Marks & Spencer, which has a large branch near the entrance to Edgware Road underground station where one of the bombs went off. Phone activity erupted immediately thereafter: "The Business Continuity Manager gets 20 to 25 phone calls in the first 5 to 10 minutes after a major incident has been reported," says Trevor Partridge, Head of Business Continuity at M&S. Although the company prioritizes business continuity and had a crisis management team established, the phone system failed in the immediate aftermath. The team was unable to convene for an hour because the members were in different locations—central London and Heathrow. And even though it was tested successfully beforehand, the audio-conferencing system did not work. M&S has since outsourced audio-conferencing to a managed services provider and can now connect more than 100 people together at any given time. It has also set up a large crisis management center at its data center at Heathrow, so a team can assemble there if central London is unsafe. As further measures, M&S has set up a portal for "wartime" communication for staff, and senior managers are sent on day-long courses in business continuity.

Across these industry sectors, the need for improved communications in the immediate aftermath of the event became unmistakably clear. An independent review published in June 2006[1] highlighted in particular the failures of communication between the different emergency services, as well as within their teams. Some staff were left unable to communicate with each other or with their control rooms, and rescuers at ground level could not talk to their colleagues underground. While there were variations as to the differing priorities for the varied sectors—transport, retail, finance and others—they all share one thing: a reliance on communications and networking.

DISCUSSION QUESTIONS

1. What is the business continuity plan?
2. How can a business continuity strategy itself provide a competitive advantage to an organization?
3. How might a business continuity plan help a company in case of disaster?
4. What is the role of IT staff in this plan?
5. Who are the crucial players and cooperators in creating a business continuity plan?
6. Why is it so important for continuous computing to drive business continuity?

7. What might happen if business continuoty plan was not set?
8. How does the business continuity plan affects the information system?
9. How do major server vendors address business continuity planning approaches?
10. Explain the difference between the ITIL (Information Technology Infrastructure Library) and COBIT (Control Objectives for Information and related Technology) standards.

Discussion Questions: Lessons Learned from Cases

1. What are the biggest threats to business continuity today?
2. How can a business determine its business continuity preparedness?
3. How important is to test the organizational business continuity plan?
4. How to address telecommuting possibilities within business continuity planning?
5. Explain briefly the ways how authorities of "Transport for London" ensured that further catastrophe was avoided.

ENDNOTE

[1] Compiled from Ibrahimovic, S., Bajgoric, N., Transition of the Banking Sector In BIH: Role of Information Technology in Basel II Implementation Process, ICES2006 Conference, School of Economics and Business in Sarajevo, October 2006

Chapter XIV
Business Continuity for Business Agility

CHAPTER OVERVIEW

Continuous computing technologies are employed in order to achieve business continuity from the business operations perspective. In the same time, these technologies are the main prerequisite for business agility as agility relies on available information and "always-on" information system that generates it. Business Agility and relations with business continuity technologies are briefly explained in Chapter XIV.

INTRODUCTION TO BUSINESS AGILITY

The concept of business agility or enterprise agility is introduced. The main framework for achieving business agility by employing information technologies is presented in this section.

Business agility (enterprise agility) is a term that has been coined recently as a result of the agile manufacturing paradigm which emerged in the beginning of '90s. Agility has several dimensions and contemporary businesses are seeking ways to become "agile organizations." Since the emergence of the agile manufacturing concept, information technology (IT) has been considered as one of major agility drivers. Several IT-related technologies are employed in supporting both manufacturing and management processes. This section aims at identifying major IT-based agility drivers and their features that are critical for enhancing the enterprise-wide agility.

Enterprise agility is a term that is also used today in describing accepting and implementing the "agile" philosophy in modern organizations. Several definitions of the agility exist, depending on the standpoint of authors.

According to Sanchez and Nagi (2001) agility is characterized by cooperativeness and synergism (possibly resulting in virtual corporations), by a strategic vision that enables thriving in face of continuous and unpredictable change, by the responsive creation and delivery of customer-valued, high quality and mass customized goods/services, by nimble organization structures of a knowledgeable and empowered workforce, and facilitated by an information infrastructure that links constituent partners in a unified electronic network. Sharifi and Zhang (1999) define agility as a concept comprising of two main factors: i) responding to change (anticipated or unexpected) in proper ways and due time and ii) exploring changes and taking advantage of them as opportunities. Katayama and Bennett (1999) explore the concepts of agility, adaptability and leanness and study relationships between them. Phillips and Tulandhar (2000) use the term agility or "agile response" interchangeably with the term "flexibility" and propose a model for measuring organizational flexibility.

Several agility attributes are identified and the ways of achieving them are proposed in recent research publications. Information technology has always been considered as one of major agility drivers. Different IT-related technologies are employed in supporting both manufacturing and management processes.

Sharifi and Zhang (1999) define a hypotheses in their research which says the following: information system/technology in its utmost level of timeliness, coverage, communication ability, data banking and interchange, and so forth, is a major differentiator of an agile manufacturing company compared to traditional systems. Gunasekaran (1999) emphasizes the role of information technologies in an effective integration of physically distributed firms in agile manufacturing and lists several computer-integrated systems that could be used for AM such as (i) MRP II, (ii) Internet, CAD/CAE, (iii) ERP, (iv) Multimedia, and (v) Electronic Commerce. In addition to satisfying the traditional requirements, an agile enterprise information system must be able to be reconfigured in a very short time and should be able to include parts of information systems from other companies if a virtual corporation is required to meet the market demand.

Cheng, Harrison, and Pan (1998) presented an approach in implementing agile systems based on the integration of artificial intelligence and Internet technologies with the conventional design and manufacturing techniques. Huang, Ceroni, and Nof (2000) describe the impact of modern IT on distributed, networked enterprise systems through three categories: (1) speeding up activities; (2) providing intelligent and autonomous decision-making processes; and (3) enabling distributed operations with collaboration along communication networks, claiming that all three categories lead to agility. Enterprise agility is considered in two main parts: business and organizational agility and operational and logistics agility.

Papaioannou and Edwards (1999) discuss how mobile agent technology can improve the alignment between IT systems and the real word processes they support. They argue that this technology can aid enterprise agility, particularly in distributed environments such as virtual enterprises. Yusuf, Sarhadi, and Gunasekaran (1999) define a list of the attributes of an agile organization in several decision domains such as: concurrent execution of activities, enterprise integration, information accessibility, decentralized decision making, technology awareness, continuous improvement, and so forth.

Information agility or informational efficiency represents the major prerequisite for agile management and means eliminating inefficiencies in accessing, exchanging and disseminating of all kind of information.

Simply put, business agility is an enterprise-wide response to an increasingly competitive and changing business environment, based on the following principles:

- Customer orientation and satisfaction, enriching the customer
- Reduced time-to-market
- Increased profitability
- Mastering the uncertainty
- Improving efficiency and effectiveness by continuous process improvements
- Enterprise-wide collaboration
- Cooperation
- Improving information access
- And so forth.

Information agility in contemporary business can be improved by easing and improving the information access. The job of IT people, both IT vendors, and IT staff in organizations is to make access to information seamless and easy, especially for managers. In contemporary conditions, it is not reasonable to expect the decision makers to spend their time for specialized training in order to be able to use any software. From the perspective of easiness of use it is the Web technology that can help in that sense. Web-to-host access tools are software products that ease the process of connecting to several types of data: legacy data, c/s applications, e-mails, faxes, documents, and so forth.

Both business continuity and business agility today rely on the following three sets of information technologies (Figure14.1):

Figure 14.1. Technologies for business continuity and business agility

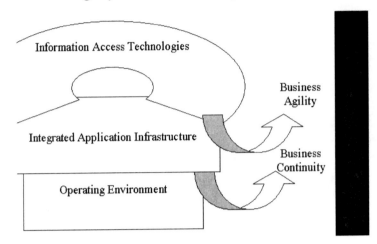

- Operating Environment Infrastructure
- Integrated application infrastructure
- Information access technologies

As can be seen from Figure 14.1, Information access technologies and integrated application infrastructure are important in boosting enterprise-wide agility while IT-solutions consisting of technologies that provide Operating Environment are critical for continuous computing and business continuity. Information access technologies and integrated application infrastructure are implemented today in the form of enterprise information systems. The newest versions of ERP suites integrate core business applications and Web-based or Portal-based access to data.

IDC (2007) defines "agile ERP" as an ERP infrastructure that possesses the ability to adjust to changing business conditions with minimal technical or business process intervention. Agile ERP applications can facilitate greater collaboration throughout the enterprise by ensuring data integrity to different project stakeholders, enabling them to update data structures on the fly and ultimately scaling the information warehouse to meet individual reporting needs even with significant increases in data volume.

INFORMATION ACCESS TECHNOLOGIES AND BUSINESS AGILITY

Information access technologies are described with regard to easing information access and enhancing business agility from managers' perspective.

Information access technologies include several solutions such as: GUI technologies, data access, data transfer, data conversion, indexing-retrieving-searching capabilities, portal-based solutions, mobile computing technologies, content transformation, and so forth. They aim at easing information access no matter where data is stored, in which format, how that data is accessed, and so forth. In that sense, an agile management support system (AMSS) can be defined as a subsystem of user interface that provides managers with an efficient and effective access to the information they need (Figure 14.2).

The primary goal of an AMSS is that the information it contains be easily accessible and retrievable by managers at the time they need it. AMSS does not have to contain all that information, rather it should provide a way of accessing it, no matter where that information is stored, and which device user connects from. Early efforts to develop such systems were limited to the implementation of terminal emulation access tools and PC/X Windows emulation programs. An extended scope of AMSS began with the advent of Internet and Web technologies. The structure of AMSS is very dynamic since it is based on the available data access technology. The lowest level of AMSS is based on using PC-terminal emulation tools, whereas the most sophisticated solutions include enterprise portal solutions and content transformation technologies.

Agility-enhancing integrated application infrastructure is based on information technologies that emerged over the last decade that helped in enterprise-wide data access and application-data integration such as: enterprise information systems for business-critical applications (ERP-SCM-CRM suites, Business Intelligence/Report-

Figure 14.2. Manager's computing devices and agile management support system

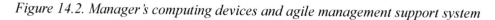

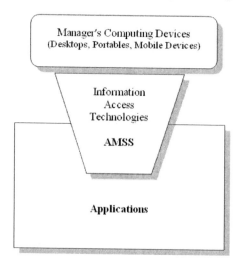

ing systems), Groupware, and videoconferencing technologies, Middleware tools, Web services and Intelligent Agents, Web-to-Host access technologies, Portable computing technologies, Content Transformation technologies, and so forth. All these technologies enable agility in a sense that they enhance information access from data integration standpoint.

Basically, there are four types of business applications: (1) transaction processing applications - applications that capture business data in the course of doing all business operations, (2) business intelligence applications that aim in improving decision making performances (3) messaging and collaboration applications, and (4) document management applications. Though these systems are separate, they are inter-related and some sort of integration is a prerequisite. Therefore, enterprise application integration tools play a critical role in every information system.

Consequently, in a virtual enterprise information system, the application platform consists of several applications such as (Figure 14.3):

- Transaction processing system
- Messaging and collaboration system
- Document management system
- Business intelligence system

Figure 14.3. Enterprise application platform

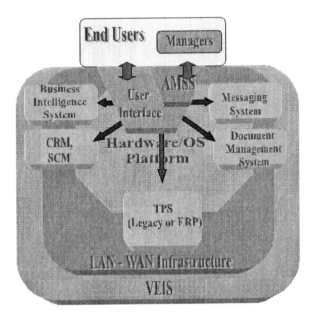

- CRM/SCM systems, as special cases of TPS for managing relations with customers and suppliers
- Enterprise application integration tools.

In the area of application platform the following technologies that emerged in the last ten years are of most importance for an efficient and effective data access:

- Web-based access to legacy systems
- Object-oriented application development paradigm and Distributed Computing
- Web-enabled applications
- ERP integrated suites
- Middleware (enterprise application integration tools)
- ASP model of running ERP applications
- SaaS

Web-based access to legacy systems. Legacy Systems (Legacy Data or Legacy Applications) refer to older or mature applications which were developed from the late '50s to the early '90s. Such systems are mainly mainframe systems, or distributed systems where the mainframe plays the major processing role and the terminals and/or PCs are used for application running and data uploading-downloading. Most companies are still relying on these platforms because mainframe systems are more secure, available, reliable, and scalable than UNIX and especially NT systems.

Ten years ago, both Gartner (www.gartner.com) and Meta Group (www.metagroup.com, acquired by Gartner in April 2005), estimated that 70–80% of all corporate data resided on legacy mainframes. This fact created a need for more efficient and effective access to legacy data. Several so-called Web-to-Host tools have been developed since then in order to ease the access to legacy data.

In information technology (IT) history, the invention of graphical user interface (GUI) was a revolutionary step in improving both efficiency and effectiveness of IT end-users. GUI interface has become dominant both in operating systems (e.g., MacOS, Windows, Linux) and in application software. After introducing Web technology in 1994, it turned out that Web browser is the most convenient way of using computers for end-users since it is completely based on a "mouse-click" operation. This became possible thanks to HTTP protocol, HTML language, and other Internet/Web related facilities.

The job of IT people, both IT vendors and IS staff in organizations is to make access to information seamless and easy, especially for managers. In contemporary conditions, it is not reasonable to expect the decision makers to spend their time for specialized training in order to be able to use any software. From the perspective of easiness of use it is the Web technology that can help in that sense. Web-to-host access tools are software products that ease the process of connecting to several types of data: legacy data, c/s applications, e-mails, faxes, documents, and so forth.

Web-to-host access tools as a specific subset of Web technology are used to improve and ease access to several types of information: legacy data, messaging system, electronic documents, business intelligence, and so on. Access to legacy data through user-friendly applications (standard client/server applications and Web-based applications for Intranets and Internet) requires a processing layer between the applications and the data. Web-to-host technology makes it possible for users to access the data stored on legacy hosts just by clicking a web link. What's more, it cuts the costs of software ownership through centralized management.

Distributed computing paradigm is a new framework within the object-oriented software engineering paradigm in which different parts of an application may be running on separate computers on LAN, WAN, or even Internet. There exist two main standards that are used for providing such application environments:

- CORBA (common object request broker architecture) is an architecture and specification for creating, distributing, and managing distributed program objects in a network. It allows programs at different locations and developed by different vendors to communicate in a network through an "interface broker." CORBA was developed by a consortium of vendors through the Object Management Group (www.omg.org).
- DCOM (distributed component object model) is a set of Microsoft concepts and program interfaces in which client program objects can request services from server program objects on other computers in a network. DCOM is based on the component object model (COM), which provides a set of interfaces allowing clients and servers to communicate within the same computer. Creators of CORBA and Microsoft have agreed on a gateway approach so that a client object developed with DCOM will be able to communicate with a CORBA server, and vice versa.

By introducing new approaches in application development, object-oriented paradigm has contributed to the overall agility within information systems. Applications have become more flexible, application components more reusable and scalable, as Dove (1995) pointed out "… Adaptability (Agility) actually became a reasoned focus with the advent of object-oriented software interests in the early 80s."

Web-enabled applications. With the increased deployment of client/server applications, system administration and version control have become a significant problem for IT professionals. One of the main advantages of legacy mainframe systems was that the application resided on a single system. There was no need of any software on the client side. This made the process of software upgrades much easier to manage. Web applications bring in a very similar advantage. In such a platform, the only software that is needed on the user's PC is the Web browser. Web-based application development paradigm can be considered in some sense as an environment very similar to a mainframe paradigm. Web server plays the role of legacy system whereas the Web browser replaces a text-based terminal.

ERP integrated application suites. Enterprise Resource Planning software is today considered as a system that aims to serve as an information backbone for the whole organization. The crucial point is in an efficient integration of all business processes with an emphasis put on reporting and business intelligence capabilities important for management. Enterprise Resource Planning (ERP) provides comprehensive information management for organizations. Even though ERP projects are costly and need several months to be implemented, in the last couple of years many companies have replaced their legacy systems with these new integrated suites. ERP systems employ client/server technology within, mainly, three-tier c/s platforms. This means that a user runs an application on a client computer (first tier) that accesses information from an ERP application (finance, HR, logistics, etc.), which is on application server (second tier). Applications use data from the third-tier data server, which is running one or more databases under DBMS. ERP software vendors are rearchitecting their applications to be used over the Internet, through Web-browser interface.

The major advantages of an ERP system include: integration of data from all business processes, easier information access for managers, stable and reliable data structure, customizable and adaptable application platform, module based infrastructure, GUI and Web-based user interface. Disadvantages include: expensive and lengthy to implement, many hidden implementation costs, maintenance is costly and time consuming, commitment to a single application vendor for mission-critical applications.

ERP is an enterprise-wide solution. The successful deployment of the ERP suite results in an enterprise that has an integrated information flow between different business functions, and even different business locations. ERP applications include support for many aspects of an internationally-based business (local currencies, taxes, etc.), therefore, they are very suitable for virtual enterprises. Norrish (1996) refers to ERP system as an "agile software for agile manufacturing." Ranganathan and Brown (2006) consider two kinds of organizational integration that are associated with information systems in general and ERP systems in particular: technical integration and business integration. They researched the ERP project variables within the relations of ERP investments and the market value of the firm.

Middleware. An efficient access to legacy data is important from application developer's perspective as well. The development of new c/s applications, which will exchange data with existing legacy systems requires a sort of middleware that overcomes the differences in data formats. Different data access middleware products exist and they are specific to a single platform, for example, RMS files on OpenVMS machines, IBM mainframes, or different UNIX machines. What is more important, application developers can build new Internet-based applications which will use data from legacy systems by using data integration standards such as: UML, OLE DB, ADO, COM, DCOM, CORBA, .NET, EJB, XML, J2EE, UDDI, WSDL, SOAP, and so forth.

Attunity Connect (www.attunity.com) is an example of data access middleware tool that provides an efficient data exchange between Windows platform and several host platforms such as OpenVMS for Digital Alpha and VAX, Digital UNIX, HP-UX, Sun Solaris and IBM AIX. Attunity products enable an access to non-relational data in almost the same way that relational data is accessed. Other examples include: ACUCOBOL from Acucorp/MicroFocus (www.acucorp.com), ClientSoft's ClientBuilder Enterprise (www.clientsoft.com). Recently, the middleware vendors have added a support for the newly created standard in application infrastructure – Service Oriented Architecture (SOA). For instance, Micro Focus' "SOA Express" provides the set of capabilities to integrate mainframe-based legacy applications with modern application development suites such as Windows .Net and J2EE environments in order to add GUI-based and Web-based access to legacy data. This suite supports an integration with a number of application servers such as Microsoft Server System, Oracle Application Server platform, IBM WebSphere application platform. It extends the viability of legacy platforms (e.g., COBOL), integrates home-grown mainframe legacy applications with new client-server and Web based applications, and provides access to legacy data from within a standard Web browser.

While middleware products serve as a data gateway between legacy systems and Windows-based c/s and desktop applications, Web-based application development products support building Web-enabled c/s applications (e.g., Microsoft's Visual Studio, Inprise-Borland's Delphi, C++Builder and JBuilder). Many Web-to-host products offer APIs to host systems that developers can use to build custom intranet applications, especially for reporting. This model usually includes taking data from host systems, converting them into HTML format and placing onto Windows Server's IIS that acts as Intranet server.

Another important area of business applications in which integration is needed is implementation of ERP systems. This activity usually means a lot of customization efforts. Many companies decide to continue with some legacy code and seek for a way of connecting ERP with legacy systems. New generation of enterprise integration application (EIA) or enterprise application integration (EAI) products provide that kind of integration (e.g., Prospero—www.oberon.com, CrossWorlds—www.

crossworlds.com, Level8 EAI products—www.level8.com, etc.). ERP vendors like SAP, Oracle, Baan and others are developing their own front-office solutions in order to achieve a higher level of integration. Also there is a need of an efficient and effective integration of ERP systems with messaging system, document management system, business intelligence system, and so forth. Therefore, the vendors of these applications provide ERP-gateways to integrate their programs with ERP systems. After the successful implementation of the ERP software, companies usually add business-intelligence tools to their ERP systems to enhance access to data and improve organizational decision making. ERP vendors provide such business-intelligence products the core of which is always a data warehouse (SAP Business Information Warehouse, Oracle Business Warehouse, PeopleSoft Enterprise Warehouse).

ASP model of ERP implementation. "Rent, don't buy" is a new approach in deploying corporate-wide business-critical applications. Application Service Providers (ASPs) are the companies that rent applications-running platforms, mostly those applications that are very complex and hard to implement (ERP, data warehousing, electronic commerce, customer relationship management). Actually, they emerged recently as a result of an effort to make ERP suite an application platform for small and mid size companies. Traditional approach in implementing ERP packages was based on a single license for this software that could cost thousands of dollars per seat (mainly between $2000 and $4000), but the real expense was in implementing these programs (consulting, process rework, customization, integration, testing). ERP implementation costs should fall in the range of $3 to $10 per dollar spent on the software itself. Unlike ISP (Internet Service Providers) - the companies that provide Internet access and standard Web hosting, ASPs help companies in such a way that they install, implement and manage complex applications on their sites and bill these services usually on monthly basis. They are providing application hosting services mostly by partnering with software vendors and networking companies. Rental fees include software customization, integration with other back-end systems and ongoing maintenance of the apps at fault-tolerant data centers.

ASP model of renting ERP and other business-critical applications represents an example of virtual business, in fact, this is the version of Business specialization-based model of VE. Companies preferring to focus on their business only may decide to outsource running business applications to another company which is specialized in it - application service provider - ASP. Application and data servers are usually located in ASP company, while applications and data are accessed on remote basis. The main prerequisite for this model of VE is a high-speed and reliable communications backbone.

New generation of hosting technologies called Software-as-a-Service (SaaS) or "On-Demand" computing that are evolutionary models of the ASP paradigm provide an opportunity for small and midsize businesses to migrate from their legacy systems to a Web-delivered ERP platform for business critical applications.

ERP vendors have also entered the arena of On-Demand computing or Software-as-a-Service (SaaS) by offering their enterprise applications on hosting basis. For example, SAP's new ERP suite called SAP Business ByDesign, formerly known by its code name A1S, is aimed at the midmarket, for use by businesses with 100 to 500 employees. The modules included in the suite are: manufacturing, purchasing, sales, marketing, accounting and human resources.

Most SMBs lack the necessary resources to hire and/or retain well-educated and experienced full-time application developers to develop business-critical applications, system administrators to administer operating platforms, network administrators to manage complex network environments. Therefore, they turn to renting applications from application service providers.

Business Intelligence vendors as well offer their BI suites on on-demand basis. For example, Business Object (acquired by SAP in October 2007, www.businessobjects.com) allows customers to deploy its BI suite called "Business Objects On-Demand" over the Web without buying servers and installing software.

Business Objects' "Business Intelligence On-Demand" suite is built on the CrystalReports.com SaaS platform, which gives subscribers access to several analytical techniques of that suite. The customers can perform several types of analyses on their in-house data, generate reports and even integrate data and results with Salesforce.com, an online customer relationship management system (platform as a service). These applications provide real on-demand reporting capabilities, including formatted reporting, dashboards, ad-hoc queries and ad-hoc analyses. For example, Salesforce.com platform has more than 35,000 customers, more than 700 applications, in 14 languages. Other examples of off-premise sources include: NetSuite and WebEx.

Business Objects' Business Intelligence OnDemand Includes

- A Data warehouse hosted by Business Objects
- An automated process of moving customer data into DW
- Several types of reports based on Business Objects' reporting tools such as Crystal Reports, Web Intelligence Reports, Crystal Xcelsius documents
- Web-based interface.

In general, enterprise-wide agility depends on so-called agility-enabling technologies in two main sets of business processes: manufacturing/services and management. Unlike agile manufacturing paradigm where several IT-related and manufacturing-oriented technologies are utilized to improve the level of manufacturing agility, the techniques and tools that can be applied in order to improve manager's agility are dominantly oriented to application-data access technologies. More than ever, today's managers need a seamless access to corporate information. In an information driven economy, every kind of information should be "mouse-click-away."

According to (HP-white paper, 2002), Gartner, Giga and META Groups emphasize agility as contemporary business strategy. Gartner pointed out that, "Progressive companies have adopted workplace agility as a competitive imperative." Giga calls agility a "critical element to deal with continuing innovation. Agility must characterize the business itself as well as the IT infrastructure and applications on which it depends."

Recent IDC Report (2006) states that architecting for agility can be a whole new mindset regarding how to think about designing and maintaining systems. Some practices that contribute to agility include establishing enterprise-wide standards, centralizing control and accountability of IT investments and services, utilizing automated change and configuration technologies at all levels of the environment, and establishing repeatable (and collaborative) processes.

IDC (2007) states that organizations should map their strategies to the following approaches:

- Organizational agility has to start with an integrated and robust business system that is scalable, easy to maintain in-house, and flexible enough to harness available resources to better forecast, execute, and extend corporate objectives.
- The emphasis on agility calls for continuous business process improvement that works best in small teams with ready access to real-time information and reliable data to anticipate change, generate innovative ideas, and reach decisions that are based on market-driven feedback and enterprise-wide collaboration.
- Legacy systems will have to be replaced if they fail to provide the flexibility to adapt to the latest market conditions resulting from mergers, consolidations, demand shifts, or other changes that require constant adjustments of business processes and IT resources to support them

In short, an agile business is characterized by:

- Continuous data processing and data access operations.
- Easy, continuous, reliable, secure, and company-wide (local and remote) data access from decision makers' and other knowledge workers' computing devices.
- Continuous, reliable, and secure data access from customers within CRM platforms.

- Multi-platform data access, including support for all commonly used computing devices (desktops, portable computing devices, mobile phones).
- Better decisions through better access to business-critical information wherever and whenever required.

AGILITY DRIVERS

Information technologies are used in order to enhance business agility. This section explores such technologies in the form of agility drivers.

Unlike agile manufacturing paradigm in which several IT-related and manufacturing-oriented technologies are utilized to improve the level of manufacturing agility, the techniques and tools that can be applied in order to improve manager's agility are dominantly oriented to application-data access technologies. More than ever, today's managers need a seamless access to corporate information. That access is determined by several factors such as: a) computing device that is used, b) operating system's user interface, c) application interface, d) data/application availability, e) server's reliability, and so forth. Consequently, several IT-related factors can be identified in order to focus on those technologies that can enhance the level of manager's agility. Here, they are identified as "agile management IT drivers," or simply "agility drivers—AD" and presented in Figure 14.4.

Figure 14.4. IT-related agility drivers for agile management

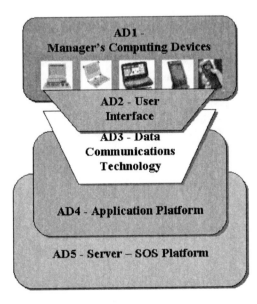

As can be seen from Figure 14.4, these five sets of information technologies that are defined as agile management drivers (AD) are as follows:

- AD1—Manager's computing devices
- AD2—User interface and data access technology
- AD3—Data communications technology
- AD4—Application platform
- AD5—Server and server operating systems platform

Agility drivers are characterized by:

- Agility attributes, in other words, the ways how these drivers can enhance the level of agility and
- Facilities and/or technologies that belong to that agility dimension.

Information access is determined by several factors such as: i) computing device that is used, ii) operating system interface, iii) application interface, iv) data/application availability, v) server's availability, and so forth. Consequently, several IT-related factors can be identified in order to focus on those technologies that can enhance the level of manager's agility, as well as the agility of all knowledge workers. Here, they are identified as "agility drivers—AD" and presented in Figure 14.5.

Figure 14.5. IT-based agility drivers, attributes and technologies

Agility Drivers	Agility Attributes	Agility Enhancing Technologies
AD1: **Computing devices**	Portable computing Mobile computing Integration of communication and computing devices Pervasive computing Contextual Computing	Portable and mobile computing devices: Notebooks, Hand-held PCs, PDAs, Tablet PC, GSM devices, Smart phones, BlackBarry devices, iPhone Embedded Computing technologies GPS devices RFID
AD2: **Information access technology**	User-friendly interface Integrated information access Remote/mobile access Retrieving and Searching capabilities	GUI-based OS-app interface Browser-based interface Portals and Mobile Portals Search engines WAP technology Virtual Keyboards Multi Touch Screen

continued on following page

Figure 14.5. continued

Agility Drivers	Agility Attributes	Agility Enhancing Technologies
AD3: Fast and reliable access technologies	Faster LAN/WAN communications Wireless LAN-WAN-Internet Data/voice/video integration Remote access Groupwork and Real-time collaboration Virtual meetings Telecommuting Networked enterprise Virtual enterprise/Virtual Reaility	High-speed LAN/WAN technologies Remote access technologies Wireless technology/Wi-Fi Video conferencing/Web Conferencing Groupware technology GSM devices Smart phones IP telephony HTML/XML/WML/VRML protocols
AD4:Integrated application platform	Web-based access Thin client/server platforms Application/data integration SaaS (Software as a Service)	Internet technology Object-oriented paradigm and Distributed computing Web 2.0 Web-enabled applications ERP suites Business Intelligence, Data/Text/Web Mining Middleware ASP app platform and SaaS Web services - intelligent agents Information and Knowledge Discovery Data Visualization and Visual Interactive Modelling
AD5: Server operating platform	Reliability Availability Scalability Serviceability Integratibility Manageability	SMP-clusters 64-bit computing RAID technology VLM/VLDB support Fault tolerance ServerWare Internet bundled servers

MANAGER'S COMPUTING DEVICES, DATA ACCESS TECHNOLOGY, AND BUSINESS AGILITY

As said before, today's business computing is dominantly based on two main types of information system architectures: a) an old-style mainframe environment, and b) several models of client-server architectures. In a mainframe-based operating environment, mainframe computer does the whole processing; dumb terminals and/or emulation programs on PCs are used just to enter/get data. Client-server architectures consist of servers and clients with applications running on server computers.

When managers' computing devices are considered, in contemporary business computing the following types of information access can be used:

- An old-style terminal-based access—still in use, but mainly replaced by PC-based terminal window applications or Web-to-host tools
- Desktop PC-based access
- Portable devices-based access.

Desktop (Terminal/PC-based) Access. The vast majority of end users access corporate information from desktop computers. Depending on the application platform, the following programs are used:

- Traditional data access technology: terminal-based access and PC-terminal emulation programs in case of legacy applications, PC-X Windows programs, and standard client programs within c/s application platforms.
- Web-to-host technology: Web-to-host access tools and Web-enabled client programs within c/s application platforms.
- Portal based access: Enterprise Information Portals.

Traditionally, the access to legacy data has been based on dumb terminals and PC-based terminal emulation programs. In the same time, access to corporate data has always been determined by type of information architecture, which an information system is built on. A client/server-based information architecture divides processing into two major categories: clients and servers. Each client/server application has its own **client program** that needs to be installed and maintained on all client machines. However, today as more users wish to standardize on **Web browser**-based client access, software vendors are being pressured to provide Web-enabled versions of their applications.

PC-terminal emulation tools and PC/X-based access can help end users, particularly managers, in improving informational agility by streamlining information access from their desktops. Another set of activities that are important for extending agility in modern business is based on a "webification" of desktop operating systems and application's client programs and/or implementation of **"Web-to-host" access tools**, as in contemporary conditions, there is a requirement to standardize a client software as much as possible (see Figure 14.6).

Access to corporate data has always been determined by type of information architecture, which an information system is built on (Figure 14.7). In the mainframe environment, the processing is done by a mainframe computer while the users

Figure 14.6. Web-to-host access tools and technologies

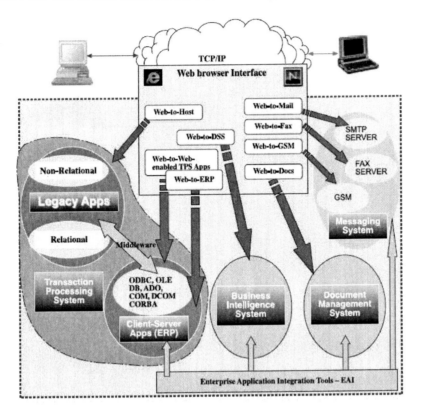

work with "dumb" terminals. The terminals are used to enter or change data and access information from the mainframe. This was the dominant architecture until the late 1980s. A version of this architecture is an architecture where PCs are used to connect to host machines through so-called PC-terminal emulation programs. Traditionally, the access to legacy data has been confined to dumb terminals and PC-based terminal emulation software. However, today as more users wish to standardize on Web browser-based client access, software vendors are being pressured to provide so-called Web-enabled versions of their applications.

PC/X Windows software serves as an emulation program that emulates UNIX graphical user interface based on X-Windows standard on desktop computers. With this software, GUI-based UNIX applications can be used directly from PC desktops.

A client/server-based information architecture divides processing into two major categories: clients and servers. A client is a computer such as a PC or a workstation attached to a computer network consisting of several dozens (hundreds or thou-

Figure 14.7. Traditional information access

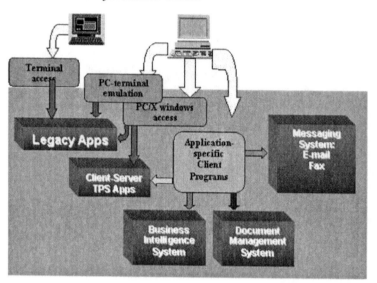

sands) clients and one or more servers. A server is a machine that provides clients with services. Examples of servers are the database server and SMTP server that provides e-mail services. Each client/server application has its own client program that needs to be installed on all client machines.

PC-terminal emulation tools and PC/X-based access can help end users, particularly managers, in improving informational agility by streamlining information access from their desktops. Another set of activities important for extending virtuality in modern business is based on implementation of so-called **Web-to-host access tools.** In contemporary conditions, there is a requirement to standardize a client software as much as possible.

Web-to-host (Web-to-legacy) tools. Access to legacy data through user-friendly applications (standard client/server applications and Web-based applications for Intranets and Internet) requires a processing layer between the applications and the data. Web-to-host technology makes it possible for users to access the data stored on legacy hosts just by clicking a web link. With the emergence of Web technology and Web browser as a unique GUI interface, independent software vendors (ISV) started working on Web-based gateway or middleware products which should provide browser-based access to corporate legacy data. Another reason for using Web browser interface for host access are cost savings that can be achieved in the total-cost-of-ownership model for client systems.

All these Web-to-host tools are created for different host/OS platforms: IBM OS/390, IBM OS/400, Digital/Compaq OpenVMS, or for specific application platforms (e.g., COBOL apps, RMS-based apps, etc). Some of them provide only access to host data, whereas some programs figure as middleware or gateway in a way that they enable adding GUI capabilities, integrating with c/s apps, converting non-DBMS data into DBMS format.

Programs are mainly based on the host-emulation server-software that runs on any Web-server platform. The emulation server is used to download Java or ActiveX applets to browser. The applets permit the browser, to establish the connection to the host using appropriate terminal emulation protocol: TN3270 for IBM mainframes, TN5250 for IBM AS/400 systems, and VT100-400 for Digital VAX/Alpha systems.

Web-to-reporting programs go a step further and provide reporting facilities applied on host data. For example, *Report.Web* (www.nsainc.com) is a Web-to-reporting program, actually an intranet report distribution tool from Network Software Associates Inc. At the heart of Report.Web is the Enterprise Server, a powerful and robust engine which automates the entire process of delivering host-generated reports to the Web from almost any host, including IBM mainframes, AS/400s, DEC VAXes, and PC LAN servers, to the corporate intranet/extranet. Report.Web also supports distributing ERP-generated reports across the corporate Intranet, without deploying ERP clients at every desktop.

Many other applications are "webified" too. Just to mention some examples:

- **Web-to-mail or mail-to-Web** program is a service, which lets users to use their POP3 email accounts through an easy Web interface.
- **Web-to-fax** program, which is very similar to Web-to-Mail, gives an opportunity of sending and receiving fax documents from Web browsers with no additional software.
- **Web-to-GSM** software allows users sending GSM messages through a Web-browser interface.
- **Web-to-document management and work flow systems.** They provide a Web-based access to user documents supporting at the same time an efficient integration with company's messaging system.
- **Web-to-business intelligence systems.** The browser-based access to Business Intelligence Systems is very important for decision makers because of its easiness of use.
- **Web-enabled desktop DSS tools.** Decision modeling by using desktop DSS tools is also available via Web browser. Decision maker can use a model, which is already created and stored on a server from his/her computer through Web browser.
- **Web-enabled EIS.** Executive information systems or integrated reporting applications provide a user-friendly access to corporate data.

- **Web-to-ERP systems.** All major ERP vendors introduced Web-enabled ERP application suites that enable ERP users to use applications via Web browser. For example, SAP introduced *System mySAP.com,* an add-on to its mySAP.com Web portal product introduced in May 1999.

Enterprise portal has been a new approach in intranet-based applications, therefore is often referred to as next-generation intranet. It goes a step further in the "webification" of applications and integration of corporate data. There have already been several "portal-based" products, particularly from business intelligence area. The concept has been extended to "enterprise information portal" which describes a system that combines company's internal data with external information.

There are several types of information portals such as: intranet portal, collaborative portal, and decision-making oriented portal, depending on the type of application. An integrated portal solution on enterprise level provides an efficient Web-based interface to all kinds of data coming from all relevant business applications (TPS, messaging system, document management system, and business intelligence system). Also, it adds an access to external information such as news services and customers/suppliers' Web sites.

The Hummingbird Enterprise Information Portal (EIP) is an example of an integrated enterprise-wide portal solution. It provides companies with Web-based interface to structured and unstructured data sources and applications. The Hummingbird emphasizes the fact that EIP promotes enterprise agility, enabling the entire organization to be flexible and to react quickly to changing market conditions (www.hummingbird.com).

There have already been several "portal-based" products, particularly from business intelligence area. Business intelligence portal is a next trend in enterprise-wide decision support. Examples include:

- Information Advantage's *MyEureka* business intelligence suite was the industry's first business intelligence portal, (now Sterling Software - www.sterling.com).
- *WebIntelligence* from Business Objects (www.businessobjects.com) includes a business-intelligence portal that gives users a single, Web entry point for both WebIntelligence and BusinessObjects, the company's client-server reporting and OLAP system.
- *Brio.Portal* from Brio Technology (www.brio.com) is another example of an integrated business intelligence portal software capable of retrieving, analyzing and reporting information over the Internet.

The concept is later extended to "enterprise information portal" which describes a system that combines company's internal data with external information.

An integrated portal solution on enterprise level provides an efficient Web-based interface to all kinds of data coming from all relevant business applications (TPS, messaging system, document management system, and business intelligence system). Also, it adds an access to external information such as news services and customers/suppliers Web sites. *The Hummingbird Enterprise Information Portal (EIP)* is an example of an integrated enterprise-wide portal solution. It provides companies with Web-based interface to structured and unstructured data sources and applications.

Portable devices-based access. There are four different forms of portable devices:

- **Standard hand-held devices or hand-held PCs**—provide the user with a screen and a small but useable keyboard. Data entry and access are provided via keyboard, function buttons, and even a mouse. These devices run mainly Windows CE operating system, which incorporates many elements of the standard desktop Windows versions. Basic Windows CE programs for hand-held PCs include pocket versions of Microsoft Office suite. By using Microsoft ActiveSync technology, Windows CE Services component automatically synchronizes information between a hand-held PC and the desktop.
- **Palm-held devices or personal digital assistants (PDAs).** These are the keyboardless devices that rely on function buttons to activate applications and access or enter information. They run operating systems such as Windows CE or 3Com's PalmOS.
- **Cellular telephone-based devices**. Even these standard phone communication devices are being enhanced from visual information access perspective enabling users with keyboards and small screens. Some GSM vendors: Nokia, Ericsson, Motorola and Psion announced forming a joint venture called Symbian which will standardize creating wireless information devices, such as smart phones and communicators.
- **Smart phones** are wireless phones with Internet capabilities. They can be used for voice mail, storing data, sending/receiving e-mail and fax messages, and using Internet via built-in mini Web browser.
- **Tablet PC** as a variant of notebook computers which brings some additional notebook features that are crucial in improving user performances of portable computing, such as: natural interface for entering data by using tablet pens with *ultra-light form factor*, speech recognition, and so forth.
- **BlackBerry devices for an integrated wireless-based communications.** It has its own operating system, GUI interface and keyboard. It supports several

standard personal productivity applications: Email, Web browser, phone, SMS, Internet faxing, calendar, address book, tasks, memo pad.

According to IAPS Report (2007), the use of mobile devices (PDAs, cell phones, laptops, tablet PCs, and cell phones) has been increased significantly. An overwhelming 89% majority of businesses users employs one or more of these devices. And as their usage grows, so do concerns about problems. Topping the list is security, data protection for business continuity, accessibility of applications, remote management and integration and interoperability with various applications and heterogeneous platforms.

From agility perspective, in the area of application platform the following ten technologies that emerged over the last decade are of most importance:

- Web-to-host access technology—Web-based access to legacy systems
- Web-enabled applications
- Object-oriented application development paradigm and distributed computing based on OO paradigm
- ERP-SCM-CRM suites
- Groupware and videoconferencing technologies

Figure 14.8. Agile management support system

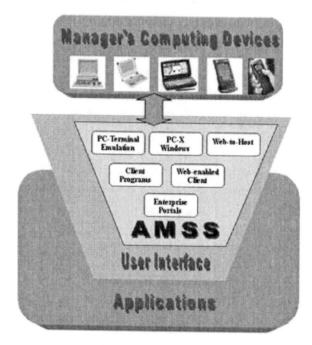

- Middleware (EAI—enterprise application integration tools)
- ASP/Utility/On-Demand/SaaS models of computing
- Web services and intelligent agents
- Portable computing
- Content transformation-content management.

Web-to-host access tools as a specific subset of Web technology are used to improve and ease access to several types of information: legacy data, messaging system, electronic documents, business intelligence, and so on. Web-to-host technology makes it possible for users to access the data stored on legacy hosts just by clicking a Web link.

Distributed computing paradigm is a new framework within the object-oriented software engineering paradigm in which different parts of an application may be running on separate computers on LAN, WAN, or even Internet. By introducing new approaches in application development, **object-oriented paradigm** has contributed to the overall agility within information systems. Applications have become more flexible, application components more reusable and scalable, as Dove (1995) pointed out "...Adaptability (Agility) actually became a reasoned focus with the advent of object-oriented software interests in the early 80s."

Enterprise resource planning, supply chain management, and customer relationships management software suites are today considered as systems that aim to serve as an information backbone for the whole organization, depending on the type of the business. The crucial point is in an efficient integration of all business data and processes in the form of an integrated information system (ERP) with an emphasis put on reporting and business intelligence capabilities important for management. The major agility-related advantages of an ERP system include: integration of data from all business processes, easier information access for managers, stable and reliable data structure, customizable and adaptable application platform, module based infrastructure, GUI and Web-based user interface, and so forth, Norrish (1996) referred to ERP system as an "agile software for agile manufacturing." Disadvantages include: expensive and lengthy to implement, many hidden implementation costs, maintenance is costly and time consuming, commitment to a single application vendor for mission-critical applications.

Groupware solutions such as Microsoft's Exchange, IBM's Lotus Domino/Notes, and Novell's Groupwise play crucial role in enhancing managers' agility when several forms of messaging systems and group work are considered. As a supplement to standard messaging technology, videoconferencing technology enables remote users not only to communicate among each other, exchange standard data, but organize virtual meetings, exchange video and audio data, and share data and applications as well.

Middleware. An efficient access to legacy data is important from end-users' perspective but from application developer's perspective as well. The development of new standard or Web-enabled c/s applications which will exchange data with existing legacy systems requires a sort of software called middleware that overcomes the differences in data formats. These products help in enhancing application platform's agility as they enable access to non-relational data in almost the same way that relational data is accessed. Application developers can build new Internet-based applications, which will use data from legacy systems by using data integration standards such as: OLE DB, ADO, COM, DCOM, CORBA, and so forth.

ASP/utility/on-demand/SaaS models of computing. New business applications delivery models developed during the last 10 years. ASP model introduced ten years ago by application service providers (ASPs) has been redefined by introducing new approaches, namely: Utility computing, on-demand computing, software as a service model. Software vendors rent the whole applications—running platforms, mostly those applications that are very complex and hard to implement (ERP, SCM, CRM, data warehousing, electronic commerce). The service level agreements are based on "pay-as-you-go" basis, or utility-like pricing.

Web services are applications that exist on the Internet; they use a common language for exchanging data and instructions. Language standards that are used in exchanging data are: SOAP (simple object access protocol), WSDL (Web services description language), and UDDI (universal description, discovery, and integration).

Portable computing. The ultimate goal in using portable computing devices that are designed as companion products to personal computers is again in improving information access of mobile users or teleworkers, firstly just for accessing and downloading data, but later on for uploading data as well. Currently, these devices are used mainly by managers and service workers for managing their schedules, contacts, and other business information. They have the utility for synchronizing information with a personal computer. In addition to standard office scheduling needs it is a customer interaction software—CIS (customer relationships management—CRM) that drives the PDA market. These are applications like: sales force automation, customer support, service support, maintenance, and so forth. In the same time, both ERP and CIS/CRM vendors are introducing non-PC links to their sites (PDAs, Windows CE-based hand-held PCs, GSM).

Content management-content transformation. Most of the existing data within enterprise-wide information Internet-based infrastructures are in HTML or XML formats. In order to have that content available on portable and wireless devices, it has to be compatible with these devices. As said before, mobile devices require data in different formats such as: WML, clipped HTML, cHTML and they all work with micro-browsers on mobile devices. As mobile computing devices have different memory sizes, screen sizes, and so forth, there has to be a solution, which should dynamically adapt the content for each device. Several approaches in content transformation exist such as: screen scrapping, content duplication, software-based transformation, conversion by wireless providers, communication device-based content transformation (e.g., Cisco's CTE-Content Transformation Engine), and so forth.

IDC (2007) defines "agile ERP" as an ERP infrastructure that possesses the ability to adjust to changing business conditions with minimal technical or business process intervention. Agile ERP applications can facilitate greater collaboration throughout the enterprise by ensuring data integrity to different project stakeholders, enabling them to update data structures on the fly and ultimately scaling the information warehouse to meet individual reporting needs even with significant increases in data volume.

CHAPTER SUMMARY

The terms of business agility or enterprise agility that have been coined recently as a result of the agile manufacturing paradigm from the beginning of 90s. Agility has several dimensions and contemporary businesses are seeking ways to become "agile organizations." Several IT-related technologies are employed in supporting both manufacturing and management processes. This chapter aimed at identifying the relations between business continuity and business agility. The major IT-based agility drivers and their features that are critical for enhancing the enterprise-wide agility are explained. Data access technologies that play crucial role in achieving the agility are briefly explained.

REFERENCES

Cheng, K., Harrison, D. K. & Pan, P. Y. (1998). Implementation of agile manufacturing ñ an AI and Internet based approach. *Journal of Materials Processing Technology, 76*, pp. 96-101.

Dove, R. (1995). Introducing principles for agile systems. *Production Magazine 8*(95), Gardner Publications, http://www.parshift.com/Essays/essay010.htm.

Gunasekaran, A. (1999). Agile manufacturing: A framework for research and development. *Int. J. Production Economics, 62*, pp. 87-105.

Huang, C. Y, Ceroni, J. A. & Nof, S. Y. (2000). Agility of networked enterprises ñ parallelism, error recovery and conflict resolution. *Computers in Industry, 42*, pp. 275-287.

IAPS Report (2007). 2007 Server Hardware and OS Deployment and Usage Survey. *Institute for Advanced Professional Studies.*

IDC Report (2007). Business process agility: The next ERP Imperative, *March 2007.*

IDC Report (2006). Thinking outside of the box: Architecting for agility, Retrieved on July 29, 2006 from http://www.theitevolution.com/content/IDC_473.pdf.

Katayama, H. & Bennet, D. (1999). Agility, adaptability, and leanness: A comparison of concepts and a study of practice. *Int. J. Production Economics, 60-61*, pp. 43-51.

Norrish, D. (1996). Agile software for agile manufacturing. *APICS - Agile Manufacturing, 6*(12), December 1996.

Papaioannou, T. & Edwards, J. (1999). Using mobile agents to improve the alignment between manufacturing and its IT sypport systems. *Robotics and Autonomous Systems, 27*, pp. 45-57.

Ranganathan, C. & Brown, C. V. (2006). ERP investments and the market value of firms: Toward an understanding of influential ERP project variables. *Information Systems Research, 17*(2), June 2006, pp. 145–161.

Phillips, F. & Tuladhar, S. (2000). Measuring organizational flexibility: An exploration and general model. *Technological Forecasting and Social Change, 64*, pp. 23-38.

Sanchez, L. M. & Nagi, R. (2001). A review of agile manyfacturing systems. *International Journal of Production research, 39*(16), pp. 3561-3600.

Sharifi, H. & Zhang, Z. (1999). A methodology for achieving agility in manufacturing organizations: An introduction. *Int. J. Production Economics, 62*, pp. 7-22.

Yusuf, Y. Y., Sarhadi, M. & Gunasekaran, A. (1999). Agile manufacturing: The drivers, concepts and attributes. *Int. J. Production Economics, 62*, 33-43.

REAL WORLD CASES

IT Agility through Automated, Policy-based Virtual Infrastructure
Compiled from: http://www.intel.com/it/pdf/it-agility-policybased-virtual-infra-structure.pdf

Enterprises such as Intel increasingly recognize agility as a key competitive advantage and look to their IT organizations to achieve it. If we can rapidly repurpose IT systems to meet new computing challenges as they arise, we can achieve greater agility by addressing business needs as quickly as possible.

Traditional bottom-up approaches to infrastructure design focused on providing powerful infrastructure based on requirements and capabilities defined by IT. This approach was effective at addressing discrete business needs. However, a purely technology focused approach suffers from a lack of integration with the future business direction of the organization. For this reason, businesses are moving to a top-down approach, where executive-level decision makers define strategic infrastructure requirements that support the business as a whole. IT then responds to strategic long-term requirements, rather than focusing on near-term issues.

DISCUSSION QUESTIONS

1. Give the brief description of an agile business.
2. Explain briefly the concepts of agile manufacturing and agile management.
3. What is the role of a continuous computing platfrom for business agility?
4. Define the concept of "Agile ERP."
5. What is the role of data access technologies in enhancing enterprise-wide agility?
6. Describe the concept of "agile management support system."
7. What is the role of middleware products in business computing?
8. List and briefly explain main business agility drivers.
9. How do Business Intelligence tools and integrated suites help in enhancing business agility?
10. Explain the role of Web-to-Host connectivity tools in modern computing.

About the Author

Nijaz Bajgoric is an associate professor of business computing and information technology management in the School of Economics and Business, University of Sarajevo, Bosnia and Herzegovina. He has a PhD from the University of Sarajevo. He teaches and conducts research in information technology, business computing, information technology management, and operating systems. He has published papers in the following peer-reviewed journals: *International Journal of Enterprise Information Systems, Kybernetes, Information Management and Computer Security, Information Systems Management, Industrial Management and Data Systems, International Journal of Production Research, European Journal of Operational Research, International Journal of Agile Management Systems, Journal of Concurrent Engineering, International Journal of Agile Manufacturing*, and has authored and co-authored chapters in the edited books published by: IGI Global, Elsevier Science, Kluwer Academic Publishers, CRC Press, and Auerbach Publications. His current areas of research include continuous computing technologies, business continuity, enterprise information systems, and information technology management.

Index